# PUBLISHING

For June Guthrie

# PUBLISHING

## PRINCIPLES & PRACTICE

## RICHARD GUTHRIE

Los Angeles | London | New Delhi
Singapore | Washington DC

SAGE Publications Ltd
1 Oliver's Yard
55 City Road
London EC1Y 1SP

SAGE Publications Inc.
2455 Teller Road
Thousand Oaks, California 91320

SAGE Publications India Pvt Ltd
B 1/I 1 Mohan Cooperative Industrial Area
Mathura Road, Post Bag 7
New Delhi 110 044

SAGE Publications Asia-Pacific Pte Ltd
33 Pekin Street #02-01
Far East Square
Singapore 048763

Library of Congress Control Number: 2010942256

British Library Cataloguing in Publication data
A catalogue record for this book is available from the British Library

ISBN 978-1-84787-014-8
ISBN 978-1-84787-015-5 (pbk)

Typeset by C&M Digitals (P) Ltd, Chennai, India
Printed in India at Replika Press Pvt Ltd.
Printed on paper from sustainable resources

# CONTENTS

# ABOUT THE AUTHOR

Richard Guthrie is a researcher of print and digital book publishing with over 20 years' experience in film and television production. He has an MA and PhD in publishing studies and lives and writes in London.

# ACKNOWLEDGEMENTS

I am grateful for all the assistance and advice Chris Rojek, Jai Seaman and Katherine Haw at Sage gave throughout the writing. I would like to thank Professor Iain Stevenson, University College London, for reading and commenting on an earlier version of this text, and providing me with many valuable insights. I am indebted to Valentina Lichtner for reading drafts and for all her suggestions for improving the text.

Many individuals, businesses and organisations were generous with their knowledge, insights, time and resources. I particularly wish to thank: John Martin (founder of Black Sparrow Press); Jason Epstein; David R. Godine Publishers; Gordon Graham (founder of Logos); Kent Carroll, Europa Editions, New York; Richard Abel (Logos); Tina Jordan, Association of American Publishers; Professor Manuel Castells and Dr Amelia Arsenault; James Spackman, Hodder & Stoughton; John Schline, Penguin USA; Tom Tivnan, *The Bookseller* (UK); Tim Coronel, *The Bookseller* (Australia); Angela Meyer, LiteraryMinded; Eckhard Gerdes, *Journal of Experimental Fiction*; Ion Trewin, Man Booker Prize; The Publishers Association UK; and *Publishers Weekly*.

# INTRODUCTION

Publishing is a process by which human communication is made public. The intention in the first human messages transmitted by the first public speech, the first musical performance, even the first marks scratched on to a cave wall or rock face, are all integral to a history that leads through time right up to the door of contemporary publishing. Publishing has been present in every personal, political, social expression of ideas, in every creative instinct, impression, emotion, thought, memory, information exchange that has ever deliberately been made public in any cultural context since humans first began to record existence.

The extraordinary breadth and longevity of publishing is matched only by the uniqueness of each and every published event. All publishing, whether a book, a music recording, television programme, film, photo, magazine or newspaper, is unique in itself. Each road taken in the writing, composition, production and marketing of every publication is different. All the roles and decisions on the way to every publishing event describe alternative routes and individual tales – no matter how similar publishing products might seem to us now on the digitised surface. So even while analogue publishing considers whether it will finally slip permanently into a digital disguise, the enduring creative constant, the original cultural purpose – the publication of the human mind – remains intact.

As the print book proceeds through a volatile age of analogue-digital media convergence, it faces questions once asked of stone tablets, clay, wood boards, the papyrus scroll and the vellum codex. Can it, should it survive? The book is the first mass medium, remaining in essence the same as it has always been throughout five hundred years of print history. In overall design it is still remarkably close to the original codex, the object its inventor created when sewing vellum pages to a leather spine two millennia ago in the ancient era of oar-driven boats, togas and temples. The demise of the printed book is a cultural shift, a paradigm change of epic proportions.

Twentieth-century methods and trends in books, newspapers, vinyl records, celluloid films transformed culture and lives. Digital content creation methods and multi-purpose digital display devices are doing the same in the twenty-first century. The world is currently imbedded in a digital software and hardware-led race towards the incredibly shrinking appliance. Every year *digital* proves itself cheaper, smaller, lighter, and easier to use. Consumption of media content has also changed before our eyes. It is now commonplace for an ordinary episode of a so-so TV series on an average mid-week night's viewing to be seen 'by more people' than all the readers of 'a book on the fiction bestseller list'.[1] Will we wake up one day to find that the print book has disappeared entirely? Or, in truth, is the current debate over the death of print just another empty prediction, pushed and led by proponents of another over-hyped media cliché, this one called *digital convergence*?

Even as little as 40 years ago, content media from different spheres led separate lives. Each medium was a discreet enterprise. It often took years for material from one medium to find its way to another. With the spread of digital media today, producers inside one vertically integrated media conglomerate can orchestrate diverse media content into patterns of integrated media sales.

The print book so far has resisted the digital onslaught. How long it can continue to survive in its present form remains book publishing's most asked question. Supporters of the paper book believe that today's siphoning of digitised content into e-readers, down broadband cables and on to mobile telephones, adds up to readers losing something culturally precious. Many readers, music lovers and cinephiles want to be just that – not digital media consumers.

Digital books are on the march. Longtime digital advocate Nicholas Negroponte is involved in the *one laptop one child project*. Sending 100 cheap laptops to African villages, each loaded with 100 digitised books, means 10,000 e-books for communities that have never seen or used a paper book.[2] It is hard to argue with this idea. What the developed world has long had, developing continents are just beginning to remember – the power of going from *zero* to *one* overnight. Bangladeshi women who never had a standard telephone now use mobile phones for all kinds of communication and business.

Looking back on the great booms of twentieth-century media, the golden eras of cinema, television, vinyl records and paperbacks, many of us can almost see, touch, feel and hear that time when newspapers were thrown onto our doorsteps, when the first black-and-white televisions appeared in shop windows. For all the dystopian sway towards digitisation, it must be heartening to many that every medium retains its distinctive nature. Media boundaries in the twenty-first century may be oddly drawn up, but a book is still a book, a film is still a film, a recorded track is still recorded music. The writing, production and sell-through of a book, film, radio or television programme are all still separate practices. For all the merging and converging in the digital paradigm, publishing principles carry on, with definable threads there for all to see in every creation, production and delivery.

*Publishing: Principles and Practice* examines how publishing roles and practices grew up, and how and why they are maintained, visiting all the major aspects of commerce and culture in the publishing trade, how it developed in the United Kingdom and the United States, to its spread into disparate territorial corners of what is now the most global of all book trades.

Written for anyone seeking knowledge on the anglophone publishing industry, *Publishing: Principles and Practice* explains how the guiding principles and practices developed over five centuries. In narrating, questioning and analysing the main historical junctures and contemporary circumstances of the anglophone book trade, this book offers a template of the possibilities the digital future presents the business and culture of content publishing.

## NOTES

1 Compaine, B. M., 'Competition in Television and Radio', in R. Rice, ed., *Media Ownership*, Cresskill, NJ, Hampton Press, 2008.
2 Cody Combs, 'Will physical books be gone in five years?', *CNN*, 18 October 2010, http://edition.cnn.com/2010/TECH/innovation/10/17/negroponte.ebooks/.

# I A HISTORY OF BOOKS

In the time of Eumenes II of Pergamum, in Asia Minor (197–159 BC), *vellum* or parchment, made from dried animal skin, was first used in the form of two-sided leaves for writing on and reading. Eumenes created the Library of Pergamum, a great advance in the ancient world.

The earliest prototype of the book, the *vellum codex*, appeared in Greece and moved on with history to Rome, where, initially, a technique of wax inscriptions on bound wooden boards was used. Known in Latin as a *codex* from *caudex*, or tree trunk, the codex progressed to using *vellum* for leaves. Around 400 AD, the codex began to overtake the papyrus scroll as the main publishing technology and product of its time.

---

### THE PAPYRUS SCROLL

The papyrus scroll was the first light, versatile, portable method for publishing script and images. Invented in ancient Egypt some 5000 years ago, papyrus scrolls were woven from papyrus leaf. Strips of the leaf were soaked in water and lain side by side and then over again at right angles. The material was then left in the sun to dry, the resin of the leaf fusing the cross strips. After the drying process, the sheet was polished and then was ready for use.

A papyrus scroll had a life of about 200 years, but only if carefully preserved in a dry place and climate. Humidity affected the longevity of papyrus. The scroll was still used extensively in the Mediterranean basin until about 1100 AD. Conceptually, the scroll lives on in roll-up maps and design documents, and in published lists such as the electoral roll.

---

## THE FIRST PARADIGM: FROM VELLUM CODEX TO PRINT BOOK

First appearing commercially in the bookshops of ancient Rome, the *vellum codex* was developed for the publication of religious tracts, creative texts, the expression of ideas, history and learning. From 400 to 1000 AD, book production grew quickly throughout the Mediterranean basin. The book figured prominently from 700 to 1300 AD in the Arabian empire stretching from Teheran to Cordoba. Due to all the handwork involved in creating books they soon became symbols of status. The tenth century Grand Vizier of Persia was said to be so proud of his book collection that he travelled everywhere with 117,000 handwritten and bound volumes, loading them alphabetically onto 400 camels, which were taught to walk in alphabetical order. At that time only 500 volumes existed in Paris.

During the Middle Ages, central and northern Europe caught up with cultural developments. *Scriptoria* (scribe or scrivener shops) sprang up throughout Europe. Hand-produced books were extremely arduous work and took months, sometimes years, to complete. Books were made to order on the *sell and produce business model*. Books were available and affordable usually only to clerics, wealthy merchants and the aristocracy, the only members of medieval European society who had any real use for them.

In the mid-fifteenth century, book production became mechanical in Europe for the first time. Already a sophisticated cottage craft industry, book production leapt forward with Johann Gutenberg's invention of the first viable industrial prototype and machine for mass printing. Moveable wood block and sand-cast type printing techniques had existed in Korea and China centuries before, but it was Gutenberg's invention that revolutionalised publishing. In a stroke of huge paradigmatic proportions, this technological shift created the world's first mass-market business model, though it was many centuries before books began selling on a truly mass scale.

Combining wine press technology and jewellery techniques (moveable metal type pieces), the Gutenberg press reduced manuscript production time and costs by a massive 90%. Printers could now print copies in numbers they believed they could sell (*the produce and sell model*), rather than producing books requested by order. *Economies of scale* now affected production decisions. Instead of being only for the powerful and wealthy few, books were now potentially available to a very wide readership. An invigorated European book trade began the search for increased custom, growing its power in the process.

Other social improvements were needed to expand the book trade, however, not only a leap forward in technology. Literacy needed to grow, and this took centuries to mature across Europe. At the dawn of the sixteenth century in England, only 10% of women and 30% of men could read to any level of proficiency. Initially, literacy tests were rudimentary, based on whether men or women could sign their names. It was only in the mid-nineteenth century, when working-class Britain began to participate in the explosion of literacy enabled by printed books, that mass sales of books became a reality.

At first, even though the printing press was welcomed, some wealthy Europeans were determined to maintain the handwritten tradition as well. Manuscript production continued against the odds right up to 1600. But by that time, printers were already able to produce over 1,200 printed sheets a day. Printers stopped imitating manuscripts and developed new formats and styles. Faced with the overwhelming success of the print book, the craft of handwritten manuscripts disappeared.

The 42-line Gutenberg Bible, itself a product of the manuscript tradition, was the initial default design. Basic book form was a work in progress and design changes came relatively slowly, but the trade in books changed radically, almost overnight. With the sell-through model, timeliness, cost and speed of information distribution to market became the driving factors of the whole trade.

The growth of printing in England followed continental Europe by a quarter of a century, but the English book trade made up for lost time. With the importation of the printing press into England in the mid-1470s, books arrived at a time of historical and cultural flux. Books helped England emerge from its isolation. At the time very few Europeans had visited England. Few continental Europeans spoke or even knew of English. The new printing press and growth of English books was the first step in an exponential growth in importance of the English language throughout the world.

## 1475–1533: THE EARLY ENGLISH TRADE

William Caxton was the pioneering English print book trader. Caxton's first publication, *The Recuyell of the Historyes of Troye*, was produced in 1475, compiled from the French original by Raoulle Fevre, first printed in France in 1464. Caxton had begun translating the text in 1468. Other printers, such as John Lettou, also set up in London at the time. In 1482, Lettou and his new partner, William de Machlinia, printed England's first law book *Tenores novelli*, a significant milestone in UK publishing history. Since then, anglophone legal publishing has grown into one of the most important and profitable sectors.[1]

The multi-tasking Caxton (translator, printer-publisher, bookseller), with his assistant Wynkyn de Worde, prepared, printed and sold books from a base near Westminster Abbey. Caxton published 80% of his books in English, among them the works of Geoffrey Chaucer (1343–1400). After Caxton's death in 1493, De Worde moved their printing establishment to Fleet Street, beginning the long tradition of the print trade in the area around St Paul's Cathedral.

The early English book trade was given significant Crown support from one of the most reviled figures in English history, Richard III. In his short but influential reign (1483–1485), Richard III promoted the trade by exempting books, publishing skills and printing paraphernalia from the anti-alien trade statute of the time. Trade from larger and much more economically active European nations, such as Italy, were always threatening to swamp England, and the Crown's exemption of books from import sanctions was important not only for printers and book traders at the time, but also gave a strategic boost to English letters, language and culture.

Authorial rights in England took a different route to the developing trade in continental Europe. The first recorded issue of authorial rights in the world was the

Senate of Venice's grant of rights in perpetuity in 1486 to Antonio Sabellico, for his *Decades Rerum Venetiarum*. By contrast, power in the English book trade was firmly vested in the printer and bookseller, not the author. English authors had to wait nearly 250 years before their rights were recognised in English law.

## 1533–1694: THE AGE OF CONTROL

Due to his own private, religious and political concerns, in 1533 Henry VIII reversed Richard III's trade exemption for books. This brought to an end the early free trade era. Henry VIII instituted a system of Privy Council oversight of books throughout England. When it became clear that the task was too onerous for the Council, members of the Stationers' Company, a scrivener guild in existence since 1403, put themselves forward as possible managers of the process. In 1542 the Company petitioned Henry for the right to oversee the trade. Henry refused the request. The Stationers must have been a little aggrieved by this rebuff as Henry had already granted a Royal Charter for printing to the University of Cambridge in 1534.

After Henry's death, his daughter and successor to the throne, Mary, concerned with creating robust Roman Catholic controls over printed materials, gave in to the Stationers' relentless lobbying. In 1557 Mary granted the Stationers' Company a sweeping Royal Charter over commercial printing throughout England. The Stationers were granted industrial privileges and a trade-wide monopoly that they guarded jealously for 150 years. In effect, Mary provided the Stationers with a sixteenth-century royal edict to print money.

The Stationers' Company shaped the early English book trade like no other force in history. Members held rights throughout the land described as *rights in copy* — tangible ownership equal to perpetual property rights under English common law. Apart from the scholarly and religious publishing rights granted by charter to the University of Cambridge (and later the University of Oxford in 1586),[2] the Stationers' position was virtually unchallengeable. The hold over the trade was absolute and except for a few isolated events of piracy, and the mid-seventeenth-century revolutionary confusion when Stationer power lapsed, the Company's control over printing ran more or less uninterrupted from 1557 to 1694.

The enduring legacy of the Stationers' Company is embedded in the UK's publishing traditions and practices — the idea that publishers have the final say, not the original authors of literary works. This differs from most continental traditions, where authors in some countries can withdraw their works, even after publication, if they so choose.

During the reign of Charles I (1625–1649) Crown monopolies and edicts grew very unpopular. Along with other traditions and practices, the Stationers' Company's monopolistic printing powers were challenged by the Long Parliament in the early 1640s. The loathed Star Chamber was abolished and, by inference, all its decrees. A tumultuous decade saw civil war, the execution of a king and, in publishing, wild, chaotic pamphleteering. Private or self-publishing exploded on to the scene.

Throughout this revolutionary period, the Stationers' Company stood quietly aside, maintaining its position, if not its entire powers.

With the conviction for treason and beheading of Charles I in 1649, Oliver Cromwell became Lord Protector (king in all but name). New printing continued to flourish, but still the Company was not abolished, its 'suspended' powers remaining intact. With Cromwell's death in 1658, the Commonwealth faltered. Cromwell's son was unable to establish his authority and the Stuarts regained the throne in 1660. The Licensing Act of 1662 returned all its prior publishing status, power and functions to the Stationers' Company.

The seeds of liberalism and desire for fundamental democratic and systemic changes in English society, however, did not die with the revolution. The Jacobeans were swept again from power in 1688. John Locke and other liberals seized the moment, soliciting support for printing and other reforms from the new Dutch-born King, William of Orange. In 1694, the English Parliament refused to renew the Licensing Act. The Stationers' monopoly was suspended again, this time, it seemed, for good. The Stationers, however, were not a spent force.

## 1694–1774: THE RISE OF 'THE PUBLISHER'

The world's first copyright act grew out of the continuing chaos in the book trade. On 10 April 1710 *The Statute of Anne* was passed by Parliament, introducing the concept of copyright terms for authors for the first time. The Statute provided 14-year terms for new works, renewable for another 14 years upon application, and a one-time term of 21 years for works under existing terms of ownership, or for those categorised as 'orphan' works (written by authors who could not be identified or who were dead).

The Act seems to us now as if it was a revolutionary political move made by the early eighteenth-century English Parliament to establish authorial rights. The main intention of the statute, however, was to bring control to an unruly trade. The 1710 Act was not introduced as a system for advancing authorial rights, even if many liberals of the day championed the idea. Authorial rights came about almost to the trade's surprise.

A new player, *the publisher*, was now needed to run the trade, a metamorphosis of the printer-bookseller figure. The publisher was the new 'middle-man', buying works from authors, managing the preparation of books for publication and finding ways of getting books to the reading public. Initially, members of the Stationers' Company ceded this main central part of their power, but they still did not believe history had abandoned them. Wealthy stationers had political support and they were still the printers and booksellers.

The 1710 law established a registration process of copyright for published works, a service the Stationers oversaw and for which they charged a fee. Significantly, though, the Company could not refuse registration. If for some reason they did, copyright could be established by a direct announcement by the author in the general press. Monopoly conditions in the trade were now legally, if not wholly, over.

The unhappy Stationers fought on for the reinstatement of their powers by other means. Company members began to challenge the new copyright law in the courts, setting out to establish a common law property rights precedent over statute law. Initially the courts supported the Stationers. The issue was finally settled in a dramatic 1774 House of Lords' ruling in *Donaldson v. Becket*. Eleven law lords, in a majority vote of one, supported statutory superiority in published works. Common law rights remained for unpublished manuscripts. In a rousing speech that had his fellow lords on the edge of their seats, Lord Camden denounced 'the patents privileges, Star-chamber decrees, and the bye-laws of the Stationers' Company: all of them the effects of grossest tyranny and usurpation'.[3] This decision by the House of Lords cemented statute control over copyright law. The age of direct Stationers' Company control over the trade was now truly gone for ever.

---

### THE HOUSE OF LONGMAN

An early example of a modern British publisher was Thomas Longman I, who founded a family business in 1724. With an outlay of £2,282 9s 6d, Longman bought a premises in the Paternoster Row near St Paul's Cathedral. The house included a new and used book production and warehouse on the ground floor, with living quarters on the first floor. Longman bought it from printer and publisher, William Taylor, paying a separate sum of £230 18s for Taylor's copyrights. In October of the same year Longman was made a Freeman of the Stationers' Company.

A published title that Longman did not acquire in his purchase of Taylor's copyrights, was the *Life and Strange Surprizing Adventures of Robinson Crusoe of York, Mariner*, by Daniel Defoe. Taylor had earned £1,000 profit from the original publication, with copies initially selling at five shillings each. *Robinson Crusoe* was reprinted many times, going on into sequels. The book's success made Taylor the envy of other publishers in London at the time. Finally, in 1753, Thomas Longman was able to buy a ninth share in the rights to the tenth edition of the sequel to the original *Robinson Crusoe*. Publishers of the day bought shares in each other's productions, in much the way a film producer or studio might buy a share in a film production these days. The struggle Longman had in getting his hands on Defoe's classic works did not seem to hurt him or the Longman 'house'. Longman went on to be one of the three great names in British publishing, with two and half centuries in the business of books.

---

## 1774–1935: THE ERA OF THE PUBLISHING FIRM

'The publisher' soon became synonymous with the publishing process, growing into the central role within the entire anglophone book business. Copyright law granted the solid judicial support the trade had been lacking, with the levers of control no longer centred in printers and booksellers. The new publisher and authors were now the two ends of an axis on which the whole business revolved.

The United States caught up with English copyright law by passing its own Act in 1790. The US law reflected much of what had been established by the Statute of Anne, providing terms of 14 years, but the US law went one crucial step further, by enshrining freedom of expression in the first amendment of the US Constitution.

After the French revolution of 1789, the French passed a copyright law, *droit d'auteur*, in 1793, extending copyright terms to life plus five years. The French legislators grappled with issues such as *the public domain*, and the social and cultural responsibilities of publishing, differing from the thrust of English copyright law, with its emphasis on business.

In the UK, family-owned firms began to flourish. The early great names of English publishing, Longman (Thomas Longman, his nephew Thomas, and his son, Thomas Norton, 1724–1842), the first John Murray (1737–1793) and Macmillan (brothers John and Daniel 1843–1896), became synonymous with publishing in this period. The word 'publisher' described the person at the helm of the firm, and the house. Decisions and control were taken by editorial departments. Editors represented the views of publishers, dealt with acquisitions and filtered out 'dubious or commercially unsound material'. During the nineteenth century a gentrified and prosperous British publishing industry grew into an integral part of the British establishment. The provision of information was 'in safe hands'.

Even if the book trade was a modest enterprise by comparison to the commodities trades of cotton or wool, the nineteenth-century growth in publishing showed it was more than just a good business. It was culturally and politically important as well. Publishing's growth was spurred on by:

- steam power improvements in printing technology
- new techniques in paper production
- mechanical typesetting and illustration methods
- improved paper costs (falling from 20% of a book's cost in 1740 to 7% in 1910)
- the use of cloth casing instead of leather binding.

The industry grew rapidly in efficiency and profitability. Population growth throughout the industrially revolutionised world grew massively, doubling in Europe and rising fifteen-fold in the United States. New education policies helped facilitate a rise in literacy and with it an expanded reader base. Book publishing spoke to the cultural idealism of nationhood as well as commercial and political interests. With the rise of the novel, British publishers began producing around 100 new titles every year to 1750, a figure that had increased six-fold by 1825. By 1900, title output reached 6,000 per year.

London was the world's capital of English language publishing, but in the United States a thriving industry had also grown up. In Philadelphia, Boston and New York, 'anglomania' spread throughout the trade. English books were much sought after, servicing the new expansion in reading needs in the former and extant North American colonies.

Piracy was alive and well on both sides of the Atlantic. With no international copyright agreement in place, American publishers would wait dockside to pick up new English books as they arrived by ship. The industry grew and with it cross-Atlantic conflict. Illegal American editions of British books filled the US market, with books sometimes going on sale on the American east coast the same day the book had arrived by ship. Piracy also occurred in Britain, with Harriet Beecher Stowe's 1852 novel *Uncle Tom's Cabin* selling well over a million illegal copies on British streets.

In the mid-nineteenth century, British publishing was overseen by a handful of 'leviathan houses'. The industry was corralled into a system of trade policies enforced by the big houses, an arrangement described by *The Times* as 'imperious' and 'absolute'. Smaller houses, such as Chapman's (the first publisher of Charles Dickens with *Pickwick Papers* in 1836), pushed for lower, or even a free setting of, book retail prices. The 'rule' of the day, set by powerful publishers, was that book retail prices were 15 shillings. Booksellers were 'allowed' to buy books for 10 shillings, giving them a profit of 5 shillings on each sale.

There were also great and often unexpected market successes, occurring by good luck more than ingenious planning. John Murray III, who was less than convinced by the value of Charles Darwin's *The Origin of the Species*, needed a lawyer with no publishing expertise, George Collock, to convince him to print 1,000 copies of Darwin's seminal work, instead of only 500. The book sold out in a few days. In 1881, less than three weeks before Benjamin Disraeli's death, Longman paid the remainder of a record-breaking advance of £10,000 to the former prime minister for his novel *Endymion*. The novel went on to create a market sensation.

Trade publishers were thriving, but so too were academic publishers. The book business was now a large and diverse industry. The world's largest academic publisher, Oxford University Press, officially became an exported brand in 1896, opening its first American office in New York. Books were catching on with vast sections of society, crossing economic and social boundaries, filling the book shelves of the expanding middle class. The formation of the UK Publishers Association in 1896, a cartel operation to protect the established houses, set the trade's rules and practices. The formation of the Association led directly in 1900 to Macmillan's successful promotion of the Net Book Agreement (NBA), a minimum price arrangement. Meant to 'promote trade stability', in effect the NBA was a profits guarantee for the major houses. Protecting books was a popular move. A judge presiding over the NBA decision made the now famous statement that 'books are different'. Unofficially, the book trade was, from then on, in Britain at least, not just an enterprise but 'officially' a protected cultural activity. To the principle that *books are a business first and foremost* was added the notion of *cultural value*. The Association's move helped the trade achieve galloping growth in the twentieth century. Society, it seemed, had a duty to protect and promote the book trade like no other enterprise.

The United States did away with price controls in the trade in 1910, while the NBA remained in place in the UK until 1997, demonstrating that while there were shared origins, the two global leaders of the anglophone book business also had fundamental trade differences.

As the twentieth century progressed, the low-entry barriers to the trade attracted a constant stream of new small companies. The Great Depression opened up some cracks in the industry's formation and structure, but the trade also responded well. The Great Crash of 1929 soon brought cuts in consumer spending and led to a sudden decline in the American book business. This hit UK publishing hard as British publishers could no longer rely on North American sales to boost their businesses. Publishers on both sides of the Atlantic started dreaming of new ways of trading in books. Reprint book clubs grew up. In 1932, British publisher Harold Raymond invented the Book Token, allowing book consumers to exchange a token for a book. Booksellers were opposed to the idea at first but when it became a big hit at Christmas and the practice spread to other countries, almost every UK bookseller signed up to it. But more was needed. The '*recession proof*' book trade was suffering. A policy of *sale and return* was created, allowing booksellers to stay in business. Shops could order and hold publishers' books on credit for up to 90 days. Unsold books were returnable for a full credit. The policy was implemented for the tough economic times, but curiously remained after economic growth returned.

## 1935-1970: THE PAPERBACK REVOLUTION

Even more innovation was needed to keep the trade in good health. A 'new' paperback idea came about just as the world was emerging from the worst of the Great Depression. Paperbacks had already appeared in many forms from the nineteenth century onwards, but the paperback market of the 1930s introduced a whole new way of distributing paperbacks, and in the process created one of the UK's biggest names, Penguin Books.

Penguin's founder and owner, Allen Lane, borrowed his idea from a German imprint, Albatross, which had been set up in 1931 by an investor, Kurt Enoch, in Leipzig, Germany.[4] Albatross produced cheap 7⅛ inches by 4¼ inches format English-language paperbacks for the continental market. National Socialist political pressures forced Albatross to cease trading, and the German imprint's demise left the way open for the new Penguin.

Lane had to look no further than Albatross for ideas. The German company's simple designs and book size, lack of cover illustration, colour coding of jackets by genre, all ended up in Penguin's overall design. Lane even employed Kurt Enoch as Penguin's New York-based chief of Penguin's early US operations.

Coming from a strong publishing family, Allen Lane, at the time of creating Penguin, was still Publishing Director of The Bodley Head. With the means to find the necessary capital and an understanding of all aspects of the trade, Lane began Penguin Books with Hemingway's *Farewell to Arms* and nine other titles. Lane's greatest coup was to sell his paperbacks at very low prices. Convincing the UK high street store Woolworth to stock the Penguins, Lane priced the paper books at sixpence, one-twelfth of the UK hardcover price of six shillings. Sixpence fitted Woolworth's slogan of 'nothing more than sixpence'. Lane's business model meant he had to sell 18,000 copies of each title before break-even was reached. With Woolworth on board, within a year the Penguins were selling in the millions.

There is some dispute over which side of the Atlantic took the paperback revolution to its full potential. Penguin was the first to achieve mass sales, but the company had no real presence in the USA. Lane hesitated over what to do in the US market. His inflexibility with American colleagues on cover design and his aversion to populist literature selling methods meant the US market was not explored early by Penguin when it was in a perfect position to do so.

Pocket Books, created by Robert Fair deGraff, made the first big paperback move in the American paperback market. Noting how Penguin succeeded in the UK, and backed by Simon & Schuster, Pocket Books began selling its titles at 25 cents. The first copies, placed in department stores such as Macy's and Liggett's, sold out in 24 hours.

Meanwhile Lane still couldn't make up his mind. What did America want – high-brow titles or pulp novels? He wouldn't budge on his policy of no cover art. Fair deGraff, on the other hand, felt sure that to compete with pulp novels he had to decorate his books. Meanwhile, Allen Lane argued with the men he hired to advise him – Ian Ballantine, a 22-year old Columbia University and London School of Economics graduate, and Kurt Enoch, the founder of Albatross, who had already succeeded with a paperback imprint. Feuding inside Penguin US meant that Pocket Books was free to build on its initial success, cutting not only into pulp sales, but also affecting the revenues of mainstream US publishing.

The Second World War stimulated paperback sales on both sides of the Atlantic. Soldiers needed reading materials to fill in the lull between fighting. The US Council on Books in Wartime, created in 1942 from a group of trade book publishers, librarians and booksellers, set out to help the war effort, positioning books as 'idea-weapons'. Special low-cost paperbacks were sold to the Army and Navy at the cost of manufacture (six cents a copy) plus 10%. The books were made strictly for overseas distribution only, keeping them out of the US home market. Authors and publishers each received one-half of a cent per copy sold.

The book trade saw a huge paperback market suddenly opening up. Marshall Field bought Simon & Schuster and Pocket Books in 1944, and sought to buy another paperback house to cement his market plans. He chose Grosset & Dunlap, which effectively would give him a vertical monopoly – a first-print hardback, a hardback reprints and paperback reprints publisher under one roof. Seeing what Field was trying to do, Random House's Bennett Cerf blocked the purchase by organising a consortium of publishers — Little, Brown, Harpers, Scribners, World Book Encyclopedia, and Book-of-the-Month Club — to make Grosset & Dunlap a better offer. Each partner of the Random-led consortium agreed to invest $370,000, with Book-of-the-Month taking two shares at $740,000, offering Grosset & Dunlap more than $2.5 million. As Dunlap wanted out of the business, his partner Donald Grosset (who had earlier turned Fair deGraff down) accepted the consortium's proposal. Cerf then convinced Curtis Publishing Company to distribute the new paperbacks.

The new venture, Bantam Books, gave its new chief, Ian Ballantine, start-up capital of $1 million, with Curtis and Grosset & Dunlap each investing $500,000 and Ballantine adding another $100,000 of his own money (the breakdown of ownership of Bantam: Grosset & Dunlap and Curtis (42.5%), Ballantine (9%), Random House (3%)). Ballantine's Bantam bird logo acknowledged Kurt Enoch's Albatross (rather than Penguin) as the bird that led the way for all. In the meantime, Enoch, deciding he couldn't continue battling on alone with Lane without Ballantine, left Penguin US, buying out Lane's US office operation. Enoch formed The New American Library of World Literature (NAL). NAL initially produced paperback reprints of classics and scholarly books, together with pulp and hard-boiled detective fiction, later adding hardcovers to its list.

The US paperback market was expanding fast. Back in the UK, Lane kept up his own expansion plans as well, starting Penguin Classics and opening Penguin's first Australian office, in 1946. In 1949, the Canadian paperback publisher Harlequin was founded. At first in direct North American competition with Pocket Books, Harlequin produced westerns and mysteries, branching out in the 1960s to concentrate on romances. In 1952 Bennett Cerf removed Ian Ballantine as Bantam's chief. Ballantine and his wife formed Ballantine Books and went on to build a large science fiction list, publishing the works of authors such as Arthur C. Clarke.

In 1953, a young editor, Jason Epstein, convinced the management at Doubleday to let him start an up-market paperback imprint, Anchor Books, aiming the new paperback enterprise at college students and young professionals.

The paperback industry was now well established, perhaps too well established. With the post-war worldwide economic boom, many paperback imprints flooded the market and growth stalled. At the same time, paperbacks drew criticism from conservative forces for their 'racy content', but it wasn't long before the business bounced back from both setbacks. In the 1960s the market boomed again. University cafés were filled with arguing students armed with dog-eared paperback existential tracts and the novels of Camus, Sartre, Carlos Castenada, Hesse, and the 'beats', Kerouac and Ginsberg.[5] Paperbacks became essential fashion accessories, a subject for pop songs even. Like other 1960s *Zeitgeist* factors — folk, blues, rock and Pop Art — the paperback was an epitome of intellectual and cultural 'cool'. Paperback book sales exploded throughout the anglophone book world, the trade growing on average at 10% annually through to the early 1970s.

## 1965-NOW: CONGLOMERATE PUBLISHING

From the mid-1960s onwards book publishing began to leave its cottage industry status behind as book publishing firms began to be absorbed into multinational cross-media corporate empires. Motivated by publishing revenues and profits accumulated in the paperback boom, and the looming promise of a computer-led revolution in learning, corporations started the process of reconfiguring and dismembering old-style publishers.

Radio Corporation of America (RCA) set the ball rolling in the USA by buying the respected and successful trade publisher Random House for $40 million. IBM, ITT, Litton, Raytheon, Xerox, General Electric, GTE and CBS followed suit, acquiring other established publishing houses. The conglomerates began a race to own and control information and leisure book assets and markets. In the UK, famous names and imprints – Jonathan Cape, Chatto & Windus, The Bodley Head and Hutchinson – all changed hands. Many great brand names, such as Longman, eventually disappeared altogether.

Marketing and sales decisions began to replace editorial management as the main focus of the business. A lull in takeovers came in the mid to late 1970s, due to an economic downturn, but then a new phase of acquisitions started up all over again. In 1980, RCA sold Random House to the Newhouse magazine empire. CBS bought into publishing and then sold out again. Simon & Schuster bought the textbook publisher, Prentice Hall. In the UK Pearson, which merged with Longmans in 1968, bought Penguin in 1970. Other multinationals entered the fray. Australia's News Corporation bought Harper & Row in 1987, then Collins in 1989, forming HarperCollins in 1990. Holland's Elsevier merged with the UK's Reed. The German giant Holtzbrinck bought Macmillan. Time Warner, the world's largest media corporation, bought Little Brown and created Warner Books. Germany's Bertelsmann absorbed Bantam, Doubleday and Dell, becoming the biggest trade publisher in the United States when it bought Random House from Newhouse in 1998.

The conglomerates reshaped book publishing, shifting the focus from incremental backlist sales management to explosive frontlist sales promotion. The corporations decided to focus most of their efforts on bestselling star authors, promoting them heavily in periodical media outlets and on television (some of which they began to acquire). On the surface and on paper this almost seemed a sound approach. Fewer authors each selling larger numbers of books would cut costs substantially. The books business, however, did not always readily pan out as if it were selling supermarket products. When the new owners took a closer look at their acquisitions and their markets, they didn't seem quite as attractive. Initially attracted to the potential that book publishing offered integrated media investment, executives realised that early expectations for synergy-reformation of the entire model had been overly optimistic. The book industry could be rationalised but not changed completely. More books could be produced by fewer authors and midlist authors could be forced to disappear, but an ignored backlist was a poor use of an extremely valuable asset.

While the corporations sought to turn the book model into 'a global supermarket of books', books remained a discretionary purchase and as such were resistant to wholesale changes. Book buyers could be herded towards products with advertising and clever product placement in other media, but readers would not necessarily do what was expected of them.

In the 1983 edition of *The Media Monopoly*, Ben Bagdikian numbered 50 dominant companies. In 1987 that number was down to 29. In 1997, it had fallen to ten. In 2000 it was six. Finally, in 2004, five big media companies were left.[6] From the 1990s onwards, new international treaties and changes to national media regulations progressively dismantled most barriers to media conglomerate plans. Globalisation and diversification have left the media giants in charge of the book markets.[7] All the major media markets are now interdependent. Competition morphs into *co-opetition*,[8] in markets filled with synergies, collaborations and cross-overs.

Some corporations grew weary of books and sold out; others came into the industry to take their place. In the twenty-first century the book trade throughout all its sectors is now largely arranged in oligopolies – a handful of cross-media conglomerates sharing 50–80% control of all book markets in all sectors. There are also tens of thousands of small presses in existence, which provide an array of books, but the overall shift from the single dedicated book publishing firm to cross-media corporation ownership is now an accomplished fact.

The corporate consolidation of publishing is clearly the most significant event in recent times. Fifty years ago media markets were national and quite separate. Media markets are now conglomerate-led and global in scope. The decline of the dedicated, middle-sized publishing firm seems irreversible. Content now is synergised, re-used widely in diverse locations and contexts. For some observers this means less diversity of content owned by fewer entities. Another point of view maintains that the conglomerate-led globalisation of markets provides a more cost-efficient and effective industry, giving consumers what they want when they want it.

Compaine and Gomery argue that any threat presented by the corporate consolidation of publishing has been overstated, that ownership is fluid and ever-changing. Competition is open and fierce and will continue to be.[9] Robert McChesney takes the opposing view, stating that consolidation is a threat to democracy. He argues that large corporations' control of markets is based on political favours, stimulated by political donations; the control exerted by 'transnational giants' such as Time Warner, Disney, Bertelsmann, Sony, CBS-Viacom, Lagardère/Hachette, GE (NBC) and News Corporation ultimately distorts markets, to the detriment of product diversity and democracy.[10] Financial contributions in the United States by big companies to the political process between 1998 and 2004 were over $1 billion (56.2% for the Democrats, 43.2% or the Republicans).[11] While political contributions seem not (at least then) to be biased by ideology or party, money is clearly a stimulus towards favourable legislative treatment for the biggest donors.

The first decade of the twenty-first century in publishing has also been consumed by digital developments in content provision. The main preoccupation of the late twentieth century was *who would own book publishing?* The big concern of the twenty-first century is now *how will the book survive?*

## FURTHER READING

Compaine, B. M. and Gomery, D., *Who Owns the Media: Competition and Concentration in the Mass Media (Communication)*, Mahwah, NJ, Lawrence Erlbaum Associates, 2000

Feather, J., *A History of British Publishing*, 2nd edition, London, Routledge, 2006

Hesmondhalgh, D., *The Cultural Industries*, 2nd edition, Thousand Oaks, CA, Sage, 2007

Manguel, A., *A History of Reading*, London, HarperCollins, 1996

McChesney, R., *The Problem of the Media: US Communication Politics in the 21st Century*, New York, Monthly Review Press, 2004

Rice, Ronald E., Ed., *Media Ownership: Research and Regulation*, Cresskill, NJ, Hampton Press, 2008

Tebbel, J., *A History of Book Publishing in the United States*, 4 vols, New York, R. R. Bowker, 1972–1981

Thompson, J. B., *Books in the Digital Age*, Cambridge, Polity Press, 2005

## NOTES

1  John Feather, *A History of British Publishing*, London, Routledge, 2006, p. 16.

2  Queen Elizabeth I awarded a third printing charter to the University of Oxford University in 1586.

3  Briggs, A., *A History of Longmans and Their Books, 1724–1990: longevity* in *publishing*, London: Oak Knoll Press, 2008, p. 129.

4  Together with John-Holroyd-Reece and Max Weger.

5  Monteith, S., *American Culture in the 1960s*, Edinburgh, Edinburgh University Press, 2008.

6  Bagdikian, Ben H., *The Media Monopoly*, Boston, Beacon Press, 1983.

7  'The founding of the World Trade Organization (WTO) in 1995, and media privatization push by the IMF and other international regulatory bodies helped to denationalize the processes of media production and distribution.' Quote from Arsenault, A. H. and Castells, M., 'The Structure and Dynamics of Global Multi-Media Business Networks', *International Journal of Communication* 2, 2008, pp. 708–709.

8  '... [T]he business strategy of multi-media conglomerates as "American Keiretsu," an adaptation of the traditional Japanese practice of co-opting competition by creating structures of collaborations with rivals.' Quote from ibid., p. 722.

9  Compaine, B.M. and Gomery, D., *Who Owns the Media?: Concentration of Ownership in the Mass Communications Industry* (3rd revised ed). New York, Taylor & Francis, 2000.

10  McChesney, R., *The Problem of the Media: US Communication Politics in the Twenty-First Century*, New York, Monthly Review Press, 2004.

11  John Dunbar, Networks of Influence', in R. Rice, Ed., *Media Ownership*, Cresskill, NJ, Hampton Press, 2008.

# 2 THE PUBLISHING PROCESS

*publisher 1848.*

A *publisher* requires 'imagination, long-term planning, and a spirit of experimentation'[1] as well as patience and plenty of staying power. Reminiscing, the Boston-based David R. Godine posted on his own website: 'I recall that once, when I congratulated Roger Straus on his success with Bernard Malamud's *The Fixer*, he told me, coldly, "Yes, but it has taken me ten previous books that all lost money to get here".'[2]

A good description of a publisher's role is the 'director-general of the whole enterprise of publishing'.[3] Publishers develop *lists*, a collection of like or harmonious titles, of a similar style or category. Together, books in a list or lists make up a publishing company's profile. Publishers usually set out to demonstrate that they have good knowledge of the subject areas they publish on and in. Competence and knowledge of subject matter is expected and respected. A new publisher today could decide to create a list with an environmental focus and yet have no grounding or understanding of the subject. This will not be a problem if the publisher brings on board people who do know the area to help out. Publishers have always called upon and employed experts to guide and give opinions on works programmed for publication.

Publishers finance the publishing process, taking a risk in contracting and paying advances to writers. The publisher plans and oversees book pre-production and production processes, negotiating terms with writers and printers, creating and managing marketing and distribution plans. Medium to large-sized publishers will employ specialised staff to carry out many of these tasks, but in small houses a publisher will carry out all of these roles.

The publisher plays the central and fundamental, and sometimes not so delicate, gatekeeping role in the provision of entertainment and informational books. A publisher has the power of decision, with elements of open and hidden censorship built into the role. The publishing power to control the flow of ideas can be problematic, and not only for the more repressive, centrally-controlled political regimes. Publishers have a socio-political role in all societies as well as a business to build, run and make profitable.

In the twentieth century, Bennett Cerf (1898–1971) was hailed as a publisher who truly understood and loved the book business. He inhabited the role of publisher 'easily' as joint owner of Random House. Ben W. Huebsch (1876–1964), publisher of Viking Press, practised his belief that a writer's work was accepted in its entirety, without equivocation or quibbling, or heavy editing. Not surprisingly, perhaps, Huebsch won the respect, admiration and even love of Viking's writers.

Publishers have often been trailblazers. In the mid-1960s, on America's west coast, a husband and wife team, John and Barbara Martin, founded Black Sparrow Press. The couple set out to develop a 'non-commercial' publishing house. Over the years it grew to become extremely successful, both commercially and for its literary output.

## JOHN MARTIN & BLACK SPARROW PRESS

Once described by Jason Epstein as the envy of all American publishers[4] John Martin created Black Sparrow Press in 1966 in Los Angeles. Initially Martin ran a bootstrap operation on his $400 a week salary, working 80-hour weeks, 9am to 6pm, as an office supply executive, and 7pm to 1am on the press's work. Martin sold his rare collection of D. H. Lawrence first editions for $50,000 to the

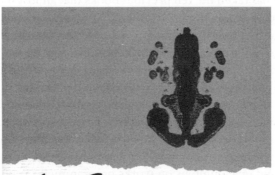

Black Sparrow Press cover image (with the kind permission of John Martin & David R. Godine Publishers, Boston)

University of California to fund the press. After taxes and fees he had $30,000 left to invest in Black Sparrow (equivalent to about $200,000 now). The seed capital kept the press active in the very early days.

Soon after starting the company, Martin attended a book party, where he met the dean of book reviewers on the west coast, *LA Times* critic, Robert Kirsch. Kirsch wished Martin luck and advised him not to publish Charles Bukowski. 'He's a cave man, disliked and feared.' Martin nodded, saying nothing of his plans. His first book of Bukowski's poems was already well underway.

Thirty copies of Charles Bukowski's poems *True Story* came out in April 1966. Martin priced copies at $10 and gave most of them away. 'I wasn't trying to sell those. They're worth a fortune now, like $2,000 or $3,000 apiece, and I would give them to my delivery boy at that office supply company or one of the secretaries.'[5]

Martin and his wife modelled the house on Black Sun, a 1920s boutique publisher, famous for its *art noveau* designs. As book designer, Barbara Martin mixed her own inks, overseeing the printing in LA of covers and colour title pages. Black Sparrow would print them and ship the pages to a printer in North Carolina who would do the rest. Martin decided on 6 × 9 inch paperbacks instead of the standard 5 × 8 inch. One distributor told him he couldn't do it because the bookstore racks were a different size. Martin replied: 'Then they'll have to buy new racks.'

From the outset Black Sparrow Press went its own way. Black Sparrow produced 16–20 page preview chapbooks of coming works, selling over 100,000 copies at 75 cents. By 1968 the press was producing 38 books annually, a rate of three a month. With the publication of *The Escaped Cock* by D. H. Lawrence in 1972, orders began to build up. Martin took on his first employee, a shipping clerk. Throughout nearly 40 years of operation, Black Sparrow Press, even at the height of its operations, had no more than a handful of employees.

From the outset, Black Sparrow's publishing focus was on America's literary outsiders. In 1969, Martin made his best publishing decision, offering Bukowski $100 a month to stop working and start writing full-time for him. Martin gambled that the poet could also produce novels. Bukowski's first novel *Post Office* was completed a little over a month after he gave up full-time postal work. By the mid-1980s more than a million copies of 15 of Bukowski's novels and books of poetry were in print in 12 languages. The writer's output accounted for 40% of Black Sparrow's $750,000 annual sales. Bukowski never forgot Martin's support, remaining fiercely loyal both to the publisher and press until his death in 1994. By 2002 Black Sparrow still had 40 Bukowski books in print, something almost no American writer could claim at any time.

Black Sparrow also cemented the careers of other now well-known writers, John Fante, Joyce Carol Oates and Paul Bowles, but it was Bukowski's novels set in East Hollywood that gave Martin's press its greatest success.

*(Continued)*

---

*(Continued)*

John Martin's publishing success story is as extraordinary as it is unique. He was the only American small publisher who dared dictate sales terms to the US book distributors, Barnes & Noble, Borders, Ingram Book Company and Baker & Taylor, telling them that his books were non-returnable. Distributors had to agree if they wanted his books. They agreed. Black Sparrow's books were that much in demand.

When John Martin retired in 2002, he handed over the rights to most of his stock (66,000 books) to the Boston publisher, David R. Godine. He also struck a deal with the HarperCollins imprint, Ecco, for 49 backlist titles by Bukowski, Fante and Bowles. Gingko Press bought the rights to titles by artist and writer Wyndham Lewis. Santa Rosa's Treehorn Books bought the rest of Black Sparrow's inventory.

Martin's advice to new publishers today: 'Find a market, keep it small and keep your day job.' Martin does not like everything he sees in today's world of publishing, but he is resolutely positive on Black Sparrow's legacy. 'The books are out there, and they'll always be there, circulating. … Whatever I've accomplished, there it is. Forever.'[6]

---

## THE VALUE CHAIN

Publishing houses manage a value chain of published information and entertainment literature, conducting operations in a linear way:

**Creation ▶ Production ▶ Distribution ▶ Retail**

A book publisher is the principal investor in the business of book production. This should not be confused with individuals and companies investing in publishing houses or buying up publishing company shares. The publisher invests in books, developing them by:

- paying writers to write books, or 'buying books' from writers
- paying for the design and production of books
- paying for the promotion and marketing of books
- allowing booksellers credit on books shipped out.

Inside the creation, production, distribution and retail process the staff of publishing houses carry out many functions and manage many processes. Among them are:

- acquisition or commissioning of content
- content development and pre-press management
- book design, typography and illustrations

- production cost analyses, estimates and budgeting, choice of paper, printing and binding
- development and management of promotion and marketing programmes
- bookselling and the management of product warehousing and distribution channels
- rights sales (foreign translations, sub-volume rights and special licensing, etc.).

Overall publishers develop and trade in two types of books, *frontlist* and *backlist* titles, with the entire business relying on three areas of activity:

- current publications, or frontlist
- past publications, or backlist
- ancillary or subsidiary rights sales.

Books released onto the market remain on the *frontlist* for 12 months when they then become part of the *backlist*. On average, trade or consumer sector backlist titles account for 80% of all sales. In the education sector they make up 50% or so of sales. To be on either the frontlist or backlist a book has to remain in print. The publishing rights of an out-of-print book return to the author, according to the terms defined by the author–publisher contract.

The *anglophone book publishing model* is made up of sectors – *trade/consumer books, reference titles, journals, academic and professional books, education, children's books* and *religious books*. Rooted in a cottage-industry tradition of preparation, production and delivery of books, book publishing has grown out of several crafts – writing, writing surface creation (papyrus, vellum and paper), printing and book binding – all of which together over time became the nucleus of today's industry.

Book publishing was the first publishing medium to emerge as a commercial enterprise. It is still based on 'unit sales'. There is no substantial reliance on advertising revenue. Even after the last 50 years of conglomerate takeovers, the cottage-industry framework endures in practical production terms. Even if the majority of leading publishing firms and imprints in all sectors now sit inside divisions of companies owned and run by international media conglomerates, the 'shop floor publishing' is still a cottage industry, operating a creation, production and sales production line. There is a clear, identifiable spine to the entire industry (Figure 2.1).

Books occupy first place in all media, both historically and in terms of cultural significance. Books are unique culturally and economically. Readers are prepared to spend disposable income on discretionary leisure book purchases in good and bad times. They invest in books for education, often in bad economic times. Few media purchases are as cheap as the cover price of a book. A book gives hours of reading pleasure and provides vital information. The sheer diversity of book production and creation outstrips all other media production. In 2009, a book was published on average every four minutes in the UK.

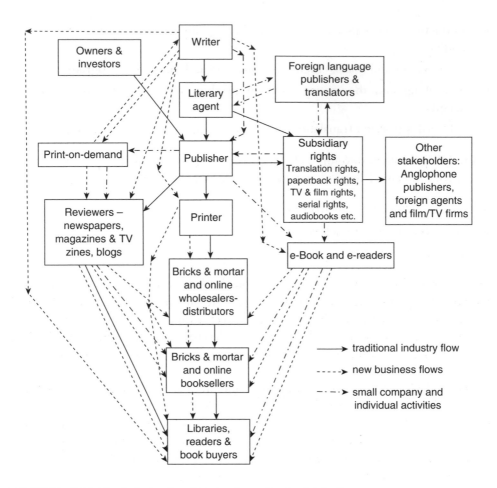

FIGURE 2.1  Publishing industry flowchart: book creation to distribution

In 2007 the UK publishing book, journal, magazine and newspaper market was estimated to be worth over £20 billion, with the three arms of print publishing employing around 175,000 people, representing 2% of gross domestic product (GDP) (see Figure 2.2).

In comparison to newspapers and magazines, overall UK book revenues have held their own well, growing 19.4% in the period 2001–2007, while newspapers and magazines grew revenue only by 9.9% and 9.8% respectively. This may seem surprising to many who perceive books as a dying medium, or at least to those who think that books are an old, fully matured market with no room left for growth. Books do very well against magazines and newspapers, which both earn advertising income, to which book markets have no access.

Publishers in the UK, the USA and China each release well over 100,000 titles annually (new titles and reprints). The UK, which is anglophone publishing's largest book exporter globally, grew export sales from £909 million in 2004 to £1,141 million

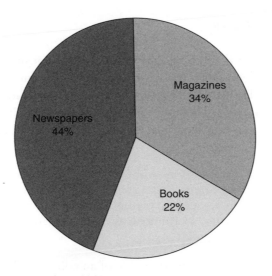

FIGURE 2.2   UK print media markets, 2007
*Source of figures*: UK Department of Media Culture and Sport

in 2008. Unit sales over the same period increased from 288 million to 357 million. The UK published more books than ever before in 2009, close to 133,000 titles, an increase of 3.2% on 2008. The previous UK output record was in 2003 with 130,000 titles; in the same year the United States published 175,000 titles. Book publishing may not break revenue records when compared to other industries such as telecommunications or pharmaceutical industries, but the book industry continues to be productive and innovative. Its overall process structure is simple:

**Writers ──────► Publishers ──────► Readers**

A writer seeks publication and/or a publisher is looking for a publishable text. To operate publishers need knowledge of the infrastructure of production, marketing and distribution in order to produce a saleable book and get it to markets of readers in the right manner at the best time. The broader step-by-step model takes in more players:

**Writer → Agent → Publisher → Printer → Distributor → Reviewer → Bookseller → Reader**

If a text is chosen, planned and commissioned by a publisher, the chain looks like this:

**Editor → Writer → Designer → Printer → Distributor → Reviewer → Bookseller → Reader**

Each book's path from writer to reader is unique and sometimes complex, taking in diverse kinds of publishing, printing, distributing and wholesaling, retailing and bookselling routes.

## THE EDITOR'S TASK

The editor's role is pivotal and is still the most respected position inside publishing. Early publishers needed a 'man-friday' to look after a manuscript, to shepherd it towards publication. The editor's role rapidly grew in importance.

What constitutes a good trade book editor? What does an editor actually do on an average day? Here is a description, from the not-so-distant past, of one editor's daily routine:

> I would busy myself, pleasantly enough, with various routines of a publishing editor's day – correcting proofs, editing a typescript, writing a blurb, puzzling over the small print in a contract, trying to make sense of an estimate or a computer print-out of sales, soothing an author's ruffled spirits, or indolently reading.[7]

This outdated description of the working life of an editor might still be relevant to a small or medium-sized publishing house, but is alien to today's corporate world where editors are expected to reach revenue targets.

Editors commission, acquire or choose a book for a house, be it an educational textbook, legal copy, a reference or trade title.[8] An editor guides an author's work through all the various levels of production, participating in a plan to promote, market and sell a published book. In a trend which began when the conglomerates started taking over large swathes of publishing, editors went from being book-guiders to dealmakers. In summary, an editor's responsibilities are:

- acquiring or commissioning publishable material
- rejecting submissions that don't meet the requirements of the list
- contracting writers
- preparing budgets, cost and profit and loss estimates
- keeping in touch with the progress of the author's work
- planning print runs and deciding on reprints of existing publications
- informing and conferring with production and design departments or professionals
- assessing subsidiary rights and how they can be exploited
- developing co-editions and making distribution plans
- planning release dates
- preparing pre-publication publicity and marketing plans  ·
- writing copy for catalogue, promotion and jacket copy
- preparing presentations for sales conferences

Editors must find publishable materials and authors for the house. Editors want their choices to be successful. They will therefore take as few risks on untried writers as possible, especially in difficult economic periods. In publicity-driven sectors such as trade or consumer books, this is even more pronounced, as a writer's profile is a crucial factor in sales.

Editors usually choose writers on recommendations, not guesswork. Editors might have first-hand knowledge of the writer, but if not, they will rely on expert advice or tips from trusted sources.

Overall, editors make judgements about books based on their understanding of markets – what books will sell. Once writers are chosen, editors need to develop and maintain a good relationship with them. One famous trade fiction editor in the early twentieth century was Maxwell Perkins. As a young editor for Scribner's, he discovered F. Scott Fitzgerald. He went on to work closely with Ernest Hemingway, Thomas Wolfe and many others, getting the best from writers and their work. Perkins knew how to befriend and nurture writers, displaying an uncanny ability for identifying what was good and bad in a text. Perkins understood *the hard part* of being an editor: 'You can learn all the technical stuff in six months; the rest takes a lifetime.'[9]

The publishing historian John Tebbel points out that in recent times actual text editing and author nurturing happen only rarely.[10] There are very few editors like Maxwell Perkins left. The editorial role has become more title management than text and author shepherding. Today, editors spend very little time with their authors, relative to their other duties and responsibilities. Whereas once the editor was the author's friend and confidant, that task is now undertaken by the literary agent. Once the writer and project are chosen, the editor expects the author to be professional and do the job of writing the text.

While few editors would ever admit to censorship, it occurs and for all sorts of reasons. The reasoning is sometimes personal. Experienced American editor Gerald Gross would not accept works that didn't accord with his beliefs. 'I am a devout and unconditional supporter of the First amendment. ... But I know I have to sleep at night and face my children without shame of guilt.'[11]

An important task for an editor is the promotion of the text for publication within the house, a role largely invisible to outsiders. Editors have to convince colleagues that a text or book proposal is worth the firm's investment and effort. In discovering F. Scott Fitzgerald, Maxwell Perkins had to mount a vigorous campaign within Scribner's to convince colleagues that his faith in the writer was justified. This task, particularly early on in a writer's career, can be difficult for an editor. Hollywood screenwriter William Goldman's phrase 'Nobody knows anything' haunts all cultural product decision-makers. There is usually a great deal of debate and discussion within a publishing house on *what to publish and when and how to publish*.

Editorial meetings are often lively occasions, where opinions on 'book pitches' are freely given and spirited defences are mounted for individual editorial choices. In sectors such as academic and other non-fiction publishing, *book proposals* written by authors are crucial for getting in-house acceptance of book ideas. Publishing committees want to hear how the title measures up to the competition. Participants in editorial meetings will want to know why a proposed title is needed now, why it is better than an existing title by another house, what the likely readership is and, most importantly, what kind of sales it is likely to generate.

Editors often seek books and authors that they can sell in a series. Once the market is created for a writer and his or her kind of book, subsequent similar titles will be easier to market. This applies to education, children's and academic sectors, but particularly in the consumer book market. Commercial fiction authors have long exploited the idea of the series, for example Elmore Leonard with his crime novels, John Grisham with the legal thriller, and J. K. Rowling with the Harry Potter series. Agatha Christie is probably the bestselling series author of all time with her murder mysteries. Penguin Books achieved something similar to a series effect by publishing diverse content under a single brand and uniform cover design format.

## THE PRODUCTION PROCESS

A common editorial lament is that meetings, paperwork and administration take up so much time that there is never enough time to find books to publish. Time management and project timeliness are of paramount importance. In big companies many projects compete for resources and staff time.

When the house agrees with an editor that the author and book idea is a good choice, the editor starts the editorial process. The editor will send a contract to the author. Terms are now fairly standard across the industry. Some author–publisher contracts are not standard of course, whereas others are very simple, a verbal agreement even, though this is very rare and generally unadvisable as an approach.

Once the author finishes writing and the text is accepted, the 'book' begins its production progress through the house. On average the whole process will take nine months. The text is sent out for reviews by experts, who comment on the accuracy and suitability of the content. The editor will discuss the findings with the writer and if revisions are necessary will ask the writer to implement changes. Tact is required when critiquing a manuscript and checking on facts and statistics to ensure the writer's accuracy. Editors in smaller houses often work very closely with the author, ensuring that the work is the best it can be. Editors need to make sure texts are prepared to the level of quality expected and delivered on time. Slippage – when projects fall behind schedule by more than three months – can have serious knock-on effects for more than one book in a publishing programme.

The text will then be sent to a copyeditor. Copyeditors are employed by publishers to correct textual errors, following the publisher's brief. Copyeditors will look for inconsistencies and errors in syntax, spelling, typography, style, grammar and sense. Beyond fiction – where a copyeditor, in most cases, has no business considering stylistic issues – good copyeditors will or should take care to respect the individual non-fiction style of the writer. Copyeditors may have been briefed to make texts consistent with an overall house style.

## ARCHITECTURE OF THE BOOK

Once the copyediting has been done, the publishing house and editor address the book as an *object*. A book usually conforms to certain predetermined house standards in content and design. There are messages and values a book has and projects to a reader. The design of a book (the textual structure of the book having been decided by the author in the first instance) is the task of the publishing house. While the extent (length) of the book is written into an author's contract, with book design there are pagination, fonts, illustrations, type of paper, binding, format and size all to decide. Once the design is complete and the text is set, a camera-ready copy (CRC) is prepared and sent to the printer. The printer produces galleys which will be finally proofed. At this stage a proofreader and the author check the galleys to see that the typesetter's work matches the copyedited manuscript. Then the text is printed and the book bound.

Publishing houses strive to produce distinctive designs that 'transmit' messages of the firm's brand, often trying to capture *Zeitgeist* moods and fashions of the time and era of publication. Great designs forge their own unique style. Book design and cover art are crucial elements. Covers, in particular, can sell books. This is especially true in the trade sector, although less so in the 'information sectors' where the 'pedigree of content' is often the major factor of a purchase. The ultimate success of a book will be due to a complex array of factors, but design plays a huge part, giving an exterior life to content, improving its marketability.

---

### THE BOOK DESIGNER

A book designer receives a brief and then plans the layout of the book's components (writing and images), including: typography, graphic design, illustration, photography, diagrams, tables and cartography (maps and charts). Some books are design-led, or at least are conceived or developed with book design elements uppermost in mind. Consulting with the editor — in larger firms, the art director — a book designer plans the format, size, typography and layout of the book. Designers decide how images will appear, collaborating with picture researchers, photographers and graphic artists, and overseeing the creation of the crucial cover art. The designer, in collaboration with editorial staff, decides how the book will be bound and what materials will be used. The designer oversees the whole proofing process and sends the final CRC file to the printer.

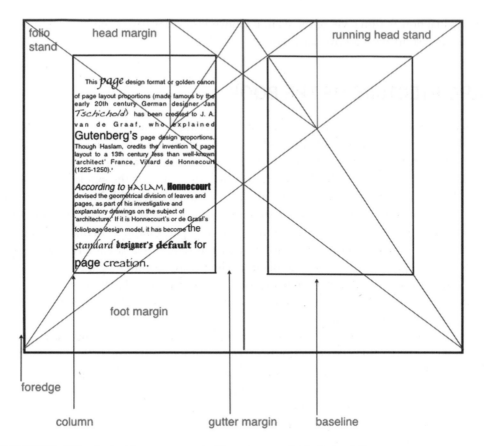

FIGURE 2.3   Villard's double-page spread with each page divided into ninths

From the earliest days of book production, book pages have been designed in grids and styles. Around 1230, a medieval French architectural designer, Villard de Honnecourt, invented the basis of today's book page design. Folding a parchment leaf in a particular way (see Figure 2.3), de Honnecourt created the golden cannon of text layout. Most western-styled print page aesthetics derive from this thirteenth-century template.

The pages of all books begin with a *recto* (the first right-side page inside the cover), followed by a *verso* (the left-side page) on the reverse of the recto, going recto verso thereafter. A book's main textual parts include:

- prelims or front matter: half-title page, full-title page, publication details, dedication, contents, list of graphs, figures, tables, maps or illustrations, preface, foreword, acknowledgements and introduction
- the text block: pagination, chapters, running heads, photos and illustrations, notes
- end matter: afterword, glossary, appendices, references, bibliography, index.

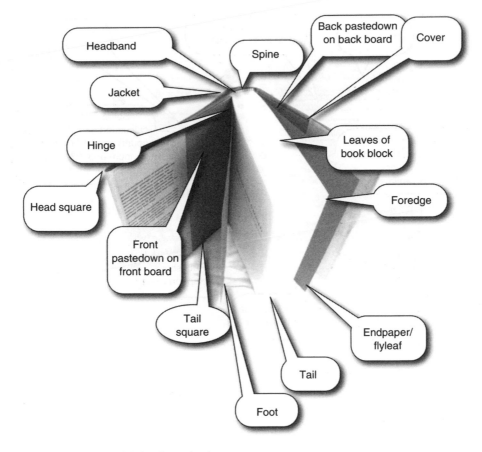

FIGURE 2.4  Terms used in book production

Production choices for an editor to ponder include the title, format, overall design, cover art, inside text block and images, and the back cover needs blurbs and endorsements (Figure 2.5).

# PRINTING, PAPER AND BOOKBINDING

## PRINTING

A printer manufactures a book according to a publisher's instructions and specifications regarding type, text layout, format size, paper, binding etc., carrying out this manufacturing task in return for payment. Printers take no risk on whether the work will sell or not. The only matter that should concern the printer is how best to print the book.[12] There are three publishing processes associated with printing:

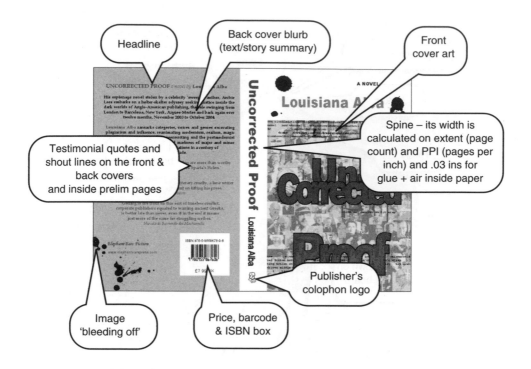

**Spine calculation example:**

312 pages ÷ 400 (ppi, pages per inch) = 0.78 + 0.03 = 0.81 inches

FIGURE 2.5   Cover art, design and copy

*Source:* Cover Image with the kind permission of ElephantEars Press ©

- Pre-press: when the content is formatted and the typography, illustrations and layout are decided.
- Press: when the content is printed (ink or toner stamped or deposited) on paper.
- Post-press: when printed sheets are cut, folded and bound into a chosen format.

## History

Printing evolved from the hand-worked wooden press to steam-driven metal presses. During the first 400 years of printing press history (1455–1885), the use of hand-composed letterpress was the dominant method. Letterpress was replaced by offset lithography[13] in the nineteenth century though letterpress techniques continued to be used.[14] Planographics, a technique invented in 1798, has evolved into today's offset lithography, with two kinds of lithographic printing methods – *sheetfed* presses using paper sheets and *web* presses printing on to large rolls of paper. With sheetfed printing, 25 feet by 38 feet sheets of paper run through the press up to

15,000 sheets per hour. Text is printed on both sides in a method called *perfecting*. Offset lithography prints more books at the lowest unit cost. Web presses can do 25,000 double-sided sheets per hour, producing over a million paperbacks in 24 hours. Newspapers, books and magazines are all printed this way.

## How it works

Pages in the form of physical artwork or digital files are transferred to a lithographic plate surface. The plates can be plastic, thin aluminium sheets, or specially coated paper. These are wrapped around the press's cylinder. Sheets of paper are fed across inked-up rubber mats.

There are now four standard kinds of printing methods: *relief*, where the ink sits on the raised surface plate or type; *planographic*, where the inks lies on a plate surface; *intaglio*, where the ink lies in grooves below the main plate surface; and *stencil*, where ink is pushed through a masking mesh. Offset lithography is the most cost-effective method. It is fast and produces a high-quality printing finish.

## Downside for editors

Offset lithography has a built-in inefficiency of process – it is virtually impossible to plan a print run according to actual market needs. Most experienced editors print short runs (fewer copies) rather than long runs (more copies). Under- and over-printing create problems. *Too many books is wasted investment; too few lose sales*.

The market share of litho offset printing is projected to decline steadily in the coming years as digital printings, currently a distant second in industry usage terms, improves and grows as a viable option. The main value of digital printing is that it allows a return to the manuscript model, of *sell and produce*, with books printed *on demand*, based on actual or near-to-actual needs rather than guesstimate projections of potential sales (see *Print on Demand* section in Chapter 8, p. 198).

## PAPER

Overall there are four kinds of paper to be chosen – *book stock* (coated or uncoated), *textured papers* and *newsprint*. Coated stock is paper with a shiny film on it; the ink soaks into the film, not to the paper stock itself, giving a very good printed text and photo-image result. Uncoated book paper comes generally in 50–60 pound weight (i.e. the US imperial weight measure for a roll of 500 sheets) of *white stock* (used for inside pages) and up to 80–100 pound stock for dust jackets.

Several factors have to be considered when choosing paper – texture, colour/shade, opacity and bulking factor (i.e. fibre content, not its weight, calculated in pages per inch or ppi). The grade of a paper refers to its type. Acid-free stock is

TABLE 2.1  Paper stock used for books

| Weight of offset white stock in lbs | Inches (thickness) | Millimetres | Weight in grams |
| --- | --- | --- | --- |
| 50 | 0.0038 | 0.097 | 75.2 |
| 60 | 0.0048 | 0.12 | 90.3 |
| 70 | 0.0058 | 0.147 | 105.35 |
| 73 | 0.0060 | 0.152 | 109.11 |
| 81 | 0.0061 | 0.155 | 116.63 |
| 90 | 0.0062 | 0.157 | 131.68 |
| 90 | 0.0068 | 0.173 | 135.45 |
| 100 | 0.0072 | 0.183 | 146.73 |
| 100 | 0.0073 | 0.185 | 150.5 |
| 110 | 0.0074 | 0.188 | 161.78 |
| 110 | 0.0076 | 0.193 | 165.55 |
| 120 | 0.0078 | 0.198 | 176.83 |

now more popular as the paper lasts longer, and recycled paper is also being used more widely. Grain in paper stock runs in one of two directions, like (but not because of) the wood it comes from. For covers it is better to have a grain parallel to the spine, though whether parallel or perpendicular, some problems can arise, such as tiny tears folding around the spine with the former and popping up with the latter.

## History

The word 'paper' derives from the papyrus reed used in the 5,000 year-old Egyptian papyrus scrolls. Paper production dates back to 200 BC in China (in some accounts, to 100 AD), when a Chinese Court official first made paper from a combination of bark and cloth.[15] The technique spread to Asia Minor in the eighth century and then to Europe.

The first European paper mills began operation in the thirteenth century. Eventually a lack of linen cloth led to experimentation with various materials, including straw, hemp, rattan and, finally, wood. In the nineteenth century softwood pulp became the preferred paper-making material. A mechanical method for pulping of wood for paper production developed in Germany in the 1840s. From the mid-nineteenth century onwards the cost of paper fell by half, leading to lower book production costs. Industrial developments led to the creation of the sulfate or 'kraft process' in 1879 in Sweden and, together with the invention of the recovery boiler in the 1930s, allowed for the recycling of chemicals used in papermaking. By the 1940s the kraft process became the dominant method.

## Acid in paper

The natural acidity in wood fibres leads to paper deterioration over time. A quarter of the 300 million books in academic libraries in the USA are currently at risk of being lost. Paper can be conservation grade, acid-free paper made from wood pulp, or it can be archival or museum grade 'rag paper' made from cotton pulp. Paper problems arise with insect infestation. Among the pests that feed off books are cockroaches, silverfish and beetles, which are attracted to the protein and starch components in book papers.

Paper products are sourced, in part at least, from endangered forests in South America (Chile), Tasmania (Australia) and Indonesia. The Book Industry Study Group (BISG) reports that 30 million trees are cut down in the USA annually to produce books, with books consuming 1.5 million metric tonnes of paper each year. The use of paper in books, though, is at the low end of timber consumption, and the American Forest and Paper Association calculates that printing and writing papers make up only about a third of the total paper market. Paper use in books accounts for less than 1% of all timber harvests.

Most publishers recognise the need to 'get environmental' on paper, but currently recycled paper fibres are too short, weak, insufficiently bulky or sturdy, and too dull in colour to be used for large-scale book production. While fully recycled paper use in books is a long way from being achieved, an environmentally sound, sustainable, renewable, recyclable paper production for books is a growing option.

Growing paper needs have produced a major paper waste recycling industry. Fifty per cent of publishers now have policies to use recycled paper. In 2006, Random House announced that it would raise the amount of recycled paper in its book production from 3% in 2006 to 30% by 2010. Simon & Schuster aims to lift recycled fibre use to 25% by 2012. Scholastic, the world's largest children's books publisher and distributor, has a five-year goal to lift its purchase of FSC-certified (Forest Stewardship Council) book paper to 30%, and to raise the use of recycled paper to 25%. By 2012 Hachette hopes to have 30% of its paper come from recycled sources. In the UK, Bloomsbury and Egmont also announced plans for the greater use of recycled paper and FSC-certified paper.

## BOOKBINDING

There are two main book products — hardbacks and softcovers. The production emphasis is now on the latter with its glued covers, called *perfect binding*. A case and sewn binding of books is still popular with readers who want a quality hardcover product, though the commercial development of paperback binding has forced a continuing decline in hardcover production.

### History

Bookbinding methods were invented in Greece and were further developed in the first century AD by Coptic Christians in Egypt. Leaves of a book were sewn together and then bound into a protective case or cover. Originally this was done by hand using parchment leaves. In 1868, David McConnell Smyth developed a sewing machine for binding books and then other machines for gluing, trimming and case-making. With hardbacks, the text block was stitched to the edges of the spine (the hinge end of a book with a rigid cover). The text block, collected in a number of machine-folded, printed sheets called signatures (gatherings or signatures comprise eight, 16 or 32 pages) was hand-sewn together with cotton thread. When the hardback is opened in the middle of a signature, the binding threads are visible. Three traditional book sizes were inherited from the hand press era (pre-nineteenth century):

- folio (largest – two leaves, four pages)
- quarto (smaller – four leaves, eight pages)
- octavo (smallest – eight leaves, 16 pages).

Signatures in hardcover books are usually octavo (8vo or 8°). A single page is printed in such an order that when the page is folded three times it produces eight leaves or 16 pages. The signatures are then sewn together into a complete text block and clamped together. When glued to the outer covers, the spine is left free, so the book opens and lays flat easily.

### Techniques today

Page and book format size today depends on two measuring standards: metric (in millimetres in the UK and most parts of the world) or imperial (inches) in the USA. The international metric standard is ISO 216, based on a standard A4 sheet size (210mm × 297mm). A5 is half of A4. Most printers trim sizes and so do not stick strictly to standard paper sizes.

Clothette, or textured paper resembling cloth, is now used widely for hardcovers, replacing actual cloth or the leather-bound book using calf skin. *Perfect bound paperbacks*, invented at the beginning of the twentieth century, became popular in the 1930s. DuPont developed a hot-melt adhesive binding process in the 1940s, making paperback bookbinding more durable.

One of the enduring myths in the hardcover/softcover debate is that hardcovers cost so much more than softcovers to produce and therefore must sell at much higher prices. Hardcovers do not cost much more to produce than softcovers. What makes hardcovers genuinely more expensive to produce are the shorter print runs, resulting in higher unit costs.

# BUDGETING A BOOK

An editor prepares a cost analysis and a production schedule, considering book and cover design, copyediting, typesetting, print, paper and binding, and proofing costs. Editors calculate costs based on the contracted book extent or length and an understanding of the content and then decide a retail price.

TABLE 2.2   Projected profit and loss statement for a hardcover (educational title)

| Print run | 5,000 copies | |
|---|---|---|
| Gross sales | 4,500 copies | 500 promotional frees |
| Returns | 900 copies | Av. 20% return rate |
| Net sales | 3,600 copies | |
| RRP | £16 | RRP – recommended retail price |
| Av. discount | 40% | Publisher nets £9.60 a copy |
| PPB | £7,500 | Print paper binding – £1.50 @ 5,000 copies |
| Prep. costs | £4,000 | Origination costs – designer, copyediting fees, etc. |
| Direct marketing | £5,000 | nominal £1 per copy for this example |
| Royalty | £7,200 | 10% or RRP |
| Subsidiary rights | £3,500 | Book club rights £2,000 (50/50% split with author), First serial rights £500 (Author 90/Publisher 10%) Second serial rights £1,000 (50/50% split with author) |

## PRICING A BOOK

Markets are often said to be price sensitive before anything else, so the price is a major decision for an editor to get right. There is often in-house debate over price. If a book is regarded as overpriced, sales will be lost. If it is thought by consumers to be underpriced, the book's quality might be doubted, also affecting sales. How book buyers respond to price is complex, and much depends on the sector, product, brand, author and 'book season' when the title is released. Book prices are generally worked out on two main factors: production costs and the market. By rule of thumb, book prices are usually set at seven to eight times costs. If a book costs $2 or £1 a copy to produce, then on this basis the rule-of-thumb book price could be $14.95 in the USA and £7.99 in the UK. But if the competition is selling a similar title at $13.95, an editor may choose to drop the price to compete head to head.

### PRICE, SUPPLY AND DEMAND

In a free market characterised by perfect competition, suppliers and consumers will share the same perfect information. Both will seek to maximise their 'utility' (satisfaction of needs and wants). Where demand and supply intersect (the quantity supplied of a product equaling its demand) the price achieves its 'equilibrium price', shown in Figure 2.6 at £22 (a nominal figure for this example only).

*(Continued)*

*(Continued)*

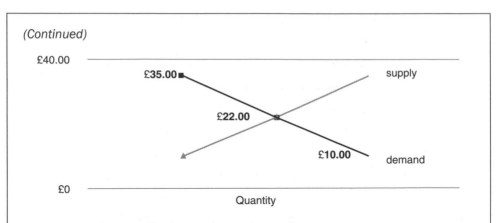

FIGURE 2.6   Behaviour of book prices in a perfect market

A change in circumstances (for example, greater consumer income) may shift the demand or the supply, quantity and prices. The demand heads downward because of the assumption of the 'law of diminishing marginal utility'. Utility increases with scarcity and diminishes with increases in the quantity of the product consumed. Price will reflect this 'law': *if the price is high, the consumer will be ready to pay only for 'high priority uses'* – those with high marginal utility. If the price diminishes, *the 'rational', 'utility-maximising' consumer will buy more*. Economic theory has moved on from Adam Smith's 'invisible hand' or self-regulating perfect competition markets. Consumer behaviour is not only dependent on 'maximising utility'. Needs are manufactured and choices are influenced by cultural and social factors. Suppliers, competitive strategies and government interventions etc., all influence the market and price (sometimes working to manufacture scarcity), and prices can become tools for market control.

Publishers set book prices, but with no expectation that these prices will be met by consumers in most circumstances. Bookselling is run on discounts. Discounts are both a book market mechanism as well as a psychological factor influencing buyer behaviour. Book consumers like 'a good deal'. Booksellers try to give them one. Publishers know that they have to participate in this market psychology, and so agree to discounts.

Book pricing operates in what economists call an imperfect market. Full information is not available to any party. In practical terms, the editor must make a judgement. A pricing decision should meet the expectations of the market mechanism while covering production, marketing, distribution, overhead and author royalty costs, i.e. all costs to the publisher. The price is set at what the market is ready to pay, which can be above, equal to, or below costs. Publishers can decide to set a price to make a profit, or use it as a strategic competition tool to forfeit profit and gain market share.

TABLE 2.3  Actual profit and loss statement for the educational title

| Book returns | £11,520 | 1200 × £9.60 |
|---|---|---|
| **Net sales** | **£20,160** | |
| Origination costs | £4,000 | |
| Print paper binding | £7,500 | |
| Royalty | £3,168 | 3,300 copies @ £9.60 × 10% |
| **Total costs** | **£14,668** | |
| Gross margin | £5,492 | Net sales *less* Production costs (17.3% gross margin) |
| Other income | £3,950 | Higher than 'projections' due to better than expected foreign translation sales + other rights sales income |
| Inventory write-off | £800 | |
| **Revised gross margin** | **£8,642** | Gross margin *plus* 'other income' *less* inventory write-off |
| Direct marketing costs | £5,000 | |
| Overhead | £1,500 | |
| **Net profit** | **£2,142** | Gross margin *less* Direct marketing *less* Overhead (10.6% net margin) |

Sales from the first printing of a title may only contribute in a modest way to the overall balance sheet of a firm. But at this stage, if a title makes a profit, it can be recorded as a success. Origination costs are now amortised – i.e., preparation costs are paid for. The market life of a commercial novel may well be over at this stage, but if the title is an educational, academic or reference book, there should be years of saleability left in backlist reprints and new editions. Unit costs fall to less than a third per unit with reprints because the printer has prepared the litho mats and will only have plant and materials to cost in for the print run.

## PLANNING PRINT RUNS

Media and publishing analyst Paul Hilts once asked the big trade publishers of fiction, how they calculated an initial print run. The best reply he received 'approximated a dart against the wall because they don't know'.[16]

In the high-octane consumer books sector, the three main sales periods are spring, autumn and the Christmas rush. Based on knowledge of the marketplace and sales statistics, editors decide how many copies of a book are needed. This method of deciding a print run is known as *just-in-case* printing, often planned on a hunch. It is an attractive option to print long (a large number of copies) in order to reduce unit costs, but this can present a problem if the sales are substantially lower than the number of copies printed. Copies shipped to booksellers will be returned to the publisher's warehouse to be remaindered or pulped.[17] Many book titles can sell over time as part of a backlist but warehousing of books is costly. Therefore the cardinal rule is never to over-print. Yet under-printing can also be problematic. Underestimating a print run of a bestseller, for instance, can leave bookshops without copies just when customers want to buy them. Consumer books are regarded by economists as a discretionary purchase, therefore sales are often lost through under-printing. Not able to get the book they want at first try, shoppers move on to spend their discretionary-purchase pounds and dollars on something else altogether.

Another method is *just-in-time* printing – books printed as and when needed to serve a specific, usually small, demand. Print-on-demand digital printing (POD) answers over- and under-printing problems created by the just-in-case printing model. With POD publishers have the option of printing when an order is placed. Book buyers can wait in the bookstore while a POD machine prints and binds the book they wish to buy.

However, just-in-time POD printing is significantly higher in unit costs. Short print runs do save publishers money, but when POD print runs rise above 400 copies the just-in-time method increasingly loses its cost-effectiveness. At 1,000 copies just-in-case printing, using traditional offset litho methods and presses, over-takes just-in-time as the best option in every way.

In terms of quality, just-in-case printing by the large photo-lithographic printing presses and binding operations still produces a far better product more reliably than POD machines, though the quality gap between the two methods is narrowing fast. Cost-ratios will undoubtedly also continue to improve for just-in-time print-on-demand solutions. Currently, major publishers only use just-in-time POD for promotional purposes, small special orders, 'boutique' publishing and uncorrected proofs.

## AUTHOR–HOUSE RELATIONS

While spending time in a well-known publishing house in London, I mentioned to a senior editor that I had read 20 books by an American crime writer the house brought out in the UK. With a look of deliberate sympathy, he said 'So you are one of them'. He proceeded to tell me of an occasion when the very same author had come to dinner at his house. 'He sat there and recounted the entire plot of his coming novel. My wife told me never to invite *that man* back again.' Writers can have complicated relations with editors.

Former editor Diana Athill, in her memoir *Stet*, abandoned her usual phlegm when describing the departure of V. S. Naipaul from the publishing house where she once worked.[18] Naipaul, it seemed, was what is known in the trade as a high-maintenance writer, at least for Athill. Her attitude on seeing him go was relief. From what has been written on this particular author–editor relationship, Athill was called upon to help the writer more than once through post-publication depression, but she must have paused when he later won the Nobel Prize.

In *Books: The Culture and Commerce of Publishing*, authors Coser, Kadushin and Powell recount the story of a young academic writer in the music field who had a very good personal and professional relationship with an editor in a publishing house. Both women respected each other and the editor readily accepted the writer's manuscript when it was offered to her. A book contract was signed. The editor gave detailed professional advice and spent quality time on the writer's work. Extremely grateful, the writer accepted the suggestions for improving the manuscript. As good as it could get, the manuscript was sent to the production department. A production editor overseeing many projects sent the manuscript out for review and copyediting to someone who, it was later discovered, claimed greater expertise than he really had. The manuscript was returned filled with error markings and gratuitous comments. Seeing the manuscript, the author went in desperation to see the original editor, but by this time the acquisitions editor had moved on to other projects. The editor promised to look into the matter. The production editor, resenting interference from the editorial department, backed his freelance reviewer and copyeditor. The young writer tried to make the necessary suggested revisions, but in the end couldn't do it, and went close to a breakdown. Luckily for her, the case was brought to the attention of the company's chief executive, who sided with the author. A new copyeditor was assigned to the task and asked for minimal changes.

The most senior manager of the house had to resolve the crisis, in the same way, as Coser et al. put it, that a Chinese autocratic ruler managed conflict in his kingdom. The regular house procedures had failed. Conflict between an author and the house at the middle management level will be damaging to the author and the work being prepared for publication.[19] But authors aren't the only victims. Editors can get rough treatment from authors as well.

Unhappy with the sales of his last book, *The Lay of the Land*, which sold less than 100,000 copies, Richard Ford, the renowned American novelist, left his editor and friend, Gary Fisketjohn at Random House's imprint Knopf, for another house, Ecco (HarperCollins). Trouble had begun when Knopf's head, Sonny Mehta, felt $750,000 was the upper limit for an advance for a Ford novel. Ecco offered Ford's agent $3 million for three books and Ford left Random House and Fisketjohn. Upset by this treatment after giving so many years of his friendship and support to the author, Fisketjohn refused to return the phone messages Ford left explaining the move. It was said that Ford had simply grown tired of Fisketjohn's editing. Ford summed up the shift this way: "'Gary has to learn he's no longer in high school." It was business, after all.'[20] For his part, Fisketjohn left the fault at the agent's door: 'I think agents often like for there to be problems, because they can be the stalwart support behind a writer.'[21]

In the same period, Cormac McCarthy also left Fisketjohn, though he didn't leave Knopf, asking Sonny Mehta to edit him instead. Mehta knew these sorts of problems well. When in 1999, Andrew Wylie, the literary agent of Mehta's close friend and one-time Knopf author, Salman Rushdie, wanted more money for Rushdie's new book, *The Ground Beneath Her Feet*, Mehta baulked at giving more than he felt he could. Holt offered $2 million and the author left Knopf. It wasn't a good move for Rushdie. The book failed and some say his career never quite recovered. Rushdie returned to Random House, though not to Knopf. Instead this time he was published under the

Little Random imprint. Matters seem to have resolved themselves fairly amicably because it was his old friend, Sonny Mehta, in 2008, who took on the role of announcing Random's publication of Rushdie last book, *The Enchantress of Florence*.

# AGENTS

An agent exists to help writers handle the business side of writing. Competent agents will help writers find the best career path and commercial arrangement for their work. The function of agents is to *sell* their clients' work to publishers. For managing the careers of writers, agents receive a percentage of all returns, usually between 10 and 20%. At times agents also provide editorial help to writers.

Outside the trade sector, most writers do not use agents. Academic, educational, journal, professional and reference writers may not even have met, let alone thought of employing, agents. Writers' associations and guilds can fulfil the agent's role for these sorts of writers, giving legal and other professional advice on various matters.

Agent placement of books involves locating the best publishing house or *home* for their writers' particular kind of writing, then making an agreement on the best terms possible. An agent also markets every associated subsidiary commercial right available outside the terms of the author–publisher contract.

An agent, in almost all cases, will know the trade far better than an author ever could, knowing where the best opportunities are for writers and their work. A good agent will know *who wants what* and, crucially, *when*. Good agents usually have specialised knowledge in certain areas of publishing, for instance a keen under-standing of particular fiction genre publishers and markets. Agents are able to assess the suitability of a work for a certain publisher as well its marketability, only passing on books and book ideas to publishers that have a reasonable expectation of success. They wouldn't stay in business long if that were not true.

Of course, agents, like the writers they represent, are not always perfect at their job. An editor at a major publishing house explained the value of agents this way: 'You have a list of agents, if some send you material you read it overnight, others in a couple of days. Others, you can wait a week, and for some on the list even longer than that. Some you have learned whatever they say to take it with a large pinch of salt.' In other words, there is a hierarchy of agents. As agents know their publishers, publishers also know their agents.

An agent needs a cool business head but also to be able to demonstrate enthusi-asm for an author's works. At a conference I once attended, New York agent Donald Maass put it like this: 'You can call an editor and say – are you looking for some-thing to fill your mystery list? Or you can say: hey, you *really* have to read this.'[22] Coser et al., reported one agent's description of the qualities all agents must have:

> One has to be very tough because the agent is caught in the middle. The agent is always wrong. The publisher says we push for too much money. The writers say we don't get them good enough deals ... so you have to be very thick-skinned.[23]

Agents need to know *how* to handle authors and publishers. By carrying out negotiations with publishers in a rational, even detached, manner agents provide a major service for writers.

## AUCTIONS

Agents spread the word on an author's work and if there is competition for it, this can lead to an auction. This kind of negotiation requires experience and skill to handle well.

If an auction is necessary and a good idea, initially an agent will contact editors at several publishing houses, explaining how the auction will work. Usually, auctions work on a *rolling* or *best bid*. When the first round of bids are received, the lowest bidder upwards is given the chance to improve the offer. This process continues until bidders drop out and the highest bidder is left. Another way is for each editor to be given a chance to offer their *best bid* without knowing what other editors or houses are bidding. This is a faster way of arriving at a buyer. In most cases it is made clear that the author has the right to accept the best overall terms, not necessarily the best bid.

On occasion, a publisher will make a pre-emptive bid (a *pre-empt*), with the offer open for one or two days and then retracted if not accepted. A pre-empt puts pressure on the agent and author to accept a deal quickly, and may even involve more rights than is usually negotiated away in any deal. It is therefore a matter of seasoned judgement for the agent to advise an author to accept or not accept. Sometimes a quick deal offering good money may be the best deal. An auction can be high-powered and high-risk, or it can be more informal and relaxed, depending on the competition and number of publishers who are interested.

Agents need to be honest with publishers. Without trust, relations, between publishers and agents will break down. Agents set up an auction to sell a title phoning several publishers, sometimes including more than one division within a single publishing house. As the auction proceeds, it is quite possible the two divisions of a single company are left bidding against each other. At that point the agent is honour-bound to inform the parties how the bidding process has developed. If it became known that an auction price was pushed up by two bidders from inside one house (one not knowing what the other was doing), the agent would lose credibility.[24]

Agents have their supporters and denigrators. Some publishers think agents just cost everyone money. Raymond Chandler has been quoted as saying agents are the 'ten per cent men'. What he actually said was:

> The agent never receipts his bill, puts his hat on and bows himself out. He stays around forever, not only for as long as you can write anything that anyone will buy, but as long as anyone will buy any portion of any right to anything that you ever did write. He just takes ten per cent of your life.[25]

Negotiations between agents, authors and publishers can go awry, even after contracts are signed. One area for potential disagreement is the book's cover. Some publishers don't like to consult with agents or authors over the market-crucial cover art. Publishers usually have control over this aspect, but contracts can have clauses over 'cover art consultation'. What this means in practice, though, can lead to a breakdown in relations between parties.

Another less publicised side of the agent's role is as the first 'line of defence' for the publishing industry, particularly in consumer book publishing. By saying yes or no to writers seeking representation, agents carry out the function most publishing houses once used to do.

Selection of new writers these days is a defensive posture. Maintenance of scarcity is in the interests of all tiers of the book trade. The risk that a rejected book will go on somewhere else and become a major bestseller is a risk that can often be readily taken because its occurrence is so rare. There are just too many writers and too much writing to assess, and editors simply don't want, or haven't the time, to ponder all day over difficult choices. Why bother when the agent is there to do this work? However, some rejected books have proven to be the book or author to crack open a market.

---

## JAY GARON

A Hollywood and Broadway actor before he decided to become a literary agent, Jay Garon first opened his agency in the 1950s. Thirty years on, he came late to 'agent fame and success' by first spotting the market value of the inventor of the legal thriller, John Grisham. Seeing pages of the writer's first novel, *A Time To Kill*, in 1987, Garon signed up the Mississippi solicitor. Garon hawked the manuscript around New York on foot. Fifteen houses turned Garon down before he convinced a small publishing house, Wynwood Press, to publish Grisham. Two years later in 1989, Grisham's first novel was published (5,000 copies), with the author purchasing 1,000 copies himself, selling them from the back of his car on weekends.

The novel only made it on to the bestseller list when Doubleday took on a later work, *The Firm*. By chance more than anything, it seems, *The Firm* was caught up in a Hollywood auction bidding war. Paramount bought the film rights for $600,000. And as the wisdom goes in Hollywood, when you spend good money on a literary property you had better make even better money with it. *The Firm* became a high-profile Hollywood film with major stars, and Garon went on to negotiate multimillion-dollar publishing and film contracts for a string of Grisham's legal thrillers. *The Client* and *The Pelican Brief* became big commercial films. Grisham's success made Garon into a 30-year overnight success. A good part of Garon's 'midas touch' was due to his pursuit of movie and book deals simultaneously.

Garon died suddenly in 1995 and the Garon–Grisham story would have ended there, if Grisham had not a year later complained over some accounting procedures. According to Grisham, Garon's company moved money from films of his books in through the back door without telling Grisham. The writer sought damages and the termination of his contract. The agency argued that Grisham was only a success because Garon took him on. The agency's lawyer, Robert N. Chan, claimed 'the so-called funneled money' represented legitimate 'fees' paid to the agency by producers, and that Grisham was fully informed on them. Michael Rudin, for Grisham, denied this: 'The payments most definitely were not disclosed to him.'[26] Whether all this added up to a lurid plot in 'agent-land' or not, nothing can wipe away the fact that it was Jay Garon who initially showed faith in the writer, leaving for posterity an image of himself as 'the man who found the man who found the legal thriller'.

# WRITERS

The writer is often at the bottom of the whole publishing process, while paradoxically being perhaps the most important participant. Some publishers see writers as trouble, and no doubt many are and have been. The truth is that publishers and writers need each other, only not always in equal measure. A good though not perfect comparison for the sometimes complicated writer–publisher relationship is the player–manager relationship in football. As with the football manager, the publisher usually calls the shots.

Writers come in many different forms. Some write fiction 'on spec' for the love of or 'calling' of the process of creative writing, and others are contracted – 'pens for hire'. Some writers – or authors, as publishers prefer to call them – are very successful commercially, others are virtually anonymous. Some win prizes, travel widely, go on TV, own houses in several countries, others have trouble finding the money for a bus fare. Some brilliant writers publish almost nothing in their lifetimes. Others publish everything they have written, even the dross in their bottom drawers. Some find success and then shun the publishing process. Others never find success and crave it all their lives. Writers come in all types, personalities and styles.

In general, publishers use the term '*author*' rather than writer because an author is the writer of a published work that a publisher finances and produces. The differences in the terms 'author' and 'writer' are practical and subtle. An author is someone a publisher chooses, produces, promotes and sells, while a writer is someone who practises the craft of writing. Market successful authors probably couldn't care less about the distinction.

Writers write and prepare texts for legal publishing updates, children's textbooks, cookbooks, biographies, journal and newspaper articles, academic studies and arguments, scientific research, fiction and so on. The list of subjects and approaches to writing is almost as endless as human thought and endeavour. In areas such as education and academic publishing, publishers like to select and develop their writers. In consumer publishing, they are often 'discovered'.

There are broadly two categories of writer: writers who write for themselves, for the art, or for self-expression or the expression of an idea, memory, argument or narrative of some sort, and writers who write on contract, for hire. The categories are not mutually exclusive but often are. Writers who write for themselves and seek publication can have a hard time finding a publisher. Publishers oversee a buyer's market. There are generally many more writers seeking publication than publishers seeking writers – though in some specialised areas of knowledge, this may not be true.

In trade publishing the odds are stacked against writers being selected by publishers without some form of help, be it from a literary agent, an introduction, a literary prize, or some unexpected and unusual contact with a publisher. Social scientists Coser et al. had this advice for writers trying to get acceptance by editors:

> If the reader who is unfamiliar with publishing takes but one message away from this book, it should be that formal channels of manuscript submission are the very last resort of would-be authors. To get a book published, recommendation through an informal circle or network is close to an absolute necessity.[27]

Being 'found from nowhere' is not unheard of, though there are only relatively a select few, if notable, examples of it happening. The author of *Ordinary People*, Judith Guest, a 'mom from Minnesota', was plucked from a slush pile in 1975.[28] Guest's novel became a bestseller and went on to become an Oscar-winning film directed by Robert Redford. Prior to the slushpile find, one publisher, in refusing the manuscript, wrote back to Guest saying the writing did not hold enough interest. Some publishers undo themselves in that expression of power – the rejection.

Stephenie Meyer, the current teenage fiction phenomenon, received many rejection letters, the final one arriving after her literary agent had just completed negotiations on a three-book deal. Her road to publication involved that crucial element of career luck that some writers experience. In 2003 she wrote to the Writers House Agency offering her 130,000-word novel on teenage vampires. An assistant reading Meyer's letter – one of the hundred or so the agency received every month – and not realising that young adult fiction was expected to be in the 40,000–60,000 word range, asked the writer to send in her manuscript. Passed on to agent Jodi Reamer, *Twilight* found approval and was eventually sold to Little Brown. In 2008, Meyer's *Breaking Dawn* sold 1.3 million copies on the day it was released. The latest film from her fiction grossed over $288 million at the box office in the USA.

Fiction can be very lucrative for the successful writer. It can be a fruitless endeavour commercially for many others, that is, if publishing books and being paid for the writing effort is the only objective of writers, which clearly it isn't, no matter what

Dr Samuel Johnson said about only blockheads writing for anything other than money. Johnson's blockheads include the fabulously unsuccessful Franz Kafka, who is now, many years after his death, still considered one of the select few of truly influential writers from the twentieth century.

The playing field of anglophone consumer book publishing is a roughhouse for most aspiring writers. Many literary writers willingly accept this challenge, spending years honing their craft and producing works that few ever read. A trade book writer fortunate enough to find a publisher usually counts him or herself very lucky. But if the book fails in the market, he or she may not be given another chance with that publisher. Yet 'pens for hire' writing for education and reference publishers can earn regular and sometimes surprisingly high sums for their efforts. One UK writer of ELT materials earned millions of pounds annually at the height of the *learn-English* boom of the 1990s.

The publisher has the power in the anglophone publishing scenario. Successful writers accrue power but, on average, a writer's income and power in most sectors of publishing is astonishingly low, considering how long it takes to research and write any booklength text. There are extraordinary stories, such as Charles Bukowski writing his first novel, *Post Office*, in a matter of a few frantic weeks and going to international success, much of it due to a publisher's faith in him. What isn't as well known is that prior to *Post Office* Bukowski had spent half his life in poverty developing his craft to a high level.

Other writers find success and desert the publisher who helped them. J. D. Salinger wrote the now annual educational blockbuster, *The Catcher in the Rye*, and after winning initial market success abandoned publishing, choosing to live as a recluse, writing for himself after that. But then with 200,000 copies sold annually of one novel alone, 65 million in total, Salinger could afford to go his own way.

There are harrowing stories as well. John Kennedy Toole's *A Confederacy of Dunces* was first published in 1980, eleven years after the writer committed suicide in 1969 at the age of 32. His novel was published due to the unyielding efforts of his mother, who after his death wouldn't give up in her quest of seeing her son's work in print. Several years after his death, she chanced upon the author and academic Walker Percy. With Percy's support, the novel was eventually published by Louisiana State University Press, Percy writing the foreword. In 1981 John Kennedy Toole was posthumously awarded the Pulitzer Prize.

Toole's novel was originally rejected by the respected editor Robert Gottlieb of Simon & Schuster. Gottlieb and Toole engaged in two years of correspondence. 'You can't stand the heartache of the correspondence', Toole's mother told the *New York Times*.[29] Approached for his comment after *A Confederacy of Dunces* won the Pulitzer, Gottlieb said he couldn't remember the writer or the book. Toole had sent in his manuscript 'unsolicited', so even getting Gottlieb's attention was an achievement. An editor engaging in correspondence with an unknown author, even back in the 1960s, was highly unusual. Today it is virtually unheard of. Today's editors, at least in the big publishing houses, approach letters from unknowns as they would a live snake in their soup. The standard response to authors offering unsolicited work is: *no unsolicited manuscript will be accepted. If the MS is not accompanied by return postage it will be held for three months and then destroyed.* It is not even that long in many cases.

There is another way of course: self-publishing. Many writers, including some very great and successful writers – William Wordsworth, Mark Twain, Gertrude Stein, James Joyce, Marcel Proust, Zane Grey, Bernard Shaw, Anais Nin, Virginia Wolff, e. e. cummings and Edgar Allen Poe, to name a few – have taken this route. Generally, the publishing industry derides self-publishing, dismissing it as little better than an exercise in authorial vanity, though the two practices – vanity and self-publishing – are quite different in reality.

Beatrix Potter self-published 250 copies of *The Tale of Peter Rabbit* in 1901 and publisher, Frederick Warne, who had rejected the author's work once, changed his mind when he saw the finished product. *Peter Rabbit* was published by Warne in 1902, and Potter's tale of Flopsy, Mopsy, Cotton-tail and Peter went on to sell over 40 million copies. *Swann's Way*, the first volume of *Remembrance of Things Past*, described by many (Graham Greene among them) as the greatest novel of the twentieth century was self-published by Proust after it was rejected by publishers. Mark Twain self-published *Huckleberry Finn*. Leo Tolstoy had *War and Peace* printed. In recent times Robert James Waller's self-published novel *The Bridges of Madison County* sold 50 million copies, becoming one of the twentieth century's biggest selling books.

In 1982, Edward Tufte, with the help of a graphic designer Howard Gralla, wrote and self-published *Visual Display*, using seed money he raised in mortgaging his house. Now a Professor Emeritus at Yale University, Tufte continues to self-publish his books through his company, Graphics Press. Tufte's works are regarded as seminal in the field of the visualisation of information and data.

In the UK, former policeman and 'motorcycling vicar' from Yorkshire, G. P. Taylor, self-published a young adult novel, *Shadowmancer*, in 2002. Printing in Finland for a few thousand pounds, Taylor faced down UK distributors and major high street bookshops which refused to stock the book. Taylor's self-belief was rewarded when the novel began selling in the thousands, on word of mouth alone. As sales kept going up, the bookshops and distributors took him on. Then Taylor received a phone call from J. K. Rowling's original editor at Bloomsbury, who advised him on how to proceed. Taylor approached the literary agent suggested to him, and was taken on by the agent on a Friday, had his novel auctioned over the weekend, and signed a multi-book deal with Faber and Faber the following Monday. Eventually, Penguin Putnam bought the US rights for six figures and the film rights were sold to Universal for a few million dollars.

In the round of all truths, publishing choices are a well-tuned mechanism. Serendipity and maverick writing choices don't fit the usual business profile. Truly innovative books have been in the past, and will continue to be, self-published (at least at first). They are sold on the slow train of reader word of mouth and the occasional critical comments, running along the informal channels we might call the *reader chat line*. This process can take decades, sometimes centuries to mature, before a maverick book hits the mainstream.

## READERS

One estimate marks the beginning of reading to about 5,000 years ago. In all probability reading of some kind goes back before then, to the interpretation of the first symbol intended to communicate meaning – a now almost incomprehensible trace of a human mark on a cave wall, rock or tree.

Some observers say the first act of reading, as we know it, began with stone slabs 900 BC–650 BC. The Olmec, in south central Mexico (1400–400 BC), reputedly developed a system of writing small stone tablets using 64 characters. The ancient world's first great collection of reading materials was Ptolemy II's creation of the Great Library of Alexandria in the third century BC, which at its height held around 700,000 scrolls, before all was lost in the fire of 640 AD.

Today, the United States Library of Congress holds around 120 million printed items in 460 languages. The British Library has around 150 million books and related print items in almost every known language on the planet, adding 3 million items annually. The world's biggest bookstore, Barnes and Noble at 105 Fifth Avenue New York, has 207,000 metres of bookshelves.[30] For all advances brought by Gutenberg's revolution, the physical act of western-styled reading remains fundamentally the same as it has always been, the eye scanning text, left to right and down a page (right to left for some cultures).

Steve Jobs, CEO of Apple, famously said in 2008: 'It doesn't matter how good or bad the product is, the fact is that people don't read anymore. ... Forty per cent of the people in the US read one book or less last year.'[31] It is fortunate, for gadget readers at least, that after 'back-handing' the culture of reading, Jobs got behind Apple's invention, the iPad. Jobs had a point to make though. A study of habits carried out by the US National Endowment of the Arts (NEA) from 1982 to 2004 found that while the population increased by 22.6%, readers of literary works over 18 years of age declined by 17.9%.

The writer–reader nexus, the linchpin and lifeblood of books, is taking a battering. Novelist Philip Roth has spoken almost in awe and gratitude of the communication he has with his 20,000 or so dedicated reader-base – far fewer than the people who buy his books. Writers want to communicate with readers. This is one of the major reasons writers write.

In the age of digital distraction there are now countless electronic alternatives to reading as a pastime. Allan Bloom argues that American students 'have lost the practice and taste for reading. They have not learned how to read, nor do they have the expectation of delight or improvement from reading.'[32] This trend is not isolated to the USA, though Americans do have many more media and leisure options than most countries. Many Americans have been pushed away from reading by an endless

TABLE 2.4   Decline in reading in the USA

| Reader groups (age) | % decline in reading in the USA 1982–2004 |
| --- | --- |
| 35–44 | Down 21.94% |
| 45–54 | Down 6% |
| 55–64 | Down 7.4% |
| 65–74 | Down 4.03% |
| Over 75 | Down 10.27% |

array of mind-numbing television and sport events, and will now read nothing weightier than the *TV Guide* or most puerile escapist fiction.[33]

Two lone facts show positive trends for reading in the future: women still read a great deal (much more than men), and the library system continues to exist. While women continue to read as much as they do, and libraries stay open, there is hope. The second-hand book market is another reader-friendly provision, though, anglophone publishers, for obvious reasons, have never warmed to it. Few, though, could fail to recognise the value of second-hand bookshops to reading and book culture overall.

In the age of celebrity authors, some successful writers complain of being besieged by intrusive readers. Looking at the equation from the other side, and 'cranks' apart, direct communication between writers and readers seems to be a vital component, one to be nurtured if the story of books is to continue.

## FURTHER READING

Blake, Carole, *From Pitch to Publication: Everything You Need to Know to Get Your Novel Published*, London, Macmillan, 1999

Bloom, Allan, *The Closing of the American Mind*, New York, Simon & Schuster, 1987

Coser, L. A., Kadushin, C. and Powell, W. W., *Books: The Culture and Commerce of Publishing*, New York, Basic Books, 1982

Greco, A. N., *The Book Publishing Industry*, Mahwah, NJ, Lawrence Erlbaum Associates, 2005

Greco, A. N., Rodríguez, C. E. and Wharton, R. M., *The Culture and Commerce of Publishing in the 21st Century*, Stanford, CA, Stanford Business Books, 2007

Haslam, A., *Book Design*, London, Laurence King, 2006

Powell, Walter A., *Getting into Print: The Decision-Making Process in Scholarly Publishing*, Chicago and London, University of Chicago Press, 1985

Vanderbilt, Arthur T., *The Making of a Bestseller: From Author to Reader*, Jefferson, NC, McFarland & Co., 1999

*And a view from an earlier era:*

Smith, Datus C., *A Guide to Book Publishing*, revised edition, University of Washington Press, 1989 (orig. published 1966)

# NOTES

1  Datus C. Smith, *A Guide to Book Publishing*, University of Washington Press, 1966. Revised edition 1989, p. 18.

2  David R. Godine, 'A Few Principles of Publishing', http://www.godine.com

3  Datus C. Smith, op. cit.

4  Phone interview with John Martin, 2010.

5  Geneviève Duboscq, 'A Flashing Heaven of Luck', 4–10 July 2002 issue of the *North Bay Bohemian*.

6  Ibid.

7  Jeremy Lewis, *Kindred Spirits: Adrift in Literary London*, London, HarperCollins, 1995.

8  In one sense acquisition and commissioning are simply two different terms for different sides of the Atlantic. Commissioning is the term often used in the UK, while acquisition is more common in the United States.

9  Powell, W. A., *Getting into Print*, Chicago and London, University of Chicago Press, 1985, pp. 140–141.

10  Tebbel, A., *History of Book Publishing in the US*. New York, R. R. Bowker, cited by Powell, op. cit. p. 11.

11  Greco, A. N., *The Book Publishing Industry*, Mahwah, NJ, Lawrence Erlbaum Associates, 1997, p. 119.

12  As with booksellers who are protected (if they do not knowingly sell 'illegal' or libellous material), a printer who does not 'knowingly' print illegal material is usually legally protected. Author–publisher contracts indemnify the publisher against illegal material, so if something in the text is illegal, the bookseller, publisher and printer can all point at the writer.

13  Also known as: litho, offset, photo-set or photolithography.

14  Haslam, A., *Book Design*, London, Laurence King, 2006, p. 210.

15  Haslam, op. cit., p. 7.

16  Besek, J. and Ginsburg, J. C., 'The Future of Electronic Publishing: A Panel Discussion', *Columbia Journal of Law and the Arts*, 25 (2/3), 2002, pp. 91–118, quote from p. 108.

17  Remaindered books are those sold at or below production cost in bargain book stores.

18  Athill, D., *Stet: An Editor's Life*, London, Grove/Atlantic, 2002.

19  Coser, L. A., Kadushin, C. and Powell, W. W., *Books: The Culture and Commerce of Publishing*, New York, Basic Books, 1982, pp. 250–251.

20  Boris Kachka, 'The End', *New York Magazine*, 14 September 2008.

21  Ibid.

22  Talk by Donald Maass at the Florida Writers' Conference 1999.

23  Coser et al., op. cit., p. 289.

24  Carole Blake, 'Selling within the English Language Markets,' *Pub Res Q*, 23, 2007: 129–136.

25  *Raymond Chandler Speaking*, ed. Dorothy Gardiner, Kathrine Sorley Walker, Boston, Houghton Mifflin, 1977. This quote is from a book of Chandler's own words, *Raymond Chandler Speaking*, first published in 1977, with © Helga Greene Literary Agency 1962 on the publishing information page. Chandler died in 1959.

26  Mathew Flamm, 'A Time to Press Charges', EW.com, 27 September 1996, http://www.ew.com/ew/article/0,,294329,00.html.

27   Coser et al., op. cit., p. 82.
28   Slush piles are made up of unsolicited manuscripts and typescripts sent into publishers by hopeful writers looking for publication. Major publishers and some agents will now not even consider unsolicited submissions.
29   Vanderbilt, Arthur T., *The Making of a Bestseller: From Author to Reader*, Jefferson, NC, McFarland & Co., 1999, p. 9; Coser et al., op. cit.
30   Haslam, op. cit., p. 9.
31   John Markoff, 'The Passion of Steve Jobs', *The New York Times*, 15 January 2008.
32   Alan Bloom, *The Closing of the American Mind*, New York, Simon & Schuster, 1987, p. 62.
33   Greco, op. cit. (2005 edition).

# 3 SECTORS IN THE ANGLOPHONE MODEL

The anglophone book publishing model is founded on the principle that the economics of the books trade is of paramount importance. Anglophone publishing is a business that contains more than one cultural mission, but is not driven primarily by any one of them. Anglophone publishing, sometimes known as the Anglo-American model, is a widely distributed and ever-changing global business of producing and selling English language books.

Anglophone publishing is divided into seven broad areas of activity: consumer/trade academic books; children's books; school books; professional books and journals; English language training materials; reference books and materials; and religious books and publications. Over time, each of these areas grew into a separate sector of the anglophone book industry, moving away from the entire industry's historic origins in early trade/consumer books. Each evolved sector now operates as a separate business. While there is considerable market overlap, a sharing of practices, expertise and knowledge across the many areas, sectors and sub-sectors of publishing, each sector has its own business method, profile and markets.

Anglophone publishing markets are now global, with English language books regularly sold in Australasia, Europe, the Indian subcontinent, Sub-Sahara Africa, North Africa, the Middle East, the other Americas, East and South East Asia,[1] as well as the two original and biggest markets – the United States and the United Kingdom. The anglophone model had a historical head start on globalisation, as it already operated in countries and geographical areas where the anglosphere's two biggest players had either once been colonial powers or exerted influence.

The USA and the UK have a shared history of approach and structure to their publishing industries. There are also differences between the two trades. The United States is the largest single book market, as well as English language book market, in the world. Larger than the UK's book market by five to six times, traditionally US publishers have viewed foreign book markets as a second priority.

By contrast, UK publishers are very active in export, being the anglophone world's largest exporter of books by value. UK publishing has always sold books to former colonies in Australasia, North America, Sub-Sahara Africa, East and South East Asia. The UK now has another major export market, right on its doorstep – Europe. While no market

TABLE 3.1   The UK's book export market in 2008

| UK export market 2008 | Exports £m | Percentage share |
|---|---|---|
| Europe | £448 | 39 |
| East & SE Asia | £160 | 14 |
| Australasia | £138 | 12 |
| North America | £124 | 11 |
| Middle East/North Africa | £113 | 10 |
| Africa/Sub-Sahara | £102 | 9 |
| Other Americas | £51 | 4.5 |
| Unspecified | £5 | 0.5 |
| **Total** | **£1141** | **100** |

*Source of figures*: UK Publishers Association

in continental Europe has English as its first language, 39% of all UK book exports go there (Table 3.1). US and UK books sales for the period 2004 to 2007 show only very modest overall increases in revenue (UK +6% and US +8%) (Figure 3.1).

The US and UK (Figures 3.2 and 3.3) book markets both broadly break down into three main areas of business:

- **Consumer or Trade books:** fiction, non-fiction/reference and children's books
- **School books** and **English Language Training (ELT)** (UK) or **El-Hi** (US)
- **Academic** (UK) or **Higher Education** (US) and **Professional Publishing:** Journals, Professional practice, Law, Science, Technical and Medical books.

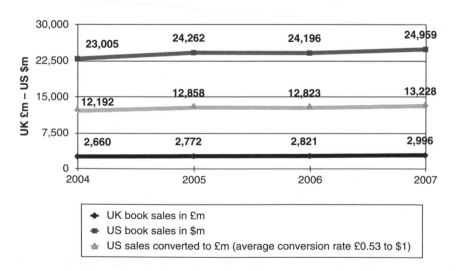

FIGURE 3.1   Comparison of US and UK book sales 2004–2007

*Source of figures*: UK Publishers Association and Association of American Publishers

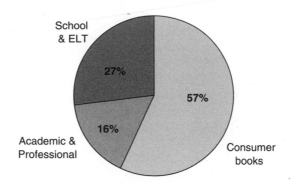

FIGURE 3.2  UK book markets aggregated into three main fields
*Source of figures*: UK Publishers Association 2008

This three-way market split is more evenly distributed in the United States (Figure 3.3).

The three-way market split of Consumer, El-Hi/School and Academic/ Higher Education/Professional is then divided into single-sector book markets:

- Consumer-trade books and materials
- Academic or Higher Education books and publishing
- Children's books
- School or El-Hi (elementary–high school) books and materials
- English Language Training (ELT) books and materials
- Professional and Journals – Law, Humanities, Science, Technical and Medical
- Reference books and publications
- Religious books and materials

Each sector has distinctive characteristics, markets and separate business models. Differences can be quite pronounced while some similarities make some sectors almost indivisible, one from the other, at times.

*Journals*, produced and sold on a pre-paid subscription model, are quite different from the *trade/consumer* books sector, which is based on unit sales. Journal content in the form of academic papers is provided free by authors trying to further their research and teaching careers. Very few trade authors are willing to 'give their work away'.

*Consumer* and *academic* publishers sell unit copies by consignment to booksellers. Writers are contracted on royalty contracts and are provided with advance payments. *Academic* and *educational* textbooks usually have longer commercial lives than trade books, and are sold into annually renewing markets. *Reference* titles remain in print for decades, sometimes centuries, after their first compilation, with texts updated on an ongoing basis to keep content current. *Law* publishing is now delivered online

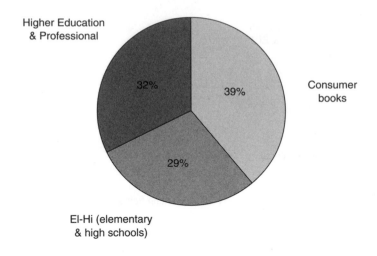

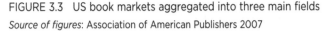

FIGURE 3.3   US book markets aggregated into three main fields
*Source of figures*: Association of American Publishers 2007

to clients, with printed law books offered as a secondary market. As the entire publishing industry evolves in the electronic age, each sector is altering its products and ways of doing business.

## CONSUMER OR TRADE BOOKS

The consumer book trade sector is the oldest market. It is still the 'front window' of book publishing. Trade/consumer books are the highly visible books on sale in bookshops and other outlets. Trade books are found in London's high street stores, online, in New York's superstores, in airports, in a small chain in a mall in an American mid-western town, in an independent bookshop café in the north of Scotland, or in the only bookshop for 500 miles in outback Australia. Consumer books are bought by the biggest group of consumers and read by book clubs big and small throughout *the anglosphere*. They are even found in book stores in cities where English is not the first language.

The Association of American Publishers' recording of consumer books sales in the USA includes religious and children's books, whereas the UK Publishers Association separates out children's books. Some UK religious sales form part of the trade sector's Mind, Body and Spirit sub-sector. Sector markets overlap. Appearance in one market does not preclude a sale in another.

Consumer books are the most discretionary of all book purchases. They can be bought as part of self-made promises for self-improvement or even to decorate a home. In a 2007 UK Publishers Association survey, the UK consumer books

TABLE 3.2  US consumer book sector in 2007

| US consumer books 2007 | $ millions | Units sold (millions) |
|---|---|---|
| Adult hardcover | 2,537.8 | 200.1 |
| Adult paperback | 1,612.2 | 220.3 |
| Adult mass market | 1,719.7 | 451.4 |
| Children's & YA hardcover | 1,127.7 | 173.2 |
| Children's & YA paperback | 732.2 | 258.2 |
| Audio books | 271.4 | 18.6 |
| Electronic books | 11.5 | 2.0 |
| Religious books | 618.4 | 88.5 |
| Other | 12.9 | 7.6 |
| **TOTAL** | **8,643.8** | **1,419.9** |

YA = Young Adult
*Source of figures*: Association of American Publishers or AAP[2]

market accounted for 88% of invoiced sales by volume, and 69% by value. Consumer books are very broad in their subject matter, approach, scope and appeal. At the high sales end, consumer books are characterised by popular subjects and high-profile celebrity authors, the often ghost-written 'authors' you thought couldn't even spell, authors you see interviewed on high-rating television programmes, or whose faces regularly stare out at us from newspapers and magazines.

Then there is the 'serious literature' and literary fiction scenes, driven by major prizes, such as the Nobel, National Book Award, Pulitzer, and Man Booker prizes. Awards are valued by publishers and writers alike and affect markets. In 2008, the first-time novelist, Aravind Adiga, with his tale *The White Tiger*, became the year's bestselling hardcover in the UK after winning the Man Booker prize.

Consumer books also include backlist perennials – the billion copy selling works of Shakespeare, and the mystery and detective novels by another 'copy billionaire', Agatha Christie. The novel is a 300-year consumer books success story, with the works of Cervantes, Dickens and Tolstoy each estimated to have also sold hundreds of millions of copies. In recent times, J. K. Rowling and Stephen King have also both achieved sales in the several hundred million copies range.

The consumer book market is highly competitive. Together with high-profile sales success stories is the *long tail* of backlist books and less well-known authors, all of which are vital revenue streams for many publishing companies. Books appear and disappear rapidly from bookshops, with a single runaway bestseller sometimes deciding whether a market for a year is up or down. Consumer books provide the highest potential rewards in the shortest period in a marketplace increasingly dictated by a mix of the vagaries of stardom and fickle mass appeal (Figure 3.4).

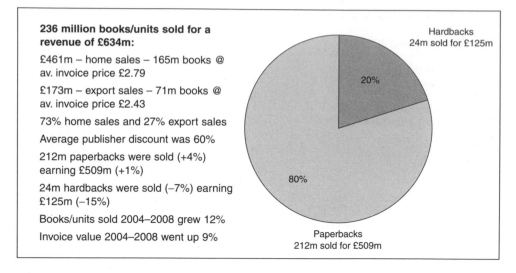

**236 million books/units sold for a revenue of £634m:**

£461m – home sales – 165m books @ av. invoice price £2.79

£173m – export sales – 71m books @ av. invoice price £2.43

73% home sales and 27% export sales

Average publisher discount was 60%

212m paperbacks were sold (+4%) earning £509m (+1%)

24m hardbacks were sold (–7%) earning £125m (–15%)

Books/units sold 2004–2008 grew 12%

Invoice value 2004–2008 went up 9%

Hardbacks
24m sold for £125m

20%

80%

Paperbacks
212m sold for £509m

FIGURE 3.4   UK fiction sales in 2008
*Source of figures*: UK Publishers Association

# ACADEMIC, SCHOLARLY OR HIGHER EDUCATION PUBLISHING

Academic or higher education publishers serve the university and college markets. These books are often required reading, recommended or promoted by teachers. Some US college courses follow specific texts for parts or the whole of an academic year, whereas a UK university course may simply present students with a recommended reading list.

Academic institutional libraries and campus bookstores stock largely according to decisions made by teaching staff. Many academic books and texts have long publishing lives, with the potential for renewed annual sales, making academic and scholarly books a far more stable and predictable proposition for publishers than consumer books.

Academic titles appear as textbooks or in single monograph studies, written by an expert on a subject of research. Academic titles are often expensive to buy, due to shorter print runs, based on smaller demand. The average UK price for a home academic/professional sale in 2008 was £12.51 and export £11.06, compared to £2.79 and £2.53 respectively in the consumer book market. Academic books draw far lower discounts than consumer books and the average percentage of returns to publishers is also much lower, in the 20% range.

In the UK, the two major academic presses are Oxford University Press (OUP) and Cambridge University Press (CUP), both global providers of academic, reference and educational (school level) materials. Other smaller UK academic publishers, such as Edinburgh University Press and Manchester University Press, produce significant titles, but OUP and CUP are by far the dominant UK players in the academic market.

Overall, OUP and CUP have helped UK academic exports into a strong position. In contrast to the 70% (home) and 30% (export) split of consumer book sales, UK academic publishers export more books and materials than they sell at home.

In the USA the major academic or higher education presses are Yale, Princeton, Harvard University and MIT (Massachusetts Institute of Technology). There are also many smaller university presses, often supported by special foundations and grants, or operating on a non-profit basis. In 2008, 96 US-based university academic presses accumulated $451 million in net revenues (gross sales minus book returns). US university presses overall are in a 'defensive' position with sales set to decline.[3] The sector is predicted to shrink by close to 4% by 2013.

By contrast, the large global commercial academic publishers – Reed Elsevier, Thomson Reuters, Wolters Kluwer, Informa, Springer, Pearson, John Wiley-Blackwell, and McGraw-Hill – are operating profitably. Backed by Wall Street, these large firms have revenue growth projections as high as 127% between now and 2013, based on sales predictions for digital products coming onstream.

There are well over 4,500 universities and colleges in the USA (426 institutions in California and 307 in New York alone). US higher education attracts over 18 million students annually, many more students now coming from previously underrepresented groups, the over 25s and women. 70% of institutions are publicly funded and 80% of students receive some form of financial aid. Recent international student enrolments were over 600,000. The US college bookstores serving these students are either owned and run by educational institutions or are private, run by large franchises.

The average price a US college student paid for a new textbook in 2009 was $57. Students can be expected to pay up to $400 for individual course materials and books. Returns on average are 20%. Savings made through digital text delivery options are becoming more attractive, though new and used textbooks selling half-price through online books are still the preferred option.

| | |
|---|---|
| **$700** | Average per annum US college student expenditure on course materials |
| **$57** | Average price of new textbooks 2007–2008 |
| **$49** | Average price for used textbooks in 2007–2008 |
| **70%** | Percentage of required texts sales from college bookstores and websites |
| **3%** | Textbooks sold as e-texts from college bookstores |

*Source of figures*: National Association of College Stores

In the UK, UCAS (the Universities and Colleges Admissions Service) lists 306 member institutions. UK student applications continue to rise. In 2010 there were 570,556 applicants, an increase of 106,389 (22.9%) on the figures for 2009. Overseas student applicants went up from 55,245 to 71,105 (+28.7%), of which percentage increases on applications from Ireland (50.4%), China (22.4%), Germany (23.7%) and Lithuania (102.3%) were the largest.

Education overall often runs counter to prevailing economic conditions. Student numbers can rise in recessions, and this in general flows to academic publishing revenues, though all this depends also on the educational policies a government puts in place. If fees rise, there can be a knock-on effect in falling admissions and academic book sales.

---

## FRANK CASS & COMPANY

Academic and journal publisher, Frank Cass, in a career spanning 1947 to 2007, went from selling books, opening his own bookshop, running a reprint academic books business, to creating military, academic and law journals, and setting a UK trend in books on media celebrities.

Inheriting his love for books from his mother, Frank Cass fell into rather than planned a book career. Born into an East London Jewish family originally from Poland, Frank attended Hackney Downs School, known as the 'Eton of the East End', where Nobel playwright Harold Pinter and Academy Award winning actor Michael Caine also attended.

Working in the The Economist Bookshop near the London School of Economics, Cass was quick to develop an understanding of the trade, engaging book buyers in long conversations. He recognised that students in 1950s London lacked all kinds of textbooks. Cass made a mental note to remedy the problem. As Britain's colonial adventure in Africa was winding down, Cass created a reprint Library of Black Studies. In the 1960s his bookshop became a source of rare books on the neglected continent. Cass also republished UK social studies. One reprint success was *A Merseyside Town in the Industrial Revolution: St. Helen's, 1750–1900* by Theo Barker and J. R. Harris.

Determined to repay Barker for helping with the republication rights, Cass set out to promote the book by every means he could. Cass had no car and didn't even know how to drive. So he hired a van with a driver and set out from London for St Helen's (Theo's birthplace) with a load of Barker's books in the back. Cass and the driver roamed the area in a freezing November. Coming upon the biggest book-shop he could find, Frank shoved a copy into the manager's hands. Perplexed by the idea that locals would buy a study of their own town, the man laughed in his face. Frank talked the bookseller into taking 24 copies. The store sold all of them before Christmas and ordered more. Frank went back up to Liverpool, via Manchester this time, selling another 100 copies, and buying up other titles from second-hand bookshops.

When the reprint boom slowed in the late 1960s, Cass moved on to journals, identifying a niche for military, intelligence and strategic studies, then branched out into law journals. In the early 1970s, he grew interested in books on show business personalities, publishing the scripts by the 1950s radio heroes, the Goons, and then a book on Britain's stand-up television comic duo of the 1960s and 1970s, Morecambe and Wise. In 1971, Cass took over Vallentine Mitchell, the Jewish Studies imprint. It never made a profit in all the years he ran it, but he kept the imprint going even after selling the rest of Frank Cass & Company in 2003.

Throughout his career Cass was quick to decide on a strategy. His natural charm and business acumen helped him maintain his financial and business independence. Unlike most publishers, Cass refused to remainder books, believing that patience for 'arriving' sales was a necessary factor in good publishing. Frank's dealing with the US book market also went against the trend. Rather than do co-editions with US publishers, a method that guaranteed a respectable, if unspectacular, return on investment, Frank decided to distribute his books in North America himself. First he used the US distribution firm, the International Specialised Book Service (ISBS), and when it ran into financial trouble, he took it over. His early investment in journal publishing also paid off very well by the late 1990s, with revenues from Cass Journals bringing in 70% of company earnings.

In 2002, after 50 years in the book business, Frank Cass & Company reported sales of £3.8 million and £400,000 in pre-tax profits. Cass ran his company like a family. Two staff had been with him for more than 30 years, one for over 20, five for 15 years and ten for more than five years. Cass employed 17 journal and books editors, nine marketing and publicity staff, and sundry others in various other functions.

In 2003, Taylor & Francis bought the company for £11.3 million (plus £3.7 million if the firm maintained some performance targets). Cass kept Vallentine Mitchell, Irish Academic Press and the US distribution arm. Taylor & Francis had 30 vacancies available after the purchase and gave preference to Cass staff. Ten employees took advantage of the offer. It was a fitting epitaph to the respect Frank Cass generated in his working life as a bookseller and publisher.[4]

## PROFESSIONAL AND JOURNAL PUBLISHING

The professional publishing sector produces books and materials on fields such as finance, business, accountancy, engineering, any publications in fact that aid, explore and explain professional careers and activities. Professional publishing includes the high-profile areas of law, journals and science, covering practices and guides for practitioners in the workplace, and continuing professional education outside academic and educational environments.

The second oldest area of publishing after trade *law publishing* is a very successful sub-sector of professional publishing. The main companies which publish anglophone law materials today are Thomson, Elsevier and Wolters Kluwer.

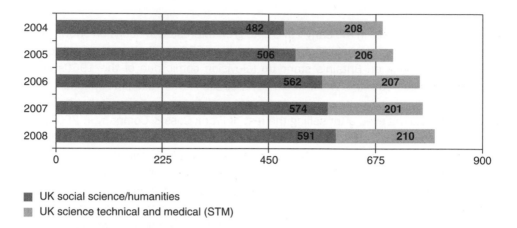

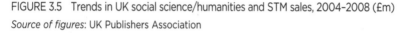
- UK social science/humanities
- UK science technical and medical (STM)

FIGURE 3.5   Trends in UK social science/humanities and STM sales, 2004–2008 (£m)
*Source of figures*: UK Publishers Association

Butterworths (now owned by Reed Elsevier) was a pioneer UK law publisher in the early twentieth century. In recent times it has been a digital pioneer with its LexisNexis database, one of the first companies in all sectors to embrace digital output. Case law and new statutes have been delivered online to subscribers and legal practitioners for many years. Legal firms receive most material in digital form. Print law books and reviews are in decline, though continue to be produced for legal professionals who also want bound copies.

*Science technical and medical* (STM) is another major sub-sector of professional publishing, overlapping significantly into journal publishing, with specialised STM journals often leading developments. The Anglo-Dutch company Elsevier is a world leader of STM publishing by volume.

The *social sciences/humanities* is also a huge growth area in professional journal and book publishing. In the UK from 2004 to 2008 social sciences/humanities titles did considerably better than science, technical and medical titles, the social science sub-sector growing its share of the overall combined market to 78% by volume and 74% by value (Figure 3.5).

## JOURNALS

Journals publish papers written by academics and other researchers, announcing, explaining, discussing or disputing professional and academic issues and developments. Journal papers are usually written by professional academics for other academics – be they scientists, technical personnel, humanities researchers and higher education (usually postgraduate) students. Papers are provided by authors to the journal's editor and or publisher for no remuneration, in order to advance the academic careers of the writers. Academics are expected by the universities employing them to regularly publish research in journals or books.

Journals of the past were associated mainly with science and technical matters but in recent years social sciences journals have become more and more prominent. The US University of California periodicals directory website and database, *Ulrich's*, lists around 250,000 periodicals, including 23,000 peer-reviewed scholarly journals which represent the main journals published worldwide. The University of California estimates that between 1986 and 2002, journal production increased by 58%, while book production went up by 50%. While the Consumer Price Index rose 64% over the 16-year period, journal prices shot up on average by 227%. Book prices on average over the same period rose only by 75%.

Libraries (mostly academic libraries) throughout anglophone markets buy journals on a subscription basis, in print and/or electronic form. Both forms are more common now, with a bundling of print and electronic editions. Journals represent 55% of overall library budgets in the UK (the figure is still rising), with 17% spent on electronic products (also rising). By comparison, library spending on books is static at 28%.

The journal subscription business model has proven itself commercially to be publishing's best model. The gross and net margins in journal publishing are among the highest of all sectors. Non-payment of contributors and the low salaries or fees paid to editorial staff are major factors. In the main, journal publishers only have production and distribution costs to consider. They have to gamble on subscriptions being bought by libraries and individuals, but once they have secured them, it is an annual income for the journal up front. This is the direct opposite of the consumer/trade publishing model which finances the whole process and then must wait, sometimes for a very long time, for revenue returns.

Elsevier is the largest journal publishing company in the anglosphere. It owns and produces over 2,000 individual journals, including prestigious medical titles such as *The Lancet*. With headquarters in Amsterdam, the company has more than 7,000 journal editors and 600,000 authors. Other major journal publishers include Macmillan (The Nature Group) owned by Verlagsgruppe Georg von Holtzbrinck of Stuttgart, producer of *Nature* (begun in 1869) and *Scientific American* (in print for 150 years). Wiley produces around 1,500 journals. The professional publisher Wolters Kluwer, with Lippincott Williams & Wilkins (a unit of Wolters Kluwer Health), produces 275 journals on medicine, clinical care and health matters. The publisher of this book, Sage Publications (named after the founders *Sara* and *George* McCune) started business in California in 1965. It is now reportedly the fifth largest journal publisher in the world,[5] producing 560 journals, along with book, reference works and databases in the area of business, humanities, social sciences, science, technology and medicine.

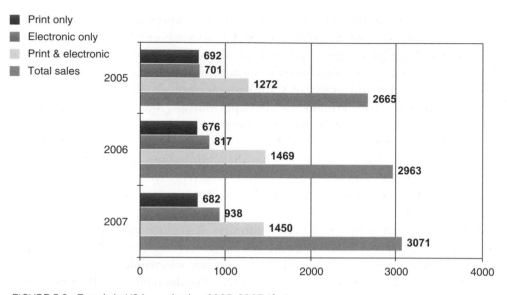

FIGURE 3.6   Trends in US journal sales, 2005–2007 ($m)
*Source of figures*: Association of American Publishers

## OPEN ACCESS

The objectives of the open access journals movement were set out in a communiqué of the 2002 Budapest Initiative, which defined open access as literature freely available

> on the public internet, permitting any users to read, download, copy, distribute, print, search, or link to the full texts of these articles, crawl them for indexing, pass them as data to software, or use them for any other lawful purpose, without financial, legal, or technical barriers other than those inseparable from gaining access to the internet itself. (Budapest Open Access Initiative)[6]

Open access has developed ten different approaches (Home page, E-print archive, Author fee, Subsidised, Dual-mode, Delayed, Partial, Per Capita, Indexing, Cooperative).[7] Effectively, it all comes down to how journals are produced and who pays for publication.

In 2003, the Bethesda Open Access Publishing initiative held at the Howard Hughes Medical Institute in Chevy Chase, Maryland, created a definition of OAP (Open Access Publication):

1   The author(s) and copyright holder(s) grant(s) to all users a free, irrevocable, worldwide, perpetual right of access to, and a license to copy, use, distribute, transmit and display the work publicly and to make and distribute derivative works, in any digital medium for any responsible

purpose, subject to proper attribution of authorship, as well as the right to make small numbers of printed copies for their personal use.

2   A complete version of the work and all supplemental materials, including a copy of the permission as stated above, in a suitable standard electronic format is deposited immediately upon initial publication in at least one online repository that is supported by an academic institution, scholarly society, government agency, or other well-established organization that seeks to enable open access, unrestricted distribution, interoperability, and long-term archiving (for the biomedical sciences, PubMed Central is such a repository).

Another development is PLoS, or Public Library of Science, begun by biochemist, Patrick Brown, at Stanford University in 2001. A supporter of the Bethesda approach, PLoS began publishing its open access peer-reviewed journals in 2003.

Before (and after) OAP, journals continue to be created and designed on the subscription model paid for by (in the main) academic libraries. Under the terms of the subscription licence, journal texts are available to staff and students at the university either in print or online. A new development inspired by OAP allows authors or university departments to pay a fee to a journal (around £1,000) to 'unlock' a paper, allowing free online access for anyone. In this way universities, departments and individuals get far wider coverage for a paper and research.

Open access means free papers for all, but the big question remains how journals are funded. All journals incur production costs, whether they appear only online or not. The methods are: subscription, direct funding by public or private grant, advertising or direct payment by authors (the pay-to-publish method used by PLoS), or a mix of all of these. The question of quality and suitable independence arises with all methods. But above all else, what is necessary and important is the academic credibility of a journal.

Academics are expected to publish in the most important journals in their field only, if they want to further their careers. But these journals can take up to two years to decide whether to publish a paper or not. So the question is – *why don't all universities start their own OAP journals?* There are several reasons. The organisation and resources required is the main one, though another major reason seems to be that if a journal doesn't rate academically – doesn't have *citation-credibility* in other words – an institution is wasting its time and money. A journal takes years to develop its profile. The quickest way to credibility is by associating with journals that already have it.

In many cases, departments and discipline areas inside universities have set up and do run journals, but usually only after making an agreement with an established journal publisher. Apart from credibility, external publisher control over academic journals brings organisation, production know-how, lists of buyers, and a well-developed brand name that creates market reach. Academic journals need strong and qualified editorial management, an independent, high-standard peer review of papers, and organised distribution.

It certainly would be possible, say, for a group of Nobel-winning scientists to start up a new journal at a 'good' university, and for it all to be paid for by a university trust fund. Editors could be found and a journal started overnight, the papers finding their way to readers within weeks, rather than years. Time-delays for publication could disappear with transparent private or public grant 'funded' OAP. But as a consequence it seems fewer journals would be available as well. A loss of control and profits would mean publishers would simply leave the field.

---

## JOURNALS PIONEER, ROBERT MAXWELL

A controversial figure throughout his working life, Robert Maxwell was born Jan Ludwik Hoch into a poor and numerous Jewish family in 1923 in Czechoslovakia. He escaped Nazism by travelling across Europe to Britain in 1939, where he joined the British army.

Speaking several languages Maxwell acted as an interpreter, rising to the rank of captain and winning the Military Cross. When the war ended Maxwell turned his talents to publishing. Knowing that the British post-war government supported the growth of science, Maxwell bought out Butterworth's co-venture with Springer Verlag for £13,000. In taking over Pergamon Press, Maxwell became a leading publisher of scientific journals in the 1950s, and he grew his company quickly.

Appreciating what a good proposition the journal publishing model was, Maxwell paid academic authors nothing, editors very little and pre-sold journal subscriptions to public and academic libraries around the world. If it wasn't a licence to print money, it was the next best thing to it. Libraries, public and academic, were bound to take science journals. By the 1960s Maxwell was doing very well. He became Member for Parliament for Buckingham. In 1966, his company made £1,331,992 before tax. Yet, by the end of the decade he had lost his company to an American investor and his parliamentary seat. Maxwell went on to receive censure of the UK High Court and find himself the subject of a damning UK Department of Trade and Industry report, doubting his character and suitability to run a company.

In a remarkable turn-around, in 1974, practically bankrupted by £2 million in legal fees fighting the American company that had bought Pergamon and forced him out, Maxwell borrowed enough money to buy back the company, at a fraction of what he sold it for. By the end of 1974, the company had earned £2 million in profit.

Maxwell then bought the British Printing Corporation in 1980, creating Maxwell Communications Corporation and acquiring the Mirror Group Newspapers from Reed in 1984. In 1988 he bought the famed Macmillan house (later acquired by Holtzbrinck).

Maxwell's rise and fall and rise again meant that in 1965 he owned 100 journals, in 1976, 200 and by 1982, 300. At the height of his empire in 1988, Maxwell's companies produced 400 journals.

The early 1990s recession pointed Maxwell's debt-laden empire into the abyss. Facing charges that he had raided his own company's pension fund, Maxwell sold Pergamon and Maxwell Directories to Elsevier for £440 million and floated his Mirror Group as a public company. At the same time (true to his counter-intuitive methods) he bought the ailing *New York Daily News* tabloid.

In November 1991, Robert Maxwell was found floating in the ocean off the Canary Islands near his yacht. His death remains a mystery, variously described as suicide, natural causes, an attack by aliens or a covert action carried out by secret agents from different countries and agencies. Maxwell's companies went bankrupt in 1992 owing £400 million.

Robert Maxwell's boundless energy and enthusiasms, his extraordinary personality, his intriguing, risk-filled and volatile, see-sawing career still inspires a range of views on him as a man and publisher. He forged markets and business relationships way beyond the anglosphere of his day, particularly early on in his career. Well before anyone even dared to think of the USSR and China as publishing opportunities, Maxwell went behind the iron and bamboo curtains in search of deals. He was the first publisher to see the value of both to scientific publishing. For all the controversy he created, Maxwell won the respect and loyalty of his journal staff, his policy of non-interference in day-to-day matters on his journals winning the lasting gratitude of his editors.

# EDUCATION

## EL-HI IN THE USA — SCHOOLS IN THE UK

The education book market covers all schools – elementary or junior school through to high or upper school levels. Books are chosen by teachers, schools or, in the USA, by city or statewide educational committees. Textbook publishers are specialist houses which study the schools markets over years and produce and sell according to the established curricula and needs projected by teachers, school bodies and committees. Publishing sales reps are 'set loose' to sell company wares, and to do that they have to convince educational committees at all levels. In the United States, having a text selected by organisers of a statewide school curricula (the system used in 22 states), means the title will:

- be used by teachers in a very large number of schools
- be bought by a huge number of students
- have a long market life.

There are 18,000 US school districts, with 64,000 elementary level schools, 24,000 public high schools and 1,800 combined schools. In the private education sector

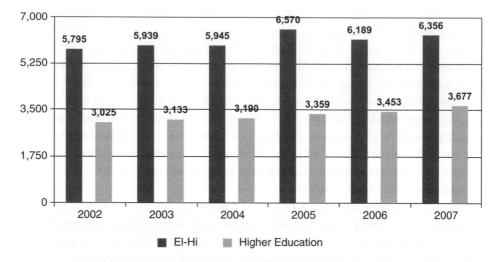

FIGURE 3.7   US El-Hi and Higher Education publishing revenues, 2002–2007 ($m)
*Source of figures*: Association of American Publishers

there are another 14,000 elementary and 4,000 high schools. In total, 2.3 million teachers are employed.

Once their books are accepted, publishers work at producing texts and materials usually in five-year cycles, shipping books on consignment to central depositories for schools, which then call on stock when and as needed.

The US education market is the second largest US book market after consumer books. In the past, educational publishing, both in the USA and the UK, provided generous operating margins, even if the books took substantial time and investment to prepare. With over a billion dollars spent on textbooks annually and competition for course acceptance now so fierce, reduced margins have convinced companies such as Wolters Kluwer and Reed Elsevier to leave the market.

Currently, the main education players in the USA are Pearson, Harcourt Education, Houghton Mifflin Company, Scholastic Inc., McGraw-Hill Companies, and Cengage Learning. Already the biggest UK educational publisher, Pearson recently also became the world's biggest educational publisher when it purchased Harcourt's international school testing and assessment business from Reed Elsevier.

As consolidated as the trade sector, the big schools publishers in the UK are Pearson, Oxford University Press (OUP), Cambridge University Press (CUP), Collins Education (News Corporation) and Hodder Education (Lagardère/ Hachette). As with trade, British educational publishers have strong presences in former colonies (the Commonwealth group of nations).

To date most UK educational book purchases have come under funding by LEAs (local education authorities), a system decided under 'capitation', a per capita educational spending quota for each student. However, with the recent change to a

Conservative/Liberal Democrat coalition government (2010), this could change to a less centralised approach.

## ENGLISH LANGUAGE TRAINING

The UK controls 43% of the global English Language Training (ELT) or English Language Learning (ELL) sector (decided by student hours), followed by the United States (18.8%), Canada (15.3%), Australia (10.4%) and New Zealand (6.3%).

More than 600,000 students travel to the UK each year to take ELT courses. Pearson, Oxford University Press, Cambridge University Press and Macmillan (Holtzbrinck) are the most prominent UK-based ELT publishers. Disney, Time LIFE, BBC, Linguaphone, Berlitz and De Agostini have also all, at one time or another, been big players in the consumer books subsector of the ELT market.

In recent years market growth has slowed for ELT publishers in both the UK and USA. Facing visa restrictions, potential students from throughout Asia have shifted their ELT study destination preference from the UK and USA to Australia and New Zealand. Recognising this growing trend, the Australian government is actively promoting its ELT and other education courses and facilities to Asian students. In targeting Asia, Australasia is becoming a serious ELT competitor for the UK publishers. The UK's share of the Australasian ELT market languishes well behind its penetration of other book sectors in Australia and New Zealand.

North America is another underperforming market for the UK's ELT products. The rate of growth for the UK's ELT exports to the USA for the period 2004–2008 was 9.1%, with Australasia 12.9% and South East and East Asia 3.5%, figures much lower than for its best performing markets: Europe 37%, Middle East/North Africa 56%, Africa/Sub-Sahara 57%, other Americas 21%.

The UK's ELT exports continued to grow, up 32% for the period 2004–2008, though the average invoiced sales price of the UK's ELT books and materials in 2008 was low at £2.86, supporting the fact that the ELT markets worldwide continue to be very competitive. While unit sales have expanded, revenue has not grown at the same pace. Overall, the rate of growth in all ELT markets has slowed over the last decade, in part as a result of a teaching trend away from specialist ELT learning materials towards an in-school learning system for English, particularly in Asia. This market trend, though, is far from settled or absolutely clear.

## REFERENCE

Reference publishing covers all sorts of informational and statistical materials in book form, CD or online. Dictionaries, encyclopedias, atlases, specialised maps, *The Guinness Book of Records*, almanacs, thesauruses, *Who's Who* and pictorial or illustrative guides are all reference publications sold either in the consumer/trade book market or under the professional book category. Reference titles usually take many years to

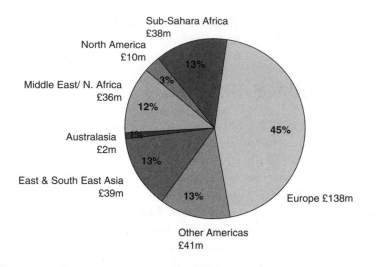

FIGURE 3.8   UK's ELT export market, 2008 (total £305m)
*Source of figures*: UK Publishers Association

develop and can be very expensive to produce. However, once they are done they can have long market lives, generating good annual sales while being relatively easy to update.

A world famous reference title is the *New English Dictionary*. In 1857, the Philological Society of London decided that no existing English language dictionary was complete or sufficient. After much discussion, in 1879, an agreement with the Oxford University Press was reached to start work on a new dictionary (later known as the *Oxford English Dictionary* or *OED*). Initially planned for completion in ten years, the project took half a century to finish, with the final OED volume being published in 1928.

There have been two editions so far of the multi-volume *Oxford English Dictionary*, the first in 1928, the second edition in 1989. In 2010, the third edition was nearly a third complete, with a team of 80 lexicographers working on it. It is predicted it will be another decade before the full third edition is published, although revisions and new entries continue to appear online every three months. There is a possibility that the third edition may only appear online, and not in print, although at the time of writing no final decision had been made by Oxford University Press.

In more recent times *The Guinness Book of Records* has been an extraordinary publishing success. First published in 1955, it began as a result of an argument over what was the fastest game bird in Europe. The reference title sold a surprising 70,000 copies in its first year in the United States alone. Today the book's website receives hits in the double-digit millions every month. *The Guinness Book of Records* is reputed to be the world's most sold book still in copyright, having sold around 100 million copies. It is now published in 27 languages. Many reference books sell as popular trade book titles, and *The Guinness Book of Records* is a prime example of how well a trade reference title sells from bookstores.

Non-fiction consumer reference sales include celebrity biographies, culture titles and war memoirs. President Barack Obama's *Dreams From My Father* sold well in the UK as it did in the USA. Madonna's brother's story of life with his famous sister also sold well.

The most significant events in contemporary reference publishing history have occurred in online delivery and databases. The online *OED* and *Encyclopedia Britannica* both now run on subscription models. The movement from paper book and foldout maps to Google maps and GPS (Global Positioning System) shows a general shift from paper books to electronic referencing methods. Apart from Google, one of the most extraordinary online growths in reference use is the free-to-edit commercially free online Wikipedia. Late in 2009 it reached a milestone of over 13 million articles appearing in 267 languages. In 2009 Wikipedia was the sixth most used and visited website in the world, standing perhaps in the way of a pay-per-view approach to online reference sites and resources. Wikipedia is part of a shift to a culture of free use and the sharing of knowledge and research, underpinning a general move towards more data and information becoming available online from all sources. Information on health issues and general advice and solutions now appear on many different sites. Critics worry about the quality of the information available across the Web, but begrudgingly admit that it is improving fast, just as most online solutions are improving. The world is still negotiating its way through an era of digital infancy.

Google and Wikipedia are actually used in many cases as a *first-call resource*, not a final point, sites where researchers of all levels can get a broad idea and description of the subject they are interested in, before being directed or moving on to better, more detailed sources and resources. Online resources such as Wikipedia could, in the end, expand all reference publishing, not coral it into one or two big online sites.

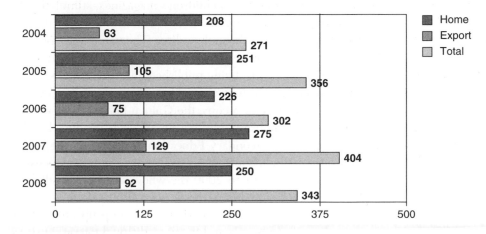

FIGURE 3.9   UK children's books sales 2004-2008 (in £m)
*Source of figures*: UK Publishers Association

# CHILDREN'S BOOKS

The history of Children's book publishing includes some of literary history's most classic tales. From the fifteenth century onward, what we now list among children's books began appearing. These included Thomas Malory's *Morte d'Arthur* and the story of Robin Hood. Great adventure epics written first for adults also interested younger readers. In the seventeenth century, Charles Perrault compiled and rewrote some traditional folk fairy tales, publishing *Cinderella*, *Little Red Riding Hood*, *Puss in Boots*, and *Sleeping Beauty* in France. Other tales such as Daniel Defoe's *The Adventures of Robinson Crusoe*, published in Britain early in 1719 and, seven years later, *Gulliver's Travels* by Jonathan Swift, in later years also became children's classics. Many of the best children's books are appreciated by all age groups.

In the nineteenth century the Brothers Grimm (Wilhelm and Jakob) published *Snow White* and *Hansel and Gretel* in Germany. At around the same time in Denmark, Hans Christian Andersen brought out *The Emperor's New Clothes* and *The Snow Queen*. In Britain Lewis Carroll published *Alice's Adventures in Wonderland* in 1865. *Heidi* was published in Switzerland in 1880. Carlo Collodi's *The Adventures of Pinocchio* was first serialised in Italy from 1881, appearing as a full story in print in 1883, the same year Robert Louis Stevenson brought out his classic tale, *Treasure Island*. Rudyard Kipling's *The Jungle Book* appeared in 1894, and in the United States, Frank Baum published *The Wonderful Wizard of Oz* in 1900.

In the twentieth century British publishers brought out Beatrix Potter's *The Tale of Peter Rabbit* (1902), Kenneth Grahame's *The Wind in the Willows* (1908), J. M. Barrie's tale of Peter Pan in *Peter and Wendy* (1911), A. A. Milne's *Winnie the Pooh* (1926), J. R. R. Tolkien's *The Hobbit* (1937) and in latter part of the twentieth century the works of C. S Lewis, Roald Dahl and J. K. Rowling.

Children's books began to become a serious publishing business in the late nineteenth century, with the serialising of novels in children's magazines, stimulating the reading habits of a far wider group of children. In 1919, Macmillan was the first company to appoint a dedicated children's books editor. The same year National Children's Book Week was created. Libraries extended their selection of children's titles. By 1935, 700 children's books were being published annually. In 1942 in the USA, Simon & Schuster brought out the first twelve titles in its *Little Golden Books* series. Sold for many years at only 25 cents a copy, the Golden Books series went on to be one of the most successful in-house publishing brands ever produced. When Congress passed the Elementary and Secondary Education Act in 1965, new book funds found their way into American schools. More and more publishers began to target the school market. From the 1970s to 2000 the whole sector expanded at a rapid pace. In the 1980s the number of children's book titles almost doubled.

Children's books now range from all manner of graphic, pop-up and activity books for the very young, through to novels and more traditional narrative story-telling for older children or young adults. The sector has seen massive growth in recent years, particularly driven by the extraordinary sales and success of the

Harry Potter series. Authors such as Beatrix Potter, Roald Dahl, A. A. Milne and Robert Louis Stevenson did much the same in the past, enthralling young readers year after year with their tales. For the last decade and more, J. K. Rowling has taken the children's book sales to new heights. Rowling's success has also created a publishing dilemma in the children's books sector, one which does not really exist in other sectors. If a Rowling book is not published any year, revenue and sales in the children's books sector fall quite dramatically. From a peak in the UK children's books sales in 2007, due largely to the success of *Harry Potter and the Deathly Hallows* (over 72 million copies were sold worldwide in the first 24 hours), in 2008 children's books sales fell 8% by value, 4.4% by volume (units sold).[8]

## RELIGION

As old as the *vellum codex* itself, religious publishing is a prodigious sector with perennial sales earning solidly on many fronts. This sector has the world's number one bestseller of all time, The Bible, which reputedly sells around 100 million copies a year. The Torah, Koran, Bhagavad Gita, and Buddhist writings (the Pali Canon, Sutras or the Dhammapada) are also bestselling holy books for devotees of Judaic, Islamic, Hindu and Buddhist religions.

Religious publications include religious discourses, discussions, debates, personal experiences, testimonies, hymn and prayer books. In the United States, religious publications grew rapidly, with a massive 50% growth from 2002 to 2003. Thereafter revenues fluctuated, with some years experiencing declines. From 2002 to 2007 the sector grew by 7.1% in the USA, compared to the 2.5% overall growth for the entire US book market over the same period. In the UK, many religious books are sold in the consumer books sub-sector of Mind, Body

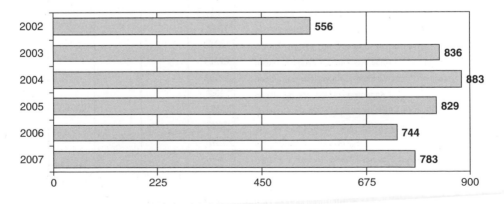

FIGURE 3.10  US sales of religious books, 2002–2007 (in $m)

*Source of figures*: Association of American Publishers

and Spirit, which has been described as being in decline due to over-publishing in
previous years, though sales of religious books – Bibles, hymn and prayer books –
continue to sell in large numbers through well-established outlets.

# LEADING REVENUES BY SECTOR (USA, UK, EUROPE AND JAPAN) IN 2009

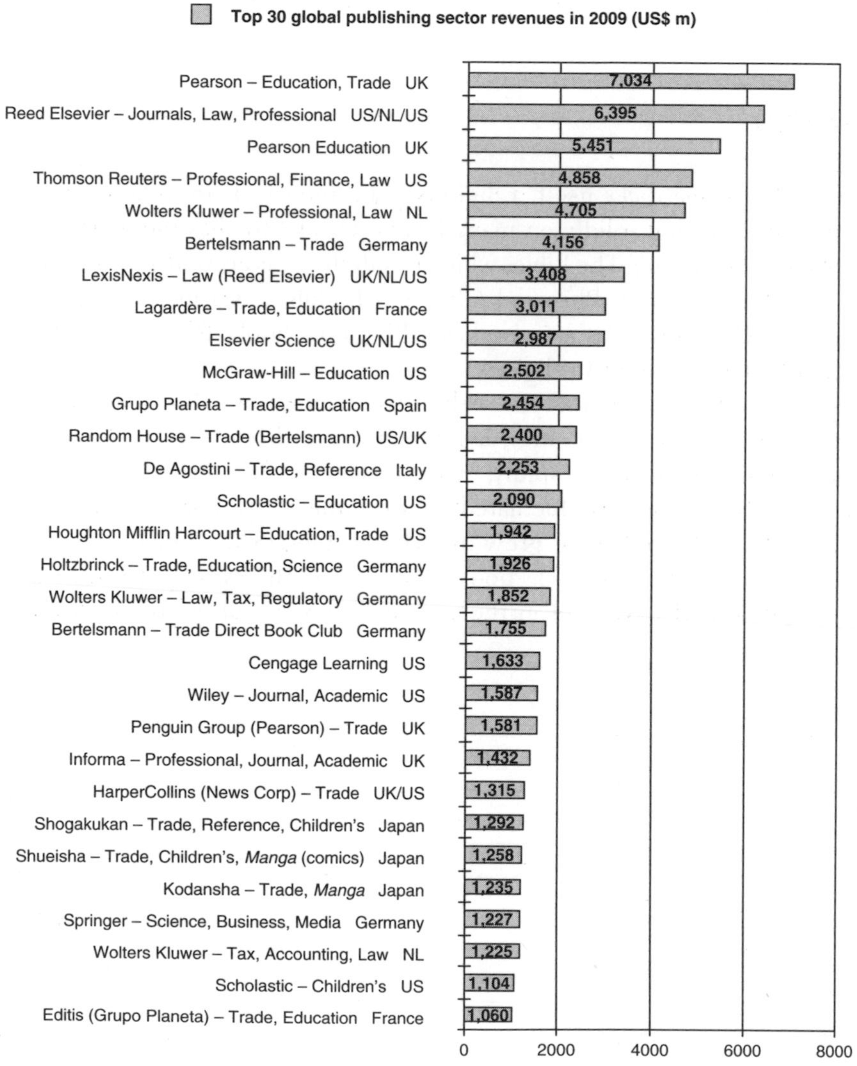

□ Top 30 global publishing sector revenues in 2009 (US$ m)

FIGURE 3.11  Top 30 global publishing sector revenues in 2009 (US$m)

Global publishing is spreading away from trade publishing, with only half of the world's top ten publishing companies now doing their main business in the consumer/trade sector. The UK–US Pearson (education, trade), the Anglo-Dutch Reed Elsevier (journal, law, science), the Canadian ThomsonReuters (professional, law, financial), and the Dutch Wolters Kluwer (professional, business, law) are now the world's most powerful publishers. Pearson grew its earnings in 2008 by 5%, with ThomsonReuters and Wiley (professional, science, journals – up from twenty-first place to fourteenth), among the most active publishing companies in recent times.

## FURTHER READING

Black, G., *Frank's Way*, London, Vallentine Mitchell, 2008

Compaine, B. M. and Gomery, D., *Who Owns the Media: Competition and Concentration in the Mass Media (Communication)*, Mahwah, NJ, Lawrence Erlbaum Associates, 2000

Coser, L. A., Kadushin, C. and Powell, W. W., *Books: The Culture and Commerce of Publishing*, New York, Basic Books, 1982

Greco, A. N., *The Book Publishing Industry*, Mahwah, NJ, Lawrence Erlbaum Associates, 2005

Greco, A. N., Ed., *The State of Scholarly Publishing*, New Brunswick, NJ, Transaction Books, 2009

Greco, A. N., Rodríguez C. E. and Wharton, R. M., *The Culture and Commerce of 21st Century Publishing*, Stanford, CA, Stanford Business Books, 2007

Thompson, J. B., *Books in the Digital Age*, Cambridge, Polity Press, 2005

## NOTES

1   The world's five largest publishing markets are, in order: the United States, Germany, Japan, China and United Kingdom.

2   The US and UK consumer book markets are surveyed and analysed differently by the respective national publisher associations.

3   Greco, A. N., ed., *The State of Scholarly Publishing*, New Brunswick, NJ, Transaction Books, 2009.

4   For a biography of Frank Cass, see Gerry Black's *Frank's Way,* London, Vallentine Mitchell, 2008.

5   http://www.researchinformation.info/news/news_story.php?news_id=179.

6   Davis, Philip M., 'How the Media Frames "Open Access"', *Journal of Electronic Publishing*, 12 (1), http://dx.doi.org/10.3998/3336451.0012.101

7   John Willinsky, *The Access Principle*, Boston, MA, MIT Press, 2006.

8   This also happened in 2010 with sales in Young Adult market. With no new Stephenie
    Meyer's *Twilight* titles, Lagardère Publishing's third quarter 2010 sales fell 7%. 'Lagardère
    Feels Full Impact of Meyer; HBG Digital Sales at 9%', *Publishers Weekly*, November 8,
    2010.
9   Original revenues were in euros – conversion rate used euro to dollar 2009 average
    1.39463.

# 4 CRAFT TO CORPORATION

Eighty per cent of book sales are controlled by a small group of very large firms. The other 20% is made by an ever-decreasing number of medium-sized companies and a fairly constant but very large disparate group of small players, entering and departing the industry almost like guests through a busy hotel's revolving door. John Martin, creator of Black Sparrow Press, identified two streams of American literature as 'the insiders conforming "to accepted standards" and the "outsiders and mavericks"'.[1] He could have been talking about book publishing itself. Most media falls into two broad categories: Big Media (centralised, vertically integrated, corporate, often oligopolistic) and Little Media (decentralised, distributed, individual, sometimes anarchic).[2]

In 1965 the first *International Directory of Little Magazines and Small Presses* listed 250 firms. In the 1990s that figure had risen to 50,000. In a 1999 survey of the R. R. Bowker Books in Print database, there were 53,000 small and independent publishers in the USA.[3]

Most publishing houses are small in size and operation. The UK's Nielsen BookData (which tracks sales and provides ISBNs to publishers) now has more than 60,000 UK and Irish imprints registered on its database. Nielsen believes about 20,000 of these are active publishers. Only 85 of these companies sell more than £5 million worth of books and only 15 companies have more than 250 employees.

In 1989 the US net book sales totalled $14 billion. Ten years later that figure had risen to $23 billion. While constantly under one sort of market pressure or another, book publishing is far from a dying industry. Reading habits may change, new technologies alter business models, production and distribution techniques, but publishing in one form or another goes on.

New independent publishers have always stimulated, even driven, the industry, often inspiring entirely new markets in tough economic times. Just after the Great Depression, new publishers used innovative publishing techniques to get new titles to readers. Two of the biggest innovators of the day are now famous brands — Random House and Penguin.

## BRANDS

The building of a brand is based on the business and gathering of cultural capital. The positioning of a market image or brand is of prime importance to the prospects of all companies, a factor more important than size or annual revenues. Many brands and logos have become household names. Many are now so well known they are almost celebrities in their own right: Random House, Penguin, HarperCollins, Simon & Schuster, Pan Macmillan, Oxford University Press, Hachette, Cambridge University Press, Harvard University Press, Yale University Press, Bloomsbury and Scholastic.

The Canadian romance publisher, Harlequin, created in 1949, is now one of the most product-focused brands, operating a rapid roll-over direct business in titles serving a large readership, often via email from its eHarlequin website. The UK's Mills and Boon pioneered the mass-market romance novel in the 1930s but, hitting lean times with the decline in lending libraries in the 1950s, it was eventually bought out by its North American distributor, Harlequin, in 1971. Both Harlequin's and Mills and Boon's market strengths are and were to publish a huge number of titles annually, withdrawing any unsold books quickly, as soon as after three months in many cases.

Black Sparrow Press's gathering of cultural capital made it an extremely valuable and profitable small press. Book brands represent image, value and continuity, giving the industry a social and political value as well as a commercial life. The main focus of anglophone publishing is on its commercial operation, but books also have the power to influence individuals and societies. Readers follow brands according to the products they sell, the authors that are promoted, but also often according to the firm's implicit or explicit cultural and social mission. It is always important for a publishing firm to maintain *reader-faith* by keeping the brand true to its core and stated values.

## THE BUSINESS OF PUBLISHING

Like other cultural product businesses, book publishing is highly unpredictable. Books – particularly in its largest sector, trade – rely on consumer whims and tastes. But unlike other media such as *newspapers, film* or *Broadway / West End theatre shows*, books are a quiet medium. The business of books is not the 'urgent media' business that other mass entertainment participation event-businesses can be. Books don't have the pizzazz of film, television or even radio. Books are not programmed participatory media. They are a solitary, private and meditative media experience. The business reflects this.

To succeed publishers must create an aura, a sense of 'specialness' around their books, and it usually takes time to pass the word or circulate this aura. Books, of course, can be a rowdy, controversial consumer product at times as well. In recent times, James Frey's *A Million Little Pieces* made the author rich and infamous. D. H. Lawrence's banned book, *Lady Chatterley's Lover*, was the focus of a lurid court case in the late 1950s. It is almost axiomatic: what good society says is 'bad behaviour' will lift sales. Of course, books don't have to create a moral controversy in order to build up a head of steam. The Harry Potter series, almost from the very outset, created its own special urgency among young readers, though the queues of children and adults that formed at bookshops and readings to see J. K. Rowling are rare. It usually takes something very special, or a long time, for books to achieve market fame. Film stars regularly attract crowds, authors only rarely so.

Publishing is described as an accidental profession, attracting young publishing staff to the trade for a cultural experience, similar to the one readers are seeking. Publishing personnel can make good salaries, but if big money is the main objective, it is safe to say they are in the wrong business.

## ENTRY BARRIERS FOR NEW PUBLISHERS

There are no direct visible obstacles to entering anglophone publishing. The field requires no publishing licence in order to practise. In terms of legal or regulatory constraints, there is no direct censorship of published materials in either the UK or the USA, or in any of the major democratically free anglophone territories around the globe. There are no pricing controls (any more) or direct quality controls on books. Books escape most goods or VAT taxes.

There is no official regulatory approval process for books going out on to the market, not even in education. There is no major body that inspects a publisher's premises to determine whether publishing standards are being maintained. Anglophone publishing is an enterprise free from most official interference. The only statutes a publishing firm must abide by are:

- general trading standards, price fixing, monopolies etc.
- copyright, libel, and obscenity laws.

A publisher needs some capital for general costs, such as the printing of books or online preparation of an e-text, the contracting of an author with a text worth publishing, and paying for a valid International Standard Book Number (ISBN). In truth, all a publisher needs is a book to print, a modest amount of money to do it and an understanding of, or better still *a flair* for, book marketing and promotion.

There are, however, some not-so-visible hurdles to get over. The capacity to distribute is a major factor that restrains newcomers. Most small companies don't have the money to buy their way into markets and most distributors and booksellers are (in the main) only interested in the bigger established clients. New publishers need to learn how to forge the necessary business relationships in order to succeed commercially. It depends on the product provided for sale, and often this will mean a long, slow lifting of business year after year. A lucky new firm can achieve a 'market breakout' with a new book and rapidly climb the sales ladder, but this, particularly in the trade sector, is like winning the lottery.

New publishers need to be competent, courageous, quick-witted and, above all, knowledgeable on their chosen book market. They need to develop innovative products, prices and methods of doing business. In effect, publishers need to find or create markets or unusual niche market positions, developing unique selling points (USPs).

There is very little available support from either the US or UK governments, far fewer funding grants for publishing than in dance, drama, music and the plastic arts. Anglophone publishing has always been regarded as a business, and publishing businesses are expected to stand on their own commercial feet. Publishers often say that the business of books is best learned on the job and this is generally true.

In summary, entrance barriers are low, access to markets is difficult. The success of a small publishing house will depend on a distinctive list. A new publisher needs to attract consumer, library, bookshop and critical attention to the press's books and this perhaps is best carried out by positioning the firm in its own market niche. Knowing how to market book products is crucial. Someone may be able to produce wonderful books but if readers don't hear of them or don't know they exist, all the production effort is wasted.

The question of what makes a successful book depends on many factors. De Vany and Walls' analysis of the commercial film industry can be applied to books.[4] The De Vany–Walls method uses what is known as Bose–Einstein dynamics, dual-sided uncertainty, and Pareto power law characteristics, all of which are based on a main premise that cultural industry products need rolling word-of-mouth to create an information 'cascade', a trend-effect on demand that is decentralised, adaptive, self-organising and famously hard, often impossible, to predict. De Vany and Walls found that one in ten cultural products, such as commercial films or books, are a market hit, two do moderately well and seven fail. This summary of general consumer book success patterns makes for grim statistics, and could send many a would-be publisher into the coin-operated laundry business.[5]

But most books need long sales cycles. The high-octane frontlist commercial bestseller is in many ways one business; the bulk of the trade another. Newly published books appear in the two main anglophone marketplaces every four or five minutes and rarely are any two books ever truly similar. No two books share the same genesis or production history, let alone the content, subject treatment, look, feel or author-career trajectory. Each book is unique, a story in itself, but a publishing company must make sure that this individual story is heard.

The saving grace of most books is that they don't all have to conquer the frontlist market immediately. Books form part of a backlist catalogue and as such become business and cultural items with long time spans, elements in a cultural river with many tributaries. In certain moments in history, sometimes well after its first publication, a book can create its own cultural cascade.

The stories of the Beatles in music and J. K. Rowling in books are both publishing fairy tales, but a perhaps more instructive story in literary publishing history is the tale behind the first edition of James Joyce's *Ulysses*. The 265,000-word novel was first published in its entirety in 1922 with 2,000 errors in a modest print run of 1,000 copies. The novel was soon banned in the USA and the UK for its sexual content. Half the print run was seized and burnt by the American customs officers. By the late 1960s, nearly 30 years after the author's death, *Ulysses* became a perennial seller to university literature course students. *Ulysses* probably did not net its first publisher, the legendary bookstore owner, Sylvia Beach – founder of the original Shakespeare and Company in Paris  a franc, penny or cent in profit. Beach's efforts, however, helped make publishing and literary history, galvanising if not launching the international career of perhaps the most influential anglophone writer of the twentieth century.

## THE CORPORATISATION OF BOOKS

At the end of the first decade of the twenty-first century, the book trade, throughout all its sectors, is dominated by a handful of global mixed-media corporations. Five of the 'big seven' publishing media corporations own major trade houses:

- News Corporation, Australian/US – the only truly global media company (owns HarperCollins)
- Bertelsmann AG, German (private) – biggest trade publisher in the world (owns RandomHouse)
- Holtzbrinck, German (private) – professional and trade publisher (owns Macmillan)
- Pearson Plc, UK/US – educational publisher, largest educational publisher in the world (owns Penguin)
- Thomson Reuters, Canadian – financial, professional and educational publisher
- Reed Elsevier, Netherlands/UK – journal and professional publisher
- Lagardère, French – global trade publisher (Hachette).

Other major international media and entertainment corporations also hold hugely influential positions in book and related media markets:

- *The Walt Disney Corporation* (USA) produces books and magazines for children under Disney Publishing Worldwide (DPW) – Disney Libri, Hyperion Books for Children, Jump at the Sun, Disney Press, and Disney Editions – reaching around 100 million readers every month in 75 countries

- *Wolters Kluwer* (Netherlands) is a global professional publisher and proprietor of the US literary house, Farrar, Straus and Giroux

- *Time Warner* (USA) From the mid-1990s to 2002 the world's largest media company, Time Warner has divested itself of its book publishing assets. It still operates in related media markets, producing the six Harry Potter films franchise which is reputed to be worth $15 billion in total.

Some way below the conglomerate/corporate level are smaller but still influential publishers such as *Oxford University Press* and *Cambridge University Press* – educational, academic and reference publishers which have also made a global mark. OUP and CUP have tax charity status in the UK, which makes their business models different from other larger publishers, but they also operate successfully in markets around the world. The two leading UK university presses have accumulated cultural and educational capital over their long histories, informing and bolstering their brands.

*Harvard*, *Yale* and *Princeton University* presses are the big names among a huge number of American university presses. These successfully run enterprises represent another face of publishing. With their focus firmly on education, firms like OUP, Harvard etc. represent the 'social purpose or mission' of books, a big part of publishing's past, and hopefully its future as well.

The power corporations have in book markets is rarely apparent to the average consumer. Benjamin Compaine and Douglas Gomery (*Who Owns the Media*, 2000) imply that corporate influence in media markets is overstated, an ownership-control myth even, arguing that corporations and control are uncertain by nature. The scenario is ever-shifting. Compaine and Gomery list big companies that have moved in and out of markets. In one sense, recent history supports Compaine and Gomery's thesis. Time Warner was once a big book publisher but is now no longer one. The first major American media corporation, Radio Corporation of America (RCA) – the pioneer of the corporatisation of books when it bought Random House in 1965 – no longer exists. The US television broadcaster, CBS, was once a major book publisher, then wasn't, and now is again – in its seemingly eternal dance of 'who's really in control' with its corporate twin, Viacom. The list of corporations that have moved into publishing and then out of the field is long enough to be significant. Conglomerates can lose influence, focus and power over time. Compaine and Gomery's analysis, however, devalues how corporations work in concert across media and related industries and morph into other identities.

Robert McChesney (*The Problem of the Media*) describes corporate ownership in terms of the political, regulatory, economic power that corporations accumulate.[6] This combined power works in commercial synergies, even in an *oblique concert* of related industrial aims, rather than by direct intervention in markets. This can represent an immense capacity to influence, if not dictate, market conditions across a range of media industries and sectors, and forms the underlying story of deeply embedded commercial and political power in the ties between companies.

In his 1996 book, *The Rise of the Network Society*, Manuel Castells argued that we are experiencing a multimedia fusion linking computer, communication and media industries in a convergence pattern.[7] With media power concentrated into fewer hands, enterprises are arranged into a cartel control pattern over production and distribution – an inter-corporate arrangement of 'I'll do this for you if you do that for me'. Media consumers are now *a profit mine*, the concept of societal benefit left to the 'politically naive' to consider on university campuses (see Figure 4.1).

In the mid to late twentieth century, many esteemed US and UK publishing houses with long histories were either merged with or absorbed into larger media entities. Around 600 takeovers took place between 1960 and 1990, 300 between 1990 and 1995, and 380 between 1996 and 2001. This consolidation of publishing was initially meant as a broadening of opportunities, a provision of capital for growth, a way of addressing technological advancements and improving operating efficiencies. The premise and mantra was that big is always better than small.

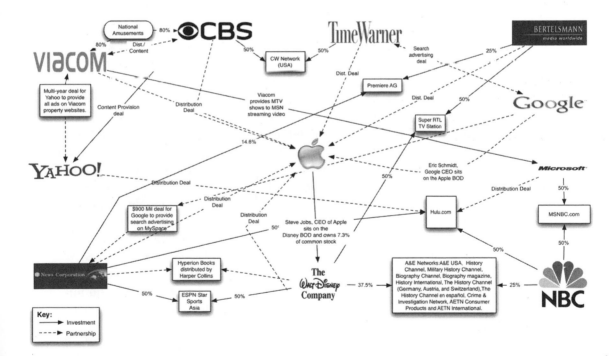

FIGURE 4.1  Key interlockings between multinational media and diversified internet corporations[8]

*Source*: 'The Structure and Dynamics of Global Multi-media Business Networks', *International Journal of Communication*, 2: 707–748. Reproduced with the kind permission of Dr Amelia H. Arsenault and Professor Manuel Castells.

## CORPORATE STRATEGIES

Competition is the natural process, the lifeblood, of the book trade, but it can be controversial at a corporate level. Companies with large sales and big brand names can be aggressive operators in the marketplace. Small companies deciding to operate in the same area and field as corporations should not be surprised to find that if by jumping into the corporate shark tank they are then subject to attack. Corporations and their operations are rarely benign. Big, medium and small publishers can coexist together until big competes with small over an asset or market, or when an abnormal market result creates interest in the smaller player.

The 'meeting of firms' may well be amicable but more often than not it is acrimonious. The ultimate objective of the corporation is to nullify market competition and increase its own market share. A soft approach may be used at first, absorbing assets via a merger arrangement, drawing the smaller company deep into a larger entity. The process is often projected as a sharing of power. Mergers can often look benign on the surface, very positive even for the smaller company, but behind the scenes the story is usually quite different. When Random House was bought by Bertelsmann in 1998, assurances were given that jobs would not be terminated. This turned out to be untrue. The Authors Guild objected and the US Justice Department filed an action against the merger but it went through regardless.

Bertelsmann's purchase of Random House, from the Newhouse-owned Advance Publications, folded the No. 1 US trade book publisher into Bertelsmann's global book publishing division, Bantam Doubleday Dell. Publishing units were closed or absorbed into other sections. Eight units became four divisions. The new Chairman of the new Random Group was Alberto Vitale, who had been the chairman of Random under Advance. Before joining Random in the early 1990s, Vitale had been head of Bantam. He originally came from the banking sector. Former editorial director of the Random imprint, André Schiffrin, Pantheon, described Vitale's early days in charge of Random – he had no books in his office only pictures of his boat.[9]

Stories circled of the new Random management's interference in editorial decisions. The company cancelled author Kim Master's contract for his book, *Keys to the Kingdom*, on the rise to power of the then Disney Chairman, Michael Eisner, even asking for part of the advance that the company had paid Masters to be returned.[10] Former Disney executive Jeffery Katzenberg's attorney, Bert Fields, said that the new Random management didn't want to offend Eisner, a man deemed useful for Random's future – Disney's ABC TV network was a good television publicity vehicle for Random's books.

## THE MECHANICS OF MERGERS

Bertelsmann's purchase of Random House trade publisher for $1.4 billion in 1998, Reed Elsevier's buyout of the non-trade college book operations of Harcourt Brace for $2.06 billion in 2000, and Pearson's pickup of the educational publishing operations at Simon & Schuster (Viacom) for $4.6 billion in 1998 all tell stories of merging. Why is a merger so attractive, especially when so many business observers say they rarely succeed? Forcing diverse company cultures to combine often has a negative effect on the operations of the new merged partners. The biggest merger in history, the 2001 AOL and Time Warner merger, didn't work for either company.

The raw truth is that the decision to merge is strategic, a question of market power, a response to the globalisation of content markets. The project is to accumulate revenue-earning content assets, not to satisfy the concerns of staff or build company cultures. Market power brings enormous benefits, even at the cost of internal conflict or the capital required to make the purchase. Bigger operations can extract better business arrangements from the market. In 2001, Random made $1.1995 bn. Regardless of staff morale, company running costs and interest payments on capital loans involved, if Random can annually earn more than its purchase price ($1.4 billion), then the deal cannot be seen as a bad purchase.

Merging problems arise when a small player doesn't react well to the attention or overtures of the larger corporation. If a straight takeover offer is not accepted, the large firm making the merger offer may adopt a wait and see approach. This is not strategically useful if values are rising in a climbing market. With consumer confidence and shares prices on an upward swing, a wait-to-see approach may prove costly. A corporation may choose to deal sooner rather than later. The rationale is: even if the price is high now, the price later will be higher again. Many mergers can appear cheap looking back. There are other reasons for merging, of course, and some mergers, whatever the reason, are never cheap, even ten years after.

## THE AOL TIME WARNER MERGER

On 10 January 2000, Time Warner (TW) and America On Line (AOL) announced a $163.4 billion merger. Among the public reasons given for the merger, both chairmen (AOL and Time Warner) cited 'perfect synergy' as a goal for the merged company. The collection of AOL and Time Warner brands looked formidable, combining *Time* magazine, Warner Bros, CNN, with America Online, the biggest online service provider of the time.

AOL was the 'archetype of the portal', boasting 27 million members, 40% of all US online subscribers, 80% of its online subscribers never going beyond AOL sites. Its closest competitors were Earthlink with 4.7 million subscribers, and Microsoft's MSN with 4 million.[11] Yet in 1998, AOL's earnings of $2.8 billion were dwarfed by Time Warner's revenues of $25 billion.

*(Continued)*

*(Continued)*

Time Warner was the world's largest media corporation, reaching that target when it merged with Turner Broadcasting (CNN) in 1996, overtaking The Walt Disney Company. Time Warner was the second largest cable operator behind AT&T, controlling 22 of the biggest 100 markets, as well as a proprietor of several cable content network providers, including CNN and HBO. TW was the second largest book publisher in the world (*Time Life Books*, *Warner Books* and *Book of the Month Club*) and owned 24 magazines, including *Sports Illustrated*, *Fortune* and *Time.* It distributed music through *Warner Music*. The list went on and on. So why did Time Warner want to merge with AOL, a much smaller and narrower-based company?

As 2000 grew nearer, informed observers were describing the internet as the next great media paradigm. The CEO of Time Warner saw AOL as the future of media. The market agreed with him. AOL's stellar share market value of $140 billion in the late 1990s meant it was worth more than CBS, Disney and Viacom put together.[12] AOL, a dial-up internet service company using ordinary bandwidth telephone lines with no real assets (badly needing Time's broadband to compete with other cable and telephone companies), was a very powerful media company.

Time Warner's CEO, Gerry Levin, believed his company, no matter how large and powerful, was poorly positioned for the internet future. He believed old media was doomed if it didn't integrate with new media.[13] In 1997 when AOL's chairman, Steve Case, offered a merger, it was said that Gerry Levin jumped on AOL's hook.

After the merger was completed in 2001, TW staff said Time Warner had been 'taken for a ride' by a sharp new media operator. AOL's stock value had reached its inflated peak and 'pannicky' TW had been 'snookered' into 'selling [its] jewels for fake currency'.[14] Time's management 'terrified of being blindsided by the Internet' jumped without looking.[15] AOL's Case sold Levin the idea that Time Warner was getting the better end of the deal, with TW caught by a 'classic sting operation'.[16]

On the surface much of this seemed true. By 2003 the merger had lost the combined company $135 billion in the falling value of stocks and shares. AOL Time Warner reported the biggest loss in US corporate history – $100 billion. Steve Case, as AOL Time Warner's Chairman, and Gerry Levin as its CEO were forced to step down, though neither suffered that much. Case was the only AOL executive allowed to sell AOL shares after the merger. He was forced out as Chairman, but remained on the combined board.[17] Levin resigned as TW's CEO, yet, together with his shareholdings, he kept a '$1 million a year' consultancy contract up to 2005.

On 16 October 2003, without ceremony, 'AOL' was officially lopped off the corporate name.[18] On 31 October 2005, Steve Case left the company, the announcement almost going unnoticed.[19] Time Warner started talking of selling off AOL – the once formidable new media outfit now languishing in a minor division inside Time Warner, not even called AOL. For AOL staff, the merger had been a disaster from day one. 'It was like the Mongolian invasion of China ... a takeover from within,' said one AOL executive at the time.[20]

The precipitous fall of AOL values began on 4 April 2000, less than three months after the new merger announcement. On that day NASDAQ dropped 575 points, losing more than 13% of its value.[21] AOL eventually lost everything, not only its stellar stock values. By contrast, Time Warner lost no real market position. While its shareholders were forced to take a financial charge, a substantial one, it was 'a paper stocks fall charge' nonetheless.

In effect, whether by intention or not, Time Warner was instrumental in destroying the first new media market boom. Time Warner achieved two things by merging: 'extravagant' new media stock valuations were gone; and Time (and other big media companies) bought themselves time – time to reposition their companies for the new media era, without an upstart digital newcomer with inflated stocks breathing down their necks.

Compaine argues that many of the companies blamed for the negative effects of mergers have themselves been victims of the corporate process.[22] Powerful media companies who were once predators, such as RCA, Vivendi, Gulf & Western and AT & T have all been absorbed into other empires at various times. Some have lost their names, some names live on.

In the US publishing industry, from 1960 to 1969, there were 183 acquisitions and mergers. Education funding growth, post-war paperback boom profits and the growing opportunities in information provision promised by computer technologies fuelled this first phase of mergers.[23] RCA acquired Random House; CBS absorbed Holt, Reinhart and Winston; Dell bought Dial Press; Doubleday acquired Laidlaw Brothers; Dun & Bradstreet bought Thomas Y. Crowell Co.; General Learning took over Silver Burdette Co.; Gulf & Western acquired Pocket Books; ITT took over Howard W. Sams; Litton Industries bought Reinhold Publishing Corporation; American Book Company merged with D. Van Nostrand Co.; National Industries acquired Bantam Books; Perfect Film & Chemical bought Popular Library Inc.; Times Mirror absorbed New American Library and Harry N. Abrams; and Xerox Corporation staged a buyout of R. R. Bowker Co. and Ginn & Co.

The 1970s merger scenario shifted as a series of economic crunches hit home. In a US economy burdened by the cost of the Vietnam war and oil crises, publishing companies were now targeted less for the market opportunities and more for the financial difficulties they were now in. American Broadcasting Corporation bought Chilton Books, Bertelsmann AG bought Bantam Books, Gulf & Western merged with Simon & Schuster, Scribner merged with Atheneum, Penguin (Pearson) bought Viking, MCA acquired G. P. Putnam, RCA bought Ballantine Books, and Time bought Book-of-the-Month Club.

As the Western World moved out of recession in the 1980s, a resurgent stock market brought back an expansionary merger and acquisition culture. Bertelsmann AG acquired Dell & Doubleday, News Corporation bought Harper and Row and then Collins, and Pearson acquired New American Library. Towards the end of the decade another recession changed the scenario again. The 1980s closed with Harcourt Brace Jovanich and Robert Maxwell's companies both fallinghard. Maxwell was forced to sell Pergamon Press and Maxwell Directories to Elsevier. In 1991, Harcourt was sold for around $1.5 billion to General Cinema Corporation. Table 4.1 details the major acquisitions and mergers from 1990 to 2003.

TABLE 4.1  Major acquisitions and mergers, 1990–2003

| |
| --- |
| News Corporation's new HarperCollins absorbed Scott Foresman, later Ecco Press & Avon and Morrow |
| General Cinema bought Harcourt Brace and Jovanich |
| McGraw-Hill bought out Macmillan/McGraw-Hill School Publishing |
| Wolters Kluwer acquired J. B. Lippincott |
| Pearson merged Penguin US with Putnam Berkley and bought Dorling Kindersley |
| Random House bought Reed Consumer Books' Adult Trade list |
| Thomson bought Reed's Harcourt Higher Education books |
| Cambridge Information acquired R. R. Bowker |
| Wolters Kluwer bought Springhouse Corporation |
| Bertelsmann acquired Random House |

## THE RISE OF THE BIG FIVE TRADE PUBLISHERS

Forty years of mergers and acquisitions radically altered the face and culture of publishing. The consumer/trade sector is now led by Random House, HarperCollins, Penguin, Hachette Livre and Simon & Schuster, their combined sales revenues representing nearly 60% of the total market (Table 4.2).

The top five UK trade publishers are a very similar list to that of the USA accounting for 54% of sales (Table 4.3). The new wild-card entrant of recent times is the Independent Alliance.[24] Other success stories include Bloomsbury, the UK publisher of Harry Potter, with 2008 revenues of £43.3 million. Medium-sized

TABLE 4.2  The top five US trade publishers, 2009

| US publisher | 2009 revenue (estimates) ($m) | US 2009 market share (%) |
| --- | --- | --- |
| Random House | 1,414 | 17.5 |
| Pearson (Penguin) | 913 | 11.3 |
| Hachette | 808 | 10.0 |
| HarperCollins | 792 | 9.8 |
| Simon & Schuster | 735 | 9.1 |

*Source of figures*: Association of American Publishers. Percentage shares from http://michaelhyatt.com[25]

TABLE 4.3  The top five UK trade publishers, 2009

| UK publisher | 2009 revenue (£m) | UK 2009 market share(%) |
|---|---|---|
| Hachette Livre UK | 287.9 | 16.4 |
| Random House | 239.4 | 13.7 |
| Penguin | 170.4 | 9.7 |
| HarperCollins | 132.3 | 7.6 |
| Independent Alliance | 57.3 | 3.3 (*+0.6% on 2008*) |
| Pan Macmillan | 57.3 | 3.3 (*no change on 2008*) |

*Source of figures: The Bookseller via Nielsen Bookscan*

firms such as Thames and Hudson (in Art), and Quarto (Illustrated publishing) have also both grown in size in recent times.

## RANDOM HOUSE

Bennett Cerf and Donald Klopfer started Random House in 1927, renaming Modern Library, a classic literature reprints house they had acquired in 1925. The name sprang from a tongue-in-cheek description by Cerf of the company's choice of titles – made 'at random'. Cerf and Klopfer soon proved themselves anything but tongue-in-cheek or random as publishers. Initially they created Modern Library Giants in 1931 – publishing 'significant' books in modern literature, including *War and Peace* by Leo Tolstoy and *Les Miserables* by Victor Hugo and an elaborate edition of *The Adventures of Tom Sawyer* by Mark Twain. The Great Depression forced them to rethink their approach.

Random began its march to the top of US trade by signing up contemporary American writers. Then, in 1932, Cerf bought US rights to the banned *Ulysses* by James Joyce. When Cerf's copy was seized by customs, he launched a legal action against the US government. On 6 December 1933, Judge John Woolsey decided in Random's favour, allowing the house to publish a wholly uncensored US version of Joyce's controversial novel. The legal victory gave Random vital nationwide publicity. The company published Joyce's novel under their Modern Library imprint in 1934.

In 1936, Random bought Robinson Smith & Robert Haas, Inc., acquiring the rights to the works of prominent authors in the process – Isak Dinesen, William Faulkner, and Jean de Brunhoff, author of the children's series *Babar*. This allowed Random to move into children's books. In 1947, after substantial investment of half a million dollars, Random published the *American College Dictionary*, the beginning of the company's successful trade reference list. With the explosion in paperback publishing in the 1950s, Random grew rapidly towards becoming the giant of US consumer books. In 1957, Random was valued at $2 million and potential mergers were discussed with Holt, Rinehart, and the then Time-Life. Random went public in 1959. With the capital accumulated from the sales of shares, Random expanded again, acquiring Alfred J. Knopf for $3 million. Cerf assured Knopf that it would maintain its editorial independence, a promise he honoured. Random then acquired the textbook publisher L. W. Singer and Pantheon Books.

In 1965 Radio Corporation of America (RCA) acquired Random House for $40 million, a price that marked a twenty-fold increase in Random House's value inside seven years. In the merger agreement Cerf insisted that RCA agree in writing not to interfere with Random's publishing programme. Bennett Cerf remained as Chairman and Company President for one year, before handing over day-to-day control of the company to his protégé, Robert Bernstein.

Random House was in very good shape, having posted record earnings. In 1966, the company published *Random House Dictionary of the English Language*, a title which had taken ten years of research and cost the company $3 million to develop. In five years the dictionary sold more than 500,000 copies. Cerf remained as Chairman until 1969, moving on to the position of senior editor, a position he held until his death in 1971 at the age of 73. By 1971, Modern Library had published over 400 titles and sold around 50 million books.

Apart from their canniness as publishers, neither Cerf or Klopfer could have realised the 'cascade effect' the RCA corporate takeover of Random would have on the publishing industry. In 1980, The Newhouse family (Advance Publications) bought Random House for $70 million. This set off another decade of Random growth, with the house acquiring Fawcett Books in 1982, creating Villard Books in 1983, and buying Times Books from the New York Times Company in 1984.

In 1985 Random started its AudioBooks division, purchased Fodor's Travel Guides in 1986, and then took over Chatto, Virago, Bodley Head and the UK's Jonathan Cape in 1987. In the same year Random merged with Pantheon Books and acquired Schocken Books. In 1988 it bought out Crown Publishing Group, adding Crown Books, Clarkson N. Potter, Inc., Harmony Books, and the Outlet Book Company to the company's already long list of assets.

In 1989, Bernstein left the company after 23 years of service. Cerf once remarked that Jason Epstein was his 'class editor' and Robert Bernstein his 'mass editor'. Bernstein was replaced by Alberto Vitale from Bantam Doubleday Dell (BDD). Vitale launched a cost-cutting regime, turning Random's focus on to the growing opportunities in electronic and multimedia publishing.

Random continued its expansion programme, buying the UK's Century Hutchinson, which together with Chatto, Virago, Bodley Head and Cape group became Random House UK. At the time, the Pantheon Books imprint, headed by André Schiffrin, was in difficulties. When Vitale set out to 'fix' the imprint, Schiffrin decided to leave the company. Pantheon's bestselling author, Studs Terkel, left as well, leading E. L. Doctorow, Barbara Ehrenreich, Kurt Vonnegut, and hundreds of others to demonstrate in the street outside Random's New York headquarters against Vitale's management and policies. The imprint's authors wrote a collectively signed letter of protest to Pantheon. Vitale went public to soothe ruffled feathers and then hired Erroll McDonald, a critic of the demonstrators, as the imprint's new executive editor. The Pantheon imprint continued on with fewer staff and titles.

Throughout the 1990s, Vitale proved a controversial and combative Random head and his electronic vision hit some snags. When Random found out in 1993 that the electronic rights to Theodor Geisel's *Dr Seuss* books were not in the company's contract, Random went on the attack, adding tough electronic rights clauses. The William Morris Agency refused to deal with Random for over a year. More authors left Random. Then Vitale got into a dispute with American Booksellers Association over the discounts the company offered the big chains.

In 1998, the privately owned German media conglomerate Bertelsmann AG (already owners of Bantam Doubleday Dell) purchased Random for $1.4 billion. Vitale remained as Chairman. Bertelsmann's acquisition of Random shocked the bookworld as the Newhouse-owned trade publisher seemed to be doing well. For the Newhouse brothers, Samuel and Donald, owners of 100% of Advance Publication's stock, Bertelsmann's offer was one they couldn't refuse. With the acquisition of Random, Bertelsmann, the third largest media conglomerate behind Time Warner and Disney, became the biggest trade publisher in the USA.

Bertelsmann sold $6 billion of books every year. Random House alone sold close to $1 billion of books annually, controlling nearly 23% of the US trade book market. The merger allowed substantial economies of scale in accounting and marketing operations to be made. In 2001, Random chief, Vitale, continued his combative approach, this time finding himself in a dispute with a small new e-book company, RosettaBooks, over the electronic rights clauses in Random author contracts. Random sued Rosetta, but a New York District Court rejected Random's arguments. Random thought of appealing the decision, then made a deal with Rosetta to produce and distribute e-books by Random's authors.

*Some key dates:*

| | |
|---|---|
| 1925 | Bennett Cerf and Donald Klopfer acquire Modern Library |
| **1927** | **Random House Inc. is formed** |
| 1934 | Random House publishes James Joyce's *Ulysses* |
| 1947 | *American College Dictionary*, Random's first reference book, is published |
| 1959 | The company goes public |
| **1965** | **Random House is acquired by RCA for $40 million** |
| 1966 | Random House *Dictionary of the English Language* is published |
| 1980 | Random House is bought by Advance Publications (Newhouse empire) for $70 million |
| 1989 | Random House UK is established |
| **1998** | **Random House acquired by German conglomerate Bertelsmann AG for $1.4 billion** |
| 2001 | Judge Stein rules against Random in digital rights dispute with RosettaBooks |

## HARPERCOLLINS

Founded by News Corporation in 1990, HarperCollins derives from two strong publishing histories on both sides of the Atlantic. In 1817, Harpers – the eventual

US arm of HarperCollins – was begun when two brothers, James and John Harper, founded Harper Brothers Company in New York City. The firm went on to publish Mark Twain, the Brontë sisters, Thackeray, Dickens, John F. Kennedy and Martin Luther King Jr.

In 1825, four Harper Brothers were shareholders of the company at $500 a share. Extremely competitive, Harpers exploited the lack of international copyright agreements, waiting on the docks for the latest editions to arrive from Britain and reprinting them, sometimes within hours of receiving a copy. By the 1830s Harpers was the largest printing company in the United States. The company's history includes great triumphs and even greater trials.

After the publication of the company's biggest project, *Harper's Illustrated and New Pictorial Bible*, in 1844, James Harper was elected Mayor of New York City. The late 1840s brought success and controversy with the publication of Thackeray's *Vanity Fair*, as well as *Jane Eyre* and *Wuthering Heights* by the Brontë sisters. *Wuthering Heights* caused a near scandal due to what some Americans regarded as its 'obscene' language. One Boston bookseller returned all copies. But with the creation of a new venture, *Harper's New Monthly Magazine*, in 1850, the company survived the ruckus, going from strength to strength. Towards the end of 1853, Harpers were running 41 presses ten hours a day, six days a week, averaging 25 volumes per minute, and achieving an annual income of nearly $2 million.

Disaster struck on 10 December 1853, when a fire destroyed their New York headquarters. Damages ran over $1 million, with the company only 20% covered by insurance. The company said it would rebuild from scratch and telegrams of support and contributions arrived from all corners of the United States. Harpers revived itself, but with a heavy price of competition in the 1870s, together with the deaths of James and Wesley Harper, by the 1890s the company was close to bankruptcy.

Bought by S. S. McClure of Doubleday & McClure, Harpers was brought back from near extinction, though still carrying unresolved debt. Costs were slashed, which led some important authors – Joseph Conrad, Theodore Dreiser and Sinclair Lewis – to leave the company. Harpers weathered the crisis and expanded, settling its debts with J. P. Morgan. By 1925 the company was again producing quality literature from writers such as Aldous Huxley, Anne Parrish, J. B. Priestly, James Thurber and E. B. White. Harpers survived low sales in the Great Depression, bringing in unknown authors to great success. By 1950 the company was again publishing literary successes and winning prizes – *The Ides of March* by Thornton Wilder, *Annie Allen* by Gwendolyn Brooks, winner of the Pulitzer Prize in 1950, and John F. Kennedy's *Profiles in Courage*, another Pulitzer Prize winner in 1957.

In 1962, Harper & Brothers merged with Row, Peterson & Company, an Illinois textbook firm, renaming itself Harper & Row Publishers, Inc. A year later, President Kennedy was assassinated and Robert Kennedy asked Harpers to publish William Manchester's *Death of a President* (with most profits earmarked for the Kennedy Library). The book inspired a legal battle over certain sections and was not published until 1967.

Image by and courtesy of Giulio Lichtner © 2010

Over the next two decades, Harper & Row embarked on a new expansion plan, acquiring T. Y. Crowell in 1977 and J. B. Lippincott in 1978, and listing the company on the New York Stock Exchange in 1983. Acquired by News Corporation in 1987 for $300 million, Harpers subsequently bought Zondervan Books in 1988 and Scott, Foresman in 1989.

The UK half of HarperCollins, William Collins and Sons, was created in 1819 by William Collins, a Presbyterian schoolmaster and millworker from Glasgow. Collins set up his press by printing and publishing pamphlets, sermons, hymn and prayer books through the early 1820s. His first book was *The Christian and Civic Economy of Large Towns*. Collins published a dictionary and in 1840 obtained permission to publish a Collins Bible. By the 1850s Collins held a monopoly of scripture publishing. In the 1870s the business expanded with the acquisition of new lithographic printing presses. Towards the end of the nineteenth century the company was under the control of William Collins III. When he died in an accident, the reins were taken up by his son William IV, and then his sons, who led the company into South America and South Africa. After the First World War, Collins expanded into publishing fiction, strengthening and diversifying the company brand. Growth continued with the paperback in the 1950s. In the 1970s, Collins renewed its printing operations. In the late 1980s, the company bought 50% of Harper & Row from News International, a collaboration that lasted until April 1989, when News acquired Collins outright, forming HarperCollins Publishers in 1990. The merger made the combined company the largest English-language publisher in the world at the time.

Despite News Corporation experiencing a severe financial crisis in 1991, HarperCollins grew fast. By 1994, it had already established itself as a world brand with global revenues of over $1 billion. Within a decade of its creation, the list of imprints HarperCollins held included Avon, Harper Perennial, Hearst Books, William Morrow, Amistad, Fourth Estate and Ecco. In 2008 News Corporation's worldwide earnings were $33 billion, HarperCollins UK contributing £147.5 million in book sales. In 2009 HarperCollins US contributed $792 million to the Corporation's $30 billion plus earnings.

*Some key dates*:

| | |
|---|---|
| **1817** | **Harper Brothers Company begins operations in New York** |
| **1819** | **William Collins begins printing religious materials in Glasgow** |
| 1841 | William Collins finds success selling Bibles |
| 1840–50 | Harpers publish *Harper's Illustrated and New Pictorial Bible*, Thackeray's *Vanity Fair*, and *Jane Eyre* and *Wuthering Heights* by the Brontë sisters. James Harper is elected Mayor of New York City. Collins publishes a Collins Bible |
| 1853 | Harper Bros' New York headquarters burns down |
| 1856 | William Collins forges a monopoly over the publishing of scripture in the UK |
| 1868 | William Collins renamed William Collins and Sons Pty Ltd |
| 1890 | Harpers bought by McLure (Doubleday) |
| 1919 | From its base in Pall Mall, London, Collins begins to publish original fiction |
| 1930s | Collins publishes *The Murder of Roger Ackroyd*, Agatha Christie's first novel, creates Crime Club list, and obtains rights to publish Walt Disney in the UK. Harpers counters the Great Depression by taking on new authors such as Thornton Wilder and Thomas Wolfe |

| 1957 | John F. Kennedy wins the Pulitzer Prize with *Profiles in Courage* for Harpers |
| **1962** | **Harper Bros** merges with **Row, Peterson & Company** to become **Harper & Row Publishers, Inc.** |
| 1983 | Harpers & Row lists itself on the New York Stock exchange |
| **1987** | **News Corporation buys Harper & Row** |
| **1989** | **News Corporations buys Collins** |
| **1990** | **HarperCollins is formed** |
| 1900–94 | HarperCollins becomes a global brand |
| 1999 | News Corporation acquires Hearst Book Group, including imprints, William Morrow & Company & Avon Books, and announces it will buy ECCO, a US literary/boutique press |
| 2000 | News Corporation buys Fourth Estate boutique literary publisher in the UK |
| 2001 | HarperCollins is the first major publisher to launch an e-book list |
| 2002 | ECCO buys Black Sparrow Press rights to Paul Bowles, Charles Bukowski, John Fante |
| 2007 | HarperCollins author, Doris Lessing, wins the Nobel Prize |

## HACHETTE

Lagardère Publishing (with Hachette as its book publishing division) is currently the world's second-largest trade-book publisher for the general public and educational markets. It is the leading publisher in French-speaking markets as well as in the United Kingdom and a major world magazine publisher. It is second in Spanish-language markets and in 2009 went from fifth to third-ranked publisher in the United States. Lagardère is the third largest magazine publisher in the USA and Italy, the largest in France and Spain, its reach making it the world's largest magazine publisher.

Lagardère/Hachette's global publishing earnings for 2010 were 2,165 €m, with a territorial split of revenue in percentages being: France 32%; United States and Canada 23%; United Kingdom and Australia 19%; Spain 9%; and other miscellaneous countries 17%. In 2010, Hachette UK titles appeared one hundred and fifty times in the UK's *Sunday Times* bestseller list, with thirty-three of those titles going to number one.

In November 2010, Hachette Livre signed an *agreement in principle* with Google, allowing the global search engine to scan Hachette's out of print titles. The intention was to end a dispute over Google's prior scanning of Hachette's out of print books held by libraries. Under the terms of the agreement in principle, Hachette Livre retained the right in the future to exploit any of titles Google had already scanned – by any means including print on demand and in any form of digital transmission. The agreement, set to progress to a fully signed contract in May 2011, did not discharge any claims Hachette believes it has or might believe it has in the future, while setting clear terms for any future scanning by Google of Hachette titles.

Lagardère is also a major French newspaper distributor, owning regional newspapers such as *Nice Matin* and *La Provence* and is the country's leading magazine publisher, producing *Paris Match*, *Elle*, *Télé 7 Jours* and *Pariscope*. Lagardère also retains a small stake in the Parti Communiste Français newspaper *L'Humanité*. Lagardère's publishing revenue in 2008 was €2.159 billion.

Lagardère acquired Hachette in 1981, a bookshop dating back to 1826. Around 51% of sales are generated outside France, with 65% of sales occurring within the European Union. In 2006, Hachette created Hachette Livre UK, buying the Time Warner Book Group and acquiring imprints such as Little, Brown and Company, Grand Central Publishing (formerly Warner Books), and Orbit, a science fiction and fantasy imprint. Hachette Livre UK (later Hachette UK) also acquired Headline, Hodder & Stoughton, Sceptre, Abacus, Sphere, Piatkus, Virago, Orion, Weidenfeld & Nicolson, Gollanz, Phoenix, Everyman, John Murray, Octopus, Cassell and Hamlyn.

*Some key dates*:

| | |
|---|---|
| 1768 | John Murray opens his publishing company in London |
| **1826** | **Louis Hachette purchases Brédif, a Paris bookstore** |
| 1837 | Little Brown established |
| 1863 | Louis Hachette publishes the *Dictionary of the French Language* |
| 1868 | Hodder & Stoughton begins publishing |
| 1945 | Matra (Mécanique Aviation TRAction) is created. Hachette launches *Elle* magazine |
| 1949 | Weidenfeld & Nicholson imprint founded |
| 1963 | Jean-Luc Lagardère is appointed CEO of Matra |
| 1971 | Octopus established |
| 1980 | Lagardère (formerly Matra) is incorporated (publishing, retail, media and aerospace) |
| **1981** | **Lagardère acquires Hachette.** Jean-Luc Lagardère takes over running the company |
| 1986 | Headline Book Publishing established |
| 1991 | Orion Publishing Group formed |
| 1992 | Headline acquires Bookpoint |
| 1993 | Headline acquires Hodder & Stoughton and forms Hodder Headline Ltd |
| 1995–96 | Time Warner acquires Little, Brown Company |
| 1996 | Hachette Livre acquires Orion and Cassell |
| 1999 | Hodder Headline acquired by WH Smith |
| 2001 | Hachette Livre acquires Octopus |
| 2002 | Lagardère buys Vivendi Universal Publishing (without Houghton Mifflin). Hodder Headline acquires John Murray |
| 2004 | Lagardère/Hachette Livre UK acquires Hodder Headline |
| 2006 | Hachette Livre UK buys Time Warner Books becoming the UK's leading consumer publisher. Time Warner Books is renamed Little Brown Book Group |
| 2007 | Hachette Book Publishing India is formed |
| 2008 | Hachette Livre UK becomes Hachette UK |

## PENGUIN (PEARSON)

Penguin Books, owned by Pearson from 1971, is probably now the world's most identifiable consumer books brand. Its distinctive logo is behind the greatest boom publishing has ever known – the trade paperback sales explosion of the mid-twentieth century. The company was created by Allen Lane in 1935, by the then director of the Lane family-created and part-owned ailing literary publishing house, The Bodley Head. Out of a dispute on how to proceed with The Bodley Head, Lane set up Penguin, leaving The Bodley Head to concentrate on his new company.

The story of Penguin is intriguing, almost a novella in itself. Waiting for a train at Exeter station after a meeting with a Bodley author, Agatha Christie, in Devon, Lane began browsing a platform bookstall for something to read on his trip back to London. Dismayed to find only magazines and old Victorian reprints on offer, Lane realised that good contemporary fiction would sell at railway stations and tobacconists, if priced reasonably. As folklore has it, Lane decided in that moment to create a new imprint.

Back in his London office, Lane's secretary came up with a name – Penguin. Lane jumped at it – it was 'dignified, but flippant' – despatching the office junior, Edward Young, to sketch penguins at the London Zoo. Young was then given the job of designing the covers for the first set of ten books. Lane was said to dislike illustrated covers (he thought them 'trashy') and laid out a simple but strict design principle – clear plain horizontal grids for jackets with colour coding to indicate genre: orange for fiction, green for crime, and blue for biography.

Lane had borrowed the entire idea from an earlier German paperback imprint, Albatross. However, while Penguin was not the first paperback, it was the first to succeed in mass terms. And that was Lane's genius, an uncanny knack for knowing how to exploit a good publishing idea. Lane also demonstrated courage, if not reck-lessness, and not a little bloody-mindedness as a businessman. Part 'missionary and part mercenary', he was described as a man who knew 'rather less Greek than his chauffeur',[26] a publisher who 'paid badly ... [and was] a compulsive hirer and firer'. Receiving help from his parents, who 'mortgaged their home to pay for the experiment', and with his brothers on board also contributing 'what they could, in time and money', Lane 'sold the paintings and the collection of books ... [his] Uncle John had left him', in order to finance the venture.[27]

After Penguin took off, hardback publisher, Jonathan Cape told Lane to his face that he was 'the bugger who ruined the trade' (animus no doubt also inspired by Lane's departure from The Bodley Head, a company of which Cape had become a partner).

Lane's starting cover price was 6d, the same as the sales call from the high street store, Woolworth – 'nothing more than 6d'. As the story went, Lane was having a hard time convincing the company's chief buyer to take on the new Penguins, when the man's wife walked in. Picking up a Penguin she found the copy fitted into her handbag. Her positive reaction convinced her husband. Woolworth bought 63,000 books, paying for Lane's investment in one order. It wasn't long before the Penguins were flying off the shelves. Within ten months the first 85 Penguin titles had sold over a million copies, the heydays of Penguin.

> The very early editorial meetings were held in a favourite Spanish restaurant, with plenty of wine to keep things cheerful. They lasted as far into the small hours as the management would permit. Those meetings were probably the happiest time of Allen's life. As Penguin grew he always regretted the loss of that experimental, mad-cap atmosphere.[28]

Penguin fiction was followed in 1937 by Penguin Shakespeare and Pelican Books (serious non-fiction studies), which was followed by a children's imprint, Puffin Books, in 1940. Opening overseas offices in America, and later in Australia in 1946, after the war the company created Penguin Classics. In the 1950s, competition grew from new paperback imprints such as Pan as the whole paperback boom broadened into a bonanza.

Perhaps sensing he needed another 'publishing coup', in 1959 Lane decided to print the banned unexpurgated version of D. H. Lawrence's *Lady Chatterley's Lover*. Lane was charged under the Obscene Publications Act. Defending the action, he won the case, overturning British censorship laws in a single stroke. Penguin sold 2 million copies of Lawrence's novel in six weeks. In 1961 the company went public, with its stock offering over-subscribed 150 times.

Even though the episode with *Lady Chatterley's Lover* might indicate otherwise, Lane's free-spirited morals had definite limits. Offended by an explicit illustrated publication by the French artist Siné, whom Lane's editorial protégé, Tony Godwin, planned to publish, Lane the risk-taker of the 1930s became Lane the old man overnight. Fighting his own board and losing, Lane loaded the Siné books into a van and took them to one of his farms and burnt the lot. Then he sacked Godwin. The talents that made Lane a maverick success seemed to have deserted him. The slowing of the paperback boom had also caught him offside. By the end of the 1960s Penguin's sales had fallen dramatically. The company found itself in severe financial difficulties. Lane died in 1970 and a battle ensued for control of Penguin. The American company McGraw-Hill bought 17% of Penguin's shares but were beaten to the goal by Longmans,[29] newly owned by the engineering-come-media corporate giant, Pearson.

A growing global media brand and software company – bringing together newspapers, education and consumer book assets – Pearson took Penguin's growth to another level, adding many other major publishing companies and imprints to the brand. The new owners expanded into the United States during the 1970s, acquiring the renowned literary house, Viking, joining the imprint to Penguin. This added John Steinbeck, Saul Bellow, Arthur Miller and Jack Kerouac to Penguin's list of writers. In its history, Viking published winners of four Nobel Prizes, seven Pulitzer Prizes in fiction and poetry, 16 National Book Awards and four Booker Prizes.

In the mid-1990s Penguin USA merged with Putnam. By 1999, 50% of the profits of Penguin's parent, Pearson Plc, were coming from its book operations and sales in the USA. Apart from PenguinPutnam, Pearson had also bought Simon & Schuster's Education and Reference divisions for $4.6 billion in 1998 (Simon & Schuster's educational and computer books business were the world's largest), which, on obtaining US government approval for the move, shot Pearson's Addison-Wesley Longman educational division to first place in the US textbook market.

*Some key dates*:

1724  Longman publishing is founded
1838  Putnam publishing created (in partnership with John Wiley until 1848)
1844  Pearson founds a civil engineering business
1856  Pearson begins railway construction in UK
1865  Frederick Warne leaves Routledge and forms Frederick Warne & Co.
1889  Scott Foresman publishing founded
1920  Pearson acquires UK newspapers, the Westminister Press and provincial newspapers, including the *Brighton Evening Argus* and *The Oxford Mail*
1931  Viking Press founded
**1935  Penguin Books begins publishing**
1936  Penguin in the UK and Putnam in the USA form a business alliance
1940  Puffin Books children's series created
1942  Addison-Wesley founded
1946  Penguin Classics launched; Penguin Australia founded
1947  Longman becomes public company
1957  Pearson buys control of *The Financial Times*
1960  Penguin is charged under the Obscene Publications Act over *Lady Chatterley's Lover*, winning the case and overturning British censorship laws, selling 2 million copies in six weeks
1961  Penguin Modern Classics is launched. Penguin becomes a public company, its share offer is 150 times oversubscribed, a record at the time for the London Stock Exchange
1967  Penguin publishes its first hardbacks under Allen Lane The Penguin Press imprint
1968  Pearson gains control of Longman publishers
1969  Pearson becomes a public company
**1970  Allen Lane dies. Pearson Longman acquires Penguin**
**1975  Penguin US merges with Viking**
1983  Penguin buys Frederick Warne, publisher of the Beatrix Potter series
1984  Penguin UK sets up the Viking imprint
1985  In Penguin's 50th year the company buys Michael Joseph and Hamish Hamilton
**1996  Pearson acquires Putnam Berkley** publishing group from Seagram for $350 million and HarperCollins US education from News Corporation for $580 million, sells Westminster Press to Newsquest for £305 million, and sells Kentish Mercury and 50% stake in UK News. Penguin buys 51% of the travel and music publisher, Rough Guides

1998    Pearson purchases Simon & Schuster education, business & professional and reference imprints for £2.9 billion. Pearson begins buy-out of children's and illustrated book publisher Dorling Kindersley for $466 million

2000    Penguin UK completes acquisition of Dorling Kindersley

## SIMON & SCHUSTER

Simon & Schuster was founded in 1924 by Richard L. Simon and M. Lincoln Schuster. The company's first publication was *The Crossword Puzzle Book*, which sold over 100,000 copies in the first year of operation. Subsequently, three other crossword puzzle books were published. By the year's end, Simon & Schuster had sold more than a million copies of the four books. When sales and interest in the crossword began to fall, Simon & Schuster diversified, finding success with its first 'serious' publication, *The Story of Philosophy*, by Will Durant, a bestseller in 1926–1927. Durant, together with his wife Ariel, went on to compile the multi-volume series *Story of Civilization* for Simon & Schuster's expanding list, which soon included Leon Trotsky's *History of the Russian Revolution*, *Ripley's Believe It or Not* newspaper cartoon features, Felix Salten's *Bambi*, Rachel Carson's *Under the Sea Wind*, and Wendell Willkie's *One World*.

In the mid-1930s, Simon & Schuster's business manager, Leon Shimkin, became a full partner and was responsible for acquiring two very successful books for the company, Dale Carnegie's *How to Win Friends and Influence People* and J. K. Lasser's *Your Income Tax*. Shimkin had begun his book publishing career in 1924, when he was hired for $25 a week by Simon and Schuster. The son of Russian immigrants, Shimkin was a freshman at New York University when he joined the company. He finished his degree by studying at night, later in his life becoming one of the university's benefactors, with a building named after him in the Washington Square campus.

In 1939, joining with Robert Fair de Graff, an experienced hardcover publisher, the three partners of Simon & Schuster provided 49% of the financing for a new American paperback venture, Pocket Books. Impressed by Allen Lane's efforts with Penguin, Fair de Graff was sure the mass-market paperback would work in the United States as well. Paperbacks in the USA went as far back as the 1770s but no one had made them work on a mass-market level.

Priced at 25¢, Pocket Book paperbacks were a huge success during the Second World War, with wartime agencies shipping 25 million copies to servicemen and women. The venture was greatly helped when Shimkin arranged for Pocket Books to take over paper quotas that other publishing companies weren't able to use during wartime. The initial eleven Pocket Books titles (and still in print) included William Shakespeare's *Five Great Tragedies*, Pearl S. Buck's *The Good Earth*, James Hilton's *Lost Horizon*, Agatha Christie's *The Murder of Roger Ackroyd*, and Felix Salten's *Bambi*. Pocket Books finally merged with Simon & Schuster in 1966. The house's greatest success was Dr Benjamin Spock's *Baby and Child Care*, published in 1946, which by 1989 had sold more than 33 million copies.

In 1942 Simon & Schuster used the Pocket Books business model to start Little Golden Books, also selling for 25¢ a copy. With costs reduced dramatically by printing 50,000 copies per title – a huge run for the time – the company's children's books saw a post-war baby boom surge in sales. Little Golden Books eventually sold over 400 million copies, spawning Big Golden Books, Giant Golden Books, the Golden Encyclopedia, and Little Golden Records.

In a corporate tale much dreamed of but not often told, in 1944, Field Enterprises, a Chicago-based communications company owned by Marshall Field, bought Simon & Schuster from Simon, Schuster, and Shimkin for $3 million. All three partners stayed with the company and in 1957, with Marshall Field's death, the executors of his estate sold Simon & Schuster back to the original partners for $1 million. In poor health, Richard Simon retired. On his death, Schuster and Shimkin each bought half his shares. Schuster retired in 1966 and sold out to Shimkin, who transformed Simon & Schuster into a publicly traded company.

Thereafter, in many ways, the progress of Simon & Schuster became almost a mirror image of the corporatisation of the publishing industry. In the 1970s, Simon & Schuster was nearly bought by Norton Simon, then by Kinney National Service Inc., and then almost merged with Harcourt Brace Jovanovich. The company was finally acquired by Gulf & Western who had also acquired Paramount. Paramount became Simon & Schuster's owner with Shimkin as Chairman. He continued to be actively connected with the company until his death at 81 years of age in 1988. Under Gulf & Western's aggressive management Simon & Schuster's sales grew from $44 million in 1975 to $1.3 billion in 1989. The company message and style was acquisitive and expansionist. When Simon & Schuster lost the distribution rights to Harlequin in the early 1980s it started its own romance imprint, Silhouette, which soon rivalled Harlequin in sales. In 1984, Harlequin's owner, Torstar, acquired Silhouette from Simon & Schuster for $10 million.

Simon & Schuster expanded again, buying the textbook publisher Esquire Inc. (no longer part of *Esquire* magazine) for $170 million, doubling staff to 2,300 and going from thirteenth US publisher in size to sixth. Then in 1985, Gulf & Western bought Prentice-Hall Inc., a major textbook publisher, for $710 million, making Simon & Schuster the biggest publisher in the USA.

There were other education purchases and mergers: Ginn & Company in 1982 ($100 million); in 1986, Silver Burdett Company ($125 million). Simon & Schuster was an early investor in the computer-driven publishing revolution. With diversification into education and information services, the company's trade division fell to about 6% of overall company sales in 1989. However, Simon & Schuster's trade assets, as with all consumer books businesses, remained high-profile, producing fiction and non-fiction books, from the very commercial to the highly literary. From the 1970s, with Bob Woodward and Carl Bernstein's *All the President's Men* and *The Final Days*, Jackie Collins's *Hollywood Wives*, to Ronald Reagan's *An American Life*, Simon & Schuster had

69 Pulitzer Prize winners. Simon & Schuster's publishing empire had expanded from consumer to education and professional assets, Macmillan Publishing USA being one notable division.

In 1996, Simon & Schuster announced a major goal to generate half of its revenues from electronic publishing by 2000. The company's Education Group created an internet resource, Edscape, a subscription-service interactive curriculum content delivery site for teachers of early grades (kindergarten through to year 12). Other electronic publishing initiatives included a college-level instructors venture by Prentice-Hall and Xilinx, Inc., supplying computer program solutions. When one of their star authors, Stephen King, decided to release his first digital book in March 2000, Simon & Schuster managed the project.

*Some key dates*:

| | |
|---|---|
| **1924** | **Simon & Schuster begins publishing** |
| 1939 | Pocket Books created with Simon & Schuster's backing |
| 1942 | Golden Books children's books launched |
| 1944 | Simon & Schuster and Pocket Books sold to Marshall for $3 million |
| 1957 | Simon, Schuster and Shimkin buy back the company for $1 million |
| 1966 | Surviving partner Shimkin takes Simon & Schuster public |
| 1971 | Viacom sells CBS and becomes a public company |
| **1975** | **Gulf & Western (Paramount) buys Simon & Schuster** |
| 1983 | Gulf & Western restructures, renaming itself Paramount |
| 1994 | Viacom launches a $9.9 billion merger with Paramount |
| 2000 | Viacom completes a $39.8 billion merger with CBS |
| 2005 | In a 'rerun of 1971', Viacom splits itself into two companies – Viacom (Paramount and MTV) and CBS, with CBS the new owner of Simon & Schuster |

## THE TWENTY-FIRST CENTURY

In March 2000, the star author of horror fiction, Stephen King, announced the first of his two online digital book experiments. Managed by his print book publisher, Simon & Schuster, King released an e-book version of a novella, *Riding the Bullet*. The experiment created a stampede among digital enthusiasts and sent shock waves through the entire anglophone publishing world.

> The frenzy was nothing short of remarkable. Never before had a story about text and electronic media penetrated so deeply. ... Grandmothers heard about it on their transistor radios ... 'It's a new book – and you can't get it in bookstores,' pronounced one anchor.[30]

Later in the same year, King launched a second online publishing experiment, this time alone. Deciding to serialise a novel online, King took a 1980s novel, *The Plant*, out of a drawer and placed chapters online for download at $1 each. After seven chapters had been posted and sold, King suddenly terminated the experiment. The author explained his reasons on his website – too many downloaders were not paying. (See Chapter 8, pp. 205–6).

Another major development in 2000 was the emergence of Gemstar. Recently merged with News Corporation's TV Guide in a $9.2 billion merger, Gemstar held a major New York publishing event in October 2000 to outline the company's plans. The company's founder, Henry C. Yuen, planned to sell bestselling authors in e-book format from Gemstar's website, to be read on Gemstar's two e-readers (REB 1100 and REB 1200) using Gemstar proprietary e-book reading software. Yuen wanted to use Gemstar's TV interactive gateway technology on cable channels[31] to create an '8 million-subscriber interactive … e-book business'.[32] It was an audacious plan. Big trade names signed up – Penguin Putnam, Simon & Schuster, St Martin's Press, Warner Books and Harlequin among them. Author brands included Patricia Cornwell, Robert Ludlum, Ed McBain and Ken Follett. Yuen had plans to sell e-books at hardcover prices. High prices would not 'deter the reader', he said, an idea not everyone agreed with at the time.[33]

In May 2001, just as Time Warner completed its merger with AOL, new media markets went into decline. The *dot.com bubble* burst in spectacular fashion. New media went into recession. Like other new media companies, Gemstar's share price plummeted. Cable operators saw an opportunity to derail Yuen's hold over them. Jonathon Fahey, writing in *Forbes*, got out his crystal ball: 'Reality is about to dissolve Yuen's vision. … Gemstar's future isn't nearly as bright as Yuen – or the market – thinks.'[34] In *Fortune*, Marc Gunther wrote that relations between Yuen and Rupert Murdoch had deteriorated badly. Gemstar's stock, $107 in 1999 before the merger, was languishing at $5, a level described 'as ridiculously undervalued'.[35] The US Security and Exchange Commission, the government regulatory body controlling stock markets, charged Gemstar with accounting irregularities. In June 2003, News Corporation closed Gemstar's e-book and e-reader operations and fired Yuen.

In all the gloom, electronic publishing continued to expand in non-trade sectors. The growing popularity of the internet search engine Google helped *New Media* climb back to its feet. Catching the traditional content firms offside, Google's free online search facility altered the whole scenario. In October 2004, Google announced Google Print, a searchable database for all books. Universities were intrigued and big publishers decidedly unimpressed.

Sony brought out a new e-reader, the Sony Librié, a major improvement on the Gemstar e-readers, introducing e-ink technology (using reflected ambient light on the screens). The electronics giant proceeded with caution, releasing the Librié into the techno-literate market in Japan only. No great demand for e-readers or electronic books seemed to exist in anglophone markets. E-books still represented barely 1% of consumer book revenues.

In September 2005, the book industry made a move to stop Google's advance into the book business. The Authors' Guild of America, backed by the Association of American Publishers, launched a class action for copyright infringement against Google Print. Describing Google's plan as 'brazen violation of copyright law',

Authors' Guild President Nick Taylor said: 'It's not up to Google or anyone other than the authors, the rightful owners of these copyrights, to decide whether and how their works will be copied.'[36] In November, Google changed the name of its project to Google Book Search, and launched a public relations offensive.

By 2007, Google had already scanned over a million books. The same year Amazon entered the e-reader market with the Kindle e-reader. A new growth phase began with e-books and e-reader devices. Continuing to use fair use to justify its actions, by 2008 Google had scanned 7 million books and placed them online for viewing. The company had 20,000 publishing firms and many universities willing to partner in the project. Consumer e-book sales were beginning to climb fast. By February 2010, Google had scanned over 12 million books. Apple released its iPad in April 2010, selling over 7 million units by October.

New Media companies – Google, Amazon and Apple – are now serious players in the publishing scenario. Google Editions is planning to offer 'device agnostic' e-books, starting with around 500,000 titles, from its storehouse of 10 million plus digitised texts.[37] The Google e-book will be usable on all hardware, available for reading on any web browser.[38] This while Amazon's Kindle and Apple's iPad use proprietary reading software, a method reflecting the Gemstar closed store model of 2000.[39]

Publishing consultant, Mike Shatzkin, wrote early in 2010 of the 'remarkable stability among big publishers since Bertelsmann acquired Random House in 1999'.[40] But is this stability another way of describing inaction, a prefiguring calm before the coming commercial storm? Are the new media companies already leading the way? Jason Epstein believes that conglomerate-owned publishing has reached a threshold: 'This is the last stage. No one is going to buy these companies again.'[41] Has big book publishing reached its full value? Are new forces about to create a new era, new market, bring more new formats, and continue developing new reading technologies? Consumer book publishing in the twenty-first century continues to face revenue and growth problems – with 2008 pin-pointed as the ultimate peak in print books sales.[42] The security of the print book seems far from assured.

Late in 2010, e-book sales from the major publishers was within a whisker of reaching 10% of the consumer book market. Is this confined to the e-reader-led boom of 2010 only, or does it tell us something fundamental about the future? Are Apple, Google and Amazon shaping up to do in the twenty-first century what publishing houses such as Penguin, Pocket Books, Simon & Schuster and Random House began to do in the 1930s?

## FURTHER READING

Arsenault, A. H. and Castells, M., 'The Structure and Dynamics of Global Multi–Media Business Networks', *International Journal of Communication* 2, 2008, pp. 707–748

Bagdikian, B., *The New Media Monopoly*, Boston, MA, Beacon Press, 2004

Compaine, B. M. and Gomery, D., *Who Owns the Media?: Competition and Concentration in the Mass Media (Communication)*, Mahwah, NJ, Lawrence Erlbaum Associates, 2000

Gasson, C., *Who Owns Whom in British Book Publishing*, London, The Bookseller, 2002

Greco, A. N., *The Book Publishing Industry*, Mahwah, NJ, Lawrence Erlbaum Associates, 2005

Greco, A. N., Rodríguez, C. E. and Wharton, R. M., *The Culture and Commerce of 21st Century Publishing*, Stanford, CA, Stanford Business Books, 2007

Hesmondhalgh, D., *The Cultural Industries*, 2nd edition, Thousand Oaks, CA, Sage, 2007

Klein, A., *Stealing Time: Steve Case, Jerry Levin and the Collapse of AOL Time Warner*, New York, Simon & Schuster, 2003

McChesney, R., *The Political Economy of Media: Enduring Issues, Emerging Dilemmas*, New York, Monthly Review Press, 2008

McChesney, R. W., Newman, R. and Scott, B., *The Future of Media: Resistance and Reform in the 21st Century*, New York, Seven Stories Press, 2005

Porter, M. E., *Competitive Strategy: Techniques for Analyzing Industries and Competitors*, London, The Free Press, 1980

Rice, R., Ed., *Media Ownership: Research and Regulation*, Cresskill, NJ, Hampton Press, 2008

Swisher, K., *There Must Be a Pony in Here Somewhere: The AOL Time Warner Debacle*, New York, Three Rivers Press, 2003

## NOTES

1   http://www.blacksparrowbooks.com/aboutbsb.htm

2   Rice, R., Ed., *Media Ownership: Research and Regulation*, Cresskill, NJ, Hampton Press, 2008, p. 50.

3   Compaine, B. M. and Gomery, D., *Who Owns the Media?: Competition and Concentration in the Mass Media (Communication)*, Mahwah, NJ, Lawrence Erlbaum Associates, 2000, p. 116.

4   De Vany, A. and Walls, D. W., 'Bose-Einstein Dynamics and Adaptive Contracting in the Motion Picture Industry', 1995 (pre-published version of paper) accessed www.wu.au. at/am/Download/ae/BoseEinstein.pdf

5   Greco, A. N., *The Book Publishing Industry*, Mahwah, NJ, Lawrence Erlbaum Associates, 2005, p. 5.

6   McChesney, R. W. *The Problem of the Media: US Communication Politics in the 21st Century*, New York, Monthly Review Press, 2004.

7   Castells, M., *The Rise of the Network Society. The Information Age: Economy, Society and Culture*, Vol. I, Cambridge, MA, Oxford, UK and Blackwell, 1996.

8   Current at Feb. 2008. This figure represents key partnerships and cross-investments. It is not exhaustive.

9   Schiffrin, A., *The Business of Books: How International Conglomerates Took Over Publishing and Changed the Way We Read*, London, Verso, 2000.

10  Compaine, op. cit., p. 87.

11  McChesney, R. W., *Rich Media, Poor Democracy: Communication Politics in Dubious Times*, Chicago, University of Illinois Press, 2000, p. 166.

12  Klein, A., *Stealing Time: Steve Case, Jerry Levin and the Collapse of AOL Time Warner*, New York, Simon & Schuster, 2003, p. 186.

13  Rosenberg, S., 'AOL and Time Warner's Marriage of Insecurity', Salon.com, http://www. salon.com/tech/col/rose/ 2000/01/10/aol_time.

14  Swisher, K., *There Must Be a Pony in Here Somewhere: The AOL Time Warner Debacle*, New York, Three Rivers Press, 2003, pp. 15, 134; Klein, op. cit., pp. 287–288.

15  McChesney, *Rich Media*, op. cit., p. 168.

16  Klein, op. cit., pp. 96, 288.

17  Yang, C. and Capell, K., 'Another Case Entirely', BusinessWeek.com, www.businessweek.com/magazine/content/05_15/b3928093.htm, 2005; Klein, op. cit., p. 298.

18  Klein, op. cit., pp. 300–307.

19  Teather, D., 'Architect of AOL Merger Quits Time Warner', *The Guardian*, 1 November 2005.

20  Klein, op. cit., pp. 291–292.

21  Swisher, op. cit., p. 168.

22  Compaine, B., 'Are the American Media Becoming More Concentrated?', in Rice, R., Ed., *Media Ownership: Research and Regulation*, Cresskill, NJ, Hampton Press Inc., 2008.

23  Under President Lyndon Johnson, education spending in the 1960s soared, providing a reason for corporations to see book publishing as a good investment.

24  Set up by Faber & Faber in 2005, the Independent Alliance now includes Faber & Faber, Atlantic Books, Canongate, Icon Books, Profile Books, Short Books, Quercus Publishing, Serpent's Tail and Granta.

25  These 2009 US percentage shares were posted by Michael Hyatt, the CEO of Thomas Nelson, the biggest US Christian publisher (accounting for 32.6% of the Christian publisher market).

26  Horatio Morpurgo, 'Lady Chatterley's Defendant – Allen Lane and the paperback revolution', *London magazine*, October–November 1999.

27  Ibid.

28  Ibid.

29  Interview with Gordon Graham, Marlow, UK, September, 2009.

30  Steven Zeitchik, 'The revolution that wasn't', *Salon*, 28 March 2000.

31  Grover, R., Lowry, T. and Armstrong, L., 'E-books: The Next Chapter', *Businessweek Online*, http://www.businessweek.com/magazine/content/01_11/b3723001.htm, 2001.

32  Higgins, J. M., 'Life Behind Royalties', Broadcasting & Cable, http://www.broadcastingcable.com/article/143309-Life_beyond_the_royalties.php [July 7 2002].

33  Rose, M. J., 'At What Cost, E-Books?', *Wired.com*. http://www.wired.com/news/culture/0,1284,39471,00.html.

34  Fahey, J., 'Screen Grab', *Forbes.com*, http://www.forbes.com/global/2001/0305/051.html.

35  Gunther, M., 'Why Gemstar May Shine Again', *Fortune*, http://money.cnn.com/magazines/fortune/fortune_archive/2002/07/22/326280/index.htm; Stone, A., 'Will Gemstar Be Our Guide to the Future?', *Businessweek Online*, http://www.businessweek.com/bwdaily/dnflash/may2000/sw00524.htm.

36  'Authors' Guild Sues Google, Citing "Massive Copyright Infringement"', 20 September, 2005, Press Release, http://www.authorsguild.org/advocacy/articles/authorsguildsuesgooglecitingmassivecopyrightinfringement.html.

37  Paul, I., 'Google Editions Embraces Universal E-book Format', *PC World*, 16 October 2009, http://www.pcworld.com/article/173789/google_editions_embraces_universal_ebook_format.html?tk=mod_rel. *Publishers Weekly* reported in December 2010 that a start date for Google Editions was imminent: Andrew Albanese, 'Google Editions Really Coming Soon', *Publishers Weekly*, 1 December 2010.

38  Google Editions, promised for the summer of 2010, has not begun operation. See p. 202.

39   Wagner, M., 'Google Editions Turns the Page on e-Books', *Computer World*, 5 May 2010, http://blogs.computerworld.com/16052/google_editions.

40   Mike Shatzkin, 'My Advice is Not Always Easy to Follow, but Sometimes it Proves Right Anyway', http://www.idealog.com/blog/my-advice-is-not-alwayseasy-to-follow-but-sometimes-it-proves-right-anyway, 29 March 2010.

41   Interview with Jason Epstein, New York, November 2004.

42   Jeffery, A. Trachtemberg, 'Authors Feel Pinch in Age of e-books', *Wall Street Journal*, 26 September 2010.

# 5 COPYRIGHT AND PUBLISHING LAW

Copyright is the bedrock of all publishing. Controlled by national law and international treaties, copyright is the legal framework that protects the creation and maintains the conditions of ownership of intellectual property. While ownership is important to creators and owners of copyright, the societal benefits associated with creative production is also of paramount importance. Copyright law sets out to balance the interests of:

- the authors, writers and creators of published and unpublished creative works
- the owners of the works who acquire ownership by agreement
- the general reading public and/or consumers of intellectual property.

Anglophone copyright began as '*rights in copy*' in sixteenth-century England. At the outset, when exclusive printing rights were granted to the Stationers' Company by the Crown, these rights were considered common law property, held in perpetuity. This charter-controlled regime ran from 1557 to 1694, when the English Parliament refused to renew the powers. A period of intense political activity resulted in a radical change to the law.

The Statute of Anne, made law by the English Parliament in 1710, was the world's first copyright act. For the first time, a statutory definition of ownership of published copy was laid down by a nation's parliament. The Statute of Anne initially covered only books and other writings, but in later years, one by one, copyright law grew to include all creative areas, output and products.

In 1790, the United States created its first copyright statute, reworking English copyright law and extending it to include original or independently created maps and charts. Since then, on both sides of the Atlantic, musical compositions, prints, engravings, musical and dramatic performances, photography, painting, drawing, sculpture, lithographs, graphic materials, architectural and fine art design, technical drawing, films, sound recordings, publishing formats, and now computer programs have also come to be protected.[1]

The initial purpose of the Statute of Anne, though, was less bound in revolutionary ideas on copyright than in an attempt to find a way of controlling a book trade wracked by infighting and politics. Legislators had to find a way of abolishing unfair *rights in copy* monopolies. This issue at the heart of copyright and still debated in the UK and the USA, is the *balance of interests* – between a creator's right (and the right of whomever copyright is passed on to, i.e. when it is sold) and what can be called *the public good*. The debate can easily slip from a delicate arrangement of stakeholder positions into a fractious dispute.

## THE STATUTE OF ANNE

In 1694 the House of Commons refused to renew the 1662 Licensing Act. Liberals led by John Locke clamoured for a new legal framework, a new ownership regime for intellectual property. The 'disempowered' Stationers had no intention of giving up their 'rights' easily, petitioning Parliament year after year for a new act. In 1703, 1704, 1706 and 1707, the Stationers lobbied Parliament. On 26 February 1707, a Stationers-sponsored bill was introduced into Parliament with the aim of 'securing property in such books as have been or shall be purchased from, or reserved to, the authors thereof'. Given the public mood against them, the Stationers decided (clearly thinking it 'politic') to emphasise the author's rights, but this deathbed conversion to the author's position fooled no one and the bill died in committee.[2]

A new bill came before Parliament on 11 January 1710. It was amended in committee in February and reappeared in the House of Commons on 14 March. The version was passed and went to the House of Lords, which amended it and recommended approval on 4 April. A conference committee on 5 April quickly agreed to a final version. With royal assent, the Statute of Anne, 'An Act for the Encouragement of Learning, by Vesting the Copies of Printed Books in the Authors or Purchasers of such Copies, during the Times therein mentioned', became law on 10 April 1710.

The Stationers were the big losers as Parliament repudiated perpetual rights, passing a law that set 14-year copyright terms for authors, renewable once upon application, and a 21-year term for works already owned, or those termed 'orphan works' (when authors were either dead or could not be found). The Statute swept away the power the Stationers had come to think was almost their birthright. For the first time in anglophone publishing history authors were granted exclusive rights over their creations.

The liberals of the day had worked hard for an end to the Stationers' Company monopoly over printing. Activist lawyer and author, Professor Lawrence Lessig, has in recent years argued for a return to the original eighteenth-century copyright term of 14 years. Lessig believes society, the arts and sciences, researchers and other authors, would benefit greatly from much more 'open access' to published works, and far sooner. It is a tough argument to win. Many authors through the ages, Mark Twain and William Wordsworth among them, have lobbied for exactly the opposite – that copyright should last for ever. One perpetual term advocate,

Jack Valenti, in his role as head of the Motion Picture Association of America, was often vociferous on the subject. Copyright should be property, Valenti said, like all other property, a common law right, plain and simple.

# TIMELINE OF COPYRIGHT AND INTELLECTUAL PROPERTY LAW

**103 AD**      The Roman poet Martial complains (in an epigram) about *plagium* of his poetry, choosing the name for someone who committed 'copytheft' as a '*plagiarius*'.

**1452**      Earliest UK litigation over a merchant mark.

**1534**      Royal Charter for printing is granted to the University of Cambridge by Henry VIII, giving the right to print and publish official religious Church of England materials, i.e. Book of Common Prayer and the authorised Bible.

**1545**      In Venice, booksellers are required to show all publications have authorial agreement.

**1557**      Queen Mary I grants a Royal Charter for printing to the **Stationers' Company**, giving them a pre-eminent position of control over printed works in England, both in terms of censorship and the commerce of the trade.

**1586**      Elizabeth I grants the University of Oxford a Royal Charter to print. As with Cambridge University, religious materials and bibles are the main publishing products in question.

**1636**      Consolidation of the Oxford University's right to print is granted by Charles I in Oxford's 'Great Charter', with the right to print the authorised version of the King James Bible.

**1637**      Decree by the Star Chamber in England declaring that all published works must be registered with the Stationers' Company.[3]

**1641**      The English (Long) Parliament closes the Star Chamber (and by inference all its decrees).

**1642**      The English Parliament reintroduces controls over 'libelous, seditious or blasphemous' publications after the Stationers argue for the restoration of previous limits.

**1643**      John Milton attacks the Stationers' arguments for regulation in *Areopatigitica*: 'Where there is much desire to learn, there of necessity will be much arguing, much writing, many opinions.' Milton calls on Parliament to rescind their Licensing Order of 16 June 1643, requiring government control with official censors, to whom authors had to submit their work for approval prior to publication. Milton felt printers and authors should be responsible for 'policing' published materials.

**1662**      **Licensing Act** restores the Stationers' Company monopoly. It is enacted two years after Charles II is restored to the throne.

1690–94  John Locke argues that knowledge resides in and is the property of the individual, not the community. He continues to lobby support from the new King, William of Orange, for a more liberal publishing scenario.

**1694**  The English Parliament refuses to renew the 1662 Licensing Act.

**1709**  **Statute of Anne** is introduced to Parliament and made law in 1710, providing authorial terms of copyright of 14 years for living authors, terms renewable for another 14 years. Prior-owned works or 'orphan' works were given a 21-year one-off term of copyright.

1765  In a case brought by former Stationers, English judge William Blackstone supports the idea that a literary property is analogous to other common law property rights.

1769  In *Millar v. Taylor* in England, a court rules that common law right in writing and/or literary property is found to be perpetual.

1773  In *Hinton v. Donaldson* in Scotland, the Court of Sessions takes an opposing view to the decision in *Millar v. Taylor* ruling.

1774  In a landmark ruling, the English Law Lords decide in **Donaldson v. Becket** that copyright for all publications is defined by statute law not common law. Common law is retained for unpublished manuscripts.

1783  Thomas Paine argues for the creation of a US copyright law.

1787  The US Constitution recognises 'intellectual property'.

**1790**  The first **US copyright law** comes into existence, almost mirroring the Statute of Anne.

1793  France's first copyright law. Works of living authors cannot be performed in a public theatre without the author's consent. Rights are passed to heirs for five years after an author's death.

1806  First copyright law in Germany.

1831  Musical compositions and notation are included in US copyright law.

1833  The UK protects performing rights for dramatic works in the Dramatic Copyright Act.

1834  The US court strikes down the common law right to intellectual property in perpetuity in *Wheaton v. Peters*, doing for US publishing what *Donaldson v. Becket* did for British publishing.

1841  *Folsom v. Marsh* landmark US ruling sets out the main principles on fair use. Involving 353 pages of a 12-volume biography of George Washington abridged to a two-volume work, the court upholds the plaintiff's case and rejects the defendant's fair use defense with the following explanation: '… what constitutes a fair and bona fide abridgment. … It is clear, that a mere selection, or different arrangement of parts of the original work, so as to bring the work into a smaller compass, will not be held to be such an abridgment. There must be real, substantial condensation of the materials, and intellectual labor and judgment bestowed thereon; and not merely the facile use of the scissors; or extracts of the essential parts, constituting the chief value of the original work …'

1842    The UK Literary Copyright Act extends terms for literary works to 42 years after publication or life plus seven years, whichever is longer.

1850    Société des Auteurs, Compositeurs et Editeurs de Musique (SACEM) is created in France, the world's first copyright collecting society.

1865    US copyright law is extended to include photography.

1866    French Copyright Act extends term to life plus 50 years.

1867    German national parliament extends copyright term to life plus 30 years.

1870    US copyright law prohibits unauthorised translations and dramatisations of works published by US publishers. Overseas publishers/authors are not protected or compensated.

1884    US Supreme Court supports copyright over photographs.

**1886**    **The Berne Convention** is the first international copyright agreement on copyright, trademark and patents. It is set up to deal with international piracy, creating the principle of mutual benefits and the protection of mutual interests. Authors of one signatory country should receive the same protections in another signatory country. The USA does not join.

1888    Pan-American agreement on international copyright. The USA does not join.

1891    Chace Act is the first US international copyright agreement to create some bilateral protection to some countries, in particular the UK and France.

1908    Berlin Convention adds photography, film and sound recordings to the original Berne Agreement.

1909    US copyright law includes prohibitions of 'unauthorized mechanical reproduction of musical compositions'.

**1911**    **UK Copyright Act**. Film, sound recordings and dramatic works are added to the UK Act. New principles include: copyright is effective upon creation without the need to register works (mandatory registration at Stationers' Hall is abolished, although registering can still be done on a voluntary basis); a published work should be provided to an official library free of charge under 'legal deposit'; protected works should display some sort of originality; terms are for author's life plus 50 years.

1928    Rome Copyright Convention protects performers, phonograms and broadcasters under the Berne Convention.

1948    Television is added to Berne Convention in the Brussels Convention.

**1952**    **Universal Copyright Convention (UCC)**. The USA leads an alternative initiative to Berne. Copyright protection is decided as a fixed, renewable term. Copyright notice is required © and copies in the USA must be registered with the US Copyright Office in Washington DC. Berne participants agree to sign up to the UCC in order to have some protection in non-Berne countries. UNESCO wants to bring the USA into Berne, but the terms of copyright (life + 50 years) and abolition of mandatory registration prove insurmountable obstacles. The US approach allows for a term of copyright for life plus 25 years and the obligatory use of the © symbol. UCC continues and some countries are still only signatories to it and not to Berne.

1956    UK Copyright Act includes film copyright, together with broadcasts.

**1976**    **US Copyright Act** is the first major revision of US copyright law since 1909. The 1976 Act remains, with amendments, the basis of US copyright law now, codifying fair use and replacing fixed terms (total 56 years) with life plus 50 years. The deposit of work is no longer mandatory, although the practice continues.

1984    *Sony Corp (America) v. Universal City Studios* (Betamax versus VHS case). Landmark decision ruling that technology is free of guilt. The precedent is set that intention behind human use of technology for copying must be established.

1985    Computer programs are considered literary works in the UK.

**1988**    **UK Copyright, Designs and Patents Act** brings the UK in line with European copyright law on Moral Right, Paternity, Integrity and the Right to Prevent False Attribution.

1989    The USA joins the Berne Convention although it does not immediately grant retrospective copyright protection to existing works from other member states.

1991    US court rules in favour of *2 Live Crew* in *Pretty Woman* parody case.

1995    GATT/TRIPS Agreement on Trade Related Aspects of Intellectual Property.

1996    World Intellectual Property Organisation (WIPO) Copyright Treaty (WCT) and WIPO Performances & Phonograms Treaty (WPPT).

1996    US Telecommunications Act removes any cap on ownership of radio stations – the prior limit was 40. Clear Channel buys 1,200 stations, reinforcing the idea of monopoly not only in radio but in all US media.

**1998**    **Digital Millennium Copyright Act (DMCA)** Enacting the WIPO Treaty, the US lays the groundwork, in section 1201, for controls over copyright materials in digital form. The DMCA represents a huge shift in the previous historical copyright tradition, providing owners with more rights and restricting fair use.

**1998**    **The Sonny Bono Copyright Term Extension Act** (a.k.a 'the Mickey Mouse Extension' Act) extends US copyright terms to the life plus 70 years and 95 years for works in copyright or made for hire before 1978.

1999    ICANN (Internet Corporation for Assigned Names and Numbers) Board accepts WIPO proposal and establishes UDRP (Uniform Domain-Name Dispute-Resolution Policy).

2001    EU Directive on Copyright & Related Rights in the Information Society 2001/29/EC harmonises copyright, implementing the 1996 WIPO Treaty. Under article 6, protection is given to 'technological measures' designed to restrict use not authorised by owners of rights (i.e. digital copying), a measure even more restrictive than the DMCA's section 1201.

2003   In *Eldred v. Ashcroft* the US Supreme Court affirms the 'Sonny Bono Act'.

2005   The US Supreme Court decides that distributors involved in file-swapping software are potentially liable for copyright infringement.

2010   Digital Economy Act (UK) is made law on 8 June 2010, with a provision to track down, and, after 12 months, to punish 'persistent' online copyright infringers with disconnection (whole households). Critics say the 'dreaded' *copyfight* measures will fail.[4]

*This timeline establishes the main events and important milestones. It is not an exhaustive list. Copyright law is likely to change further in the digital era.*

With new digital copyright law, two practical issues are at stake: the extent of ownership and the boundaries of fair use. Digitisation is seen (or is being used) by many in the publishing industry to demonstrate the opportunities pirates now have to unlawfully produce illegal, pirated copies. Digital enthusiasts, on the other hand, see digitisation as an opportunity to allow more democratisation, to roll back controls and allow more fair use.

## RANDOM HOUSE V. ROSETTABOOKS

In 2001, the world's largest trade publisher, Random House, sued a new small e-book publisher, RosettaBooks, over Rosetta's plan to publish e-books of contracted Random authors. Random House claimed that Rosetta breached existing book contacts which the company argued included electronic rights.

RosettaBooks, run by a former agent Arthur Klebanoff, had signed e-book contracts with several Random authors, including William Styron and Kurt Vonnegut. The Authors' Guild took Rosetta's side. AOL Time Warner and Viacom's Simon & Schuster expressed solidarity with the Bertelsmann/Random House position, arguing that their contracts covered both print books and e-books. 'Everyone knew what a book was when these contracts were signed,' the Guild's executive director, Paul Aiken, said. 'Volumes printed on paper. This is nothing more than a bold and baseless retroactive rights grab.'[5]

In January 2001, *Random House v. RosettaBooks* was heard by Judge Sidney Stein in the Federal District Court in New York. In July the same year, surprising many, Stein ruled in favour of RosettaBooks, deciding that the clause to 'print, publish and sell work in book form does not include the right to publish the works in the format that has come to be known as the ebook'. In his judgment, Stein wrote: 'In this case, the "new use" – the electronic digital signals sent over the Internet – is a separate medium from the original use, printed words on paper.'[6] The decision represented a major victory for e-publishers over print publishers.

Random House stood by its view that 'an e-book is a book', still believing that its contracts granted them 'the rights to publish the works in e-book form'. The company said Stein's 'decision will hinder rather than help the development of this new technology'.[7] Lloyd Weinreb, a professor of intellectual property law at Harvard Law School, believed the true significance of the decision was that courts decided not to treat the internet 'as more of the same'.[8]

In September 2001, Random filed an appeal. In October, RosettaBooks counter-filed. The appeal was never heard. The two companies settled out of court in 2002. The agreement between Random and Rosetta allowed the e-book publisher to continue with contracted Random authors under licence.

Effectively, Random House absorbed RosettaBooks into its business sphere, with the significant legal point being that the appeal did not go ahead. The issue of digital rights in author–publisher contracts was not fully tested by US courts. In the meantime many publishers scrambled to re-read the electronic clauses in existing author contracts, rewriting them more robustly in book contracts thereafter.

# COPYRIGHT TODAY

In its 300-year history, copyright has evolved in law and as a general principle. The central idea established by the Statute of Anne – exclusive rights or monopoly over intellectual property, vested in creators for a defined term – continues. A writer or creator who produces a literary or other work today has exclusive publication rights over the 'creative copy' until he or she sells or licenses the copy to a third party. In practice, and as experienced by stakeholders, copyright has a meaning way beyond this. But by the letter of the law:

- authors and creators and their descendants have a right to be protected at law and be able to profit from the fruits of their labour
- publishing firms, individuals and other bodies acquiring literary works have a right to the protection of intellectual property they have acquired
- readers, book buyers and libraries have rights accorded by the body of copyright law, under the concept of the *public domain*.

The writer's exclusive copyright, his or her monopoly, currently lasts for the term of her or his natural life plus 70 years. Whoever purchases or inherits the copy will enjoy the same monopoly privileges by law over the creative copy.

Whatever the three main participants of copyright get from the copyright tradition is often less than perfectly clear in reality. However, what cannot be copyrighted is relatively straightforward – speech and improvisational performances (unless written down), ideas, concepts, titles, phrases, works consisting only of information, weights and measures charts, tape measures and calendars. Areas of tension can appear when the author–publisher contract is not specific enough, particularly on terms dealing with:

- length of licence
- copyright ownership abuse, and if used as a means to censor
- ideas and their expression that cannot be easily divided.

A 1960s biography of Howard Hughes led Random House to fight and win against the billionaire's attempt to suppress publication of details of his life (*Rosemount Enterprises v. Random House*). In *Salinger v. Random House* (1987), the author J. D. Salinger successfully prevented a British author and biographer from quoting his unpublished letters held by academic libraries. In the case of the *Gone with the Wind* parody, *The Wind Done Gone* by Alice Randall, the US Court of Appeals reversed a lower court ruling, allowing both Randall's method and intention as permitted in writing 'a race reversal' parody of the original 1936 novel by Margaret Mitchell.[9]

To understand the problems that sometimes arise, creators, legal practitioners and public bodies overseeing the publication of cultural products and their preservation currently have to understand what copyright in the twenty-first-century digital age actually means.

Writing in *The Guardian* newspaper, Cory Doctorow described a case of photographer, Peter Zabulis, who objected to the unauthorised posting on the website of the UK newspaper *The Independent*, depicting a Zabulis photograph of a snowed-over field in Nottinghamshire, UK, that he had posted on the online photographic site Flickr.[10] Zabulis wrote a letter of complaint. In reply, *The Independent* claimed that the photo, being online, was in the public domain. As the photo carried no copyright notice, the newspaper said that Zabulis had not properly 'asserted his copyright ... and thus copyright had not been breached'.[11]

Copyright begins the instant a work is created. A legal argument ensued and the newspaper backed down and paid the photographer. It was a clear infringement and it seems *The Independent* at first simply chose to ignore its own culpability.

This case shows how the internet and World Wide Web have generated a fairly liberal approach to the use of copyright materials appearing online. Yet the law on the subject, ever since the 1998 Digital Millennium Copyright Act, has been anything but liberal. Ironically, the newspaper might well have been able to use the photo, even if there had been an 'All rights reserved' label on the photo. Copyright law and tradition allow for newspaper comment or reportage. If *The Independent* had decided to make 'a comment' on the photo itself, its appropriation may well have been allowable under fair use.

## 2 LIVE CREW AND 'PRETTY WOMAN' – CAMBELL V. ACUFF MUSIC INC.

When the rap group 2 Live Crew included the track 'Pretty Woman' in a 1989 album release 'As Clear As They Wanna Be', a group member and writer of the song in question, Luther Cambell, was sued for infringement by the rights holders of the original Roy Orbison and William Dees song, 'Oh, Pretty Woman', written in 1964.

In a self-declared parody created in 1989, Cambell reworked Orbison's musical 'hook' and the first few lines of his song into the rap group's own song. Cambell took phrases such as *pretty woman* making them *big hairy woman* and *two-timin' woman*. The rap group's version chose a street hooker as the 'pretty woman' in the song, satirising Orbison's idealisation of a 'pretty woman'.

Orbison had assigned all rights to the song to Acuff-Rose, who sued Cambell as the infringer of the copyright. The defence that the 2 Live Crew member used in the case was that his song was a parody, and was therefore protected by the fair use doctrine. The copyright factors that were called into question under section 1207 are:

- the purpose of the use, including whether it is a commercial use
- the nature of the original work
- how much of the original work was used and what portion of the work
- the effect of the copying on the market for the original work.

The US Court of Appeals supported Acuff-Rose's action, saying the 'parodic version' damaged the market value of the original. The Court held that 2 Live Crew's version was not fair use because it was produced for commercial reasons and sold for profit.

The US Supreme Court unanimously reversed this decision and returned the case for review. The Supreme Court held that commercial use is not determinative in a fair use analysis – a use may still be 'fair' under copyright law even if designed and produced for financial gain. The Court said that all four factors need to be given equal weight in any judgment of fair use, pointing out that other forms of fair use (journalism and education) are also generally work done for profit. There was also no evidence the claimants had suffered any financial harm. The Appeals court had neglected three aspects of the four-part test for fair use under the 1976 Copyright Act.

In writing the opinion, Justice David Souter argued that copying was necessary for parody to work in order to establish what was being parodied. Parody has to 'take aim at a particular original work' and to do that it has to use 'at least enough of the original to make the object of its critical wit recognizable'.[12]

# DEFAMATION AND LIBEL

US and UK legal controls over public expression of ideas grew out of the ancient Greek definition of three types of 'anti-social' speech – sedition, defamation and blasphemy, each of which is described as a libel. Libel comes from the latin *libellus* meaning 'little book'. In English common law it signifies a prohibited message. Following on from the Greek tradition, the early English laws on libel grew to include religious and moral heresies.[13]

The US and UK jurisdictions are different in many ways, though both operate in a legal environment known as common law. In the USA, due to the provisions contained in the First Amendment to the US Constitution, individuals have the right to express their opinions in public. In the UK such freedoms, though acknowledged by society and the courts, are less clear. The big difference between the UK and the USA on libel arises from the fact that the UK has no written constitution. There is no general statutory right of free speech.

Any 'published statement' – made by someone about another person to a third party (in a book, newspaper or other published media, or orally) – that is not true and damages the reputation of the person referred to can be considered defamatory. Statements are considered *libel* if printed or broadcast in any medium, and *slander* if made orally. The three factors that are considered and can assist a 'fair comment defence' are: *the facts; the comment is a genuinely held opinion and made in good faith without malice* (the comment may be biased and unfair but is defensible as long as it is an honest opinion); and *the comment is a matter of public interest*. A defamation case can be brought and can succeed if:

- a 'defamatory' statement has been published or is able to be read by the public
- the statement is untrue
- the statement includes an untrue allegation or opinion
- it is clear who the 'defamatory' statement refers to
- the statement is substantially capable of defaming the person referred to
- the statement actually defames the person referred to.

Famously, you cannot 'defame' the dead, though if, by defaming the dead, you harm the living descendants, statements can be defamatory and hence actionable. There are two privileged positions where libel law does not apply: Absolute Privilege – a statement made by a participant in the legal process in a court room; or a statement made by a Member of Parliament during sittings or legislative proceedings, known as parliamentary privilege in Commonwealth countries.

Once a defamation or libel case is brought in the UK, the onus *is on the defendant* to establish his or her innocence, whereas under American defamation and libel law *a claimant must demonstrate* that any libel referring to him or her is substantially false and damaging. For libel litigation to succeed in the USA, the plaintiff should establish that any published information is meant specifically for the plaintiff (directly or indirectly), that the statements are defamatory and affect the plaintiff's reputation, that any published statement is false, and that the defendant is at fault for the defamation.

UK law, however, assumes that the publication is false unless the defendant is able to prove otherwise. For a libel action to succeed the presiding judge must be satisfied that the defamatory statements disparage someone's public life, expose him or her to hatred, ridicule or contempt, and cause ostracism in some way – that is, substantially damages his or her reputation, socially and/or professionally, to the extent that the 'defamatory statements' cause visible, definable and even quantifiable harm.

## SEDITIOUS LIBEL

Libel in the UK is usually a civil action but can also be actionable in the criminal courts, if serious enough, such as publishing a libel against the State, the King or Queen, or a whole class of people, such as an ethnic group. Seditious libel in its most serious form is treason against the State. It has been a statutory offence in the UK (England) since 1275, referring to anything that may affect the well-being, peace and order of the State: 'tales whereby discord or occasion of discord or slander may grow between the king and his people or the great men of the realm.'[14]

It is not these days seditious to criticise the Head of State (the Queen) or the State *per se*, but if the intent were to bring down either the Queen or the State, then it could be considered seditious libel. The case for suppression of political messages under seditious libel was described by Chief Justice Holt in 1704, who gave the opinion that if writers and others making verbal statements against the Crown, government or State could not be brought to account for their ill-opinions then *no government could exist*.

Hundreds were prosecuted for sedition under English law during the sixteenth and seventeenth centuries, including John Stubbes, an English Puritan who in 1579 wrote a pamphlet that 'respectfully' criticised Queen Elizabeth. For his 'truths', Stubbes had his right hand removed with a butcher's knife. He learned his place. 'John Stubbes, so soon as his right hand was off, put off his hat with the left, and cryed aloud, God save the Queen.'[15]

In 1630, Alexander Leighton wrote and published a pamphlet, *An Appeal to Parliament*, insisting that right religion and Scripture was more important than kings. Unsurprisingly, Charles I and the Star Chamber saw matters differently, declaring Leighton's words 'seditious and scandalous'. On 16 November 1630, Leighton was taken to Westminster where he was whipped, had an ear cut off, his nose slit, and a part of his face branded. The following week he was mutilated on the other side of his face.

The English revolution and Oliver Cromwell came and went. On 20 February 1663, printer John Twyn appeared in the Old Bailey charged with high treason for a book he printed, which argued for the right of the people to create revolution, 'compassing and imagining the king's death'. The indictment against Twyn detailed his crimes as 'the printing of a seditious, poisonous and scandalous book entitled

"A Treatise of the execution of justice, wherein is clearly proved that the execution of justice is as well the people's as the magistrate's duty, and if the magistrate's pervert judgment, the people are bound by the law of God to execute judgment without them, and upon them'". Twyn was convicted by the jury. The final words of the case:

| | |
|---|---|
| **Twyn**: | I humbly beg mercy; I am a poor man, and have three small children, I never read a word of it. |
| **Lord Hyde**: | I'll tell what you shall do: Ask mercy of them that can give it; that is of God and the King. |
| **Twyn**: | I humbly beseech you to intercede with His Majesty for mercy. |
| **Cl. of Newgate**: | Tie him up, Executioner. |
| **Crier**: | O Yes! My lords the king's justices command all manner or persons to keep silence while judgment is in giving, upon pain of imprisonment. |
| **Lord Hyde**: | John Twyn ... I am heartily sorry that your carriage and grievous offences should draw me to give that Judgment upon that I must ... Yours is the most grievous and highest treason, and most complicated of all wickedness that ever I knew; for you have, as much as possibly lay in you, so reproached and reviled the king, the dead king and his posterity, on purpose to root them out from off the face of the earth ... There's nothing that pretends to religion that will avow the killing of kings, but the Jesuit on one side and the Sectary on the other ... therefore the Judgment of the court is, and the court doth award: 'That you be led back to the place from whence you came, and from thence be drawn upon an hurdle to the place of execution: and there you shall be hanged by the neck, and being alive cut down, and your privy-members shall be cut off, your entrails shall be taken out of your body, and you living, the same to be burnt before your very eyes; your head to be cut off, your body to be divided into four quarters and your head and quarters to be disposed of at the King's Majesty. And the Lord have mercy upon your soul.' |
| **Twyn**: | I most humbly beseech my lord to remember my condition and intercede for me. |
| **Lord Hyde**: | I would not intercede for my own father in this case, if he were alive.[16] |

Charles II, on regaining the throne, was said to be in a magnanimous mood. He wished no revenge on the people for his father's death. He didn't have to be in a foul mood, as others, it seemed, were heartily ready to take up that role on his behalf. After Twyn's trial, and as he awaited his own execution, he was again pressed to admit his guilt. His answer was that it was 'not his principle to betray the author'. To the end, even on the scaffold, he maintained: he knew nothing of the true nature of the text; that it had been corrected by others; and that he had been too naïve and trusting of the text and the author. The case exemplifies perhaps, at least in part, why English writers and publishers through the ages have refined the art of self-censorship.[17]

# MALICIOUS FALSEHOOD

In the UK, if published statements do not lower your public image but cause you financial harm, you may sue on the basis of a malicious falsehood has been made against you – a published statement has adversely affected your capacity to work and/or earn or do business in some way.

The legal threshold for malicious falsehood is lower than is required for a defamation in the form of a libel. Still, someone bringing an action for malicious falsehood must prove that: *the statement is untrue*; *it was published maliciously*; with the most important factor being *that it is likely to cause financial harm*.

As this aspect of the law deals primarily with financial harm, it is easier in the UK to obtain an interim injunction than in libel cases. However, the court will need to be convinced of the seriousness of the financial harm in question and that it involves malice.

A publication may also not be libellous or involve malice but represent *negligent misstatement*. The statement may simply be wrong but involve no mal-intention, yet still cause harm. False information in a publication, leading to injury or death, can be grounds for legal action (a special civil tort). A reader may be advised on diet, financial investment, pharmaceuticals, exercise or other areas of help under the heading of 'expert counsel' which could be wrong and cause harm. There is a general sense under UK law of the concept of 'duty of care', which in publishing means the welfare of the reading public can be protected against negligent publishers. For an action of this kind to succeed, it must be proved to the court that: *the publisher responsible for the negligent misstatement owed a duty of care*; *it was somehow breached*; and *the breach caused real harm, loss or damage*.

In *Hedley Byrne Co. Ltd v. Heller & Partners Ltd. 1964 House of Lords*, the Lords ruled that the advice given had been negligent and amounted to a breach of a duty of care in the contract between parties. Prior to the case other attempts to prove economic or other loss from a negligent misstatement had failed. The House of Lords overruled the previous position and introduced an *assumption of responsibility* if a special relationship of duty of care could be established between parties.

The facts of the case: Hedley Byrne had wanted to check on the creditworthiness of a prospective client, Easipower Ltd, and had asked their own bank, National Provincial Bank, to ask Easipower's bank, Heller & Partners Ltd, for an assessment. Heller & Partners replied, in a letter of advice provided for free, that Easipower was a sound business, crucially disowning responsibility for this statement in the letter. When Easipower went bankrupt, Hedley Byrne lost £17,000 from their contract with the failed company. Hedley Byrne sued Easipower's bank, Heller & Partners, for negligence, eventually winning the argument and action in the House of Lords. The issue turned on the parallel nature of a tort and a contractual responsibility. The probability of an injury arising from a misstatement, though, will usually not be enough to build a claim. Economic loss is the deciding factor and the only recoverable element under the negligent misstatement/duty of care rule. Lord Devlin made the following statement:

> ... The respondents in this case cannot deny that they were performing a service. Their sheet anchor is that they were performing it gratuitously and therefore no liability for its performance can arise. My Lords, in my opinion, this is not the law. A promise given without consideration to perform a service cannot be enforced as a contract by the promisee; but if the service is in fact performed and done negligently, the promisee can recover in an action in tort.[18]

## OBSCENITY

In the UK it is not a crime to write obscene material, only to publish it. Under the Obscene Publications Act 1959 (included also in the 1990 Broadcasting Act), a publisher of obscene publications, and persons in possession of the same for the purposes of distribution or sale, are liable for prosecution. There are obviously times where the author can be both of these as well, so if the author is also the publisher and distributor, then the author can also be liable.

Section 4 of the 1959 Act added a *'public good' defence*, allowing for the artistic merit and cultural good of a publication. The publisher must prove the argument and can call experts to the court to help the cause. This change to the Act paved the way for the Penguin release of *Lady Chatterley's Lover*, with Penguin Books successfully arguing its case. The Act also allowed for the innocent dissemination of material, meaning that if a distributor or seller had not read or looked at the work, and had no reason to believe the work obscene, he or she would not be liable.

The law on obscenity in the UK, and throughout anglophone publishing jurisdictions, turns on a publication's capacity to deprave or corrupt readers. The atmosphere in general surrounding obscene libel is more relaxed these days, and is or can be decided by general freedom of speech issues. However, there are cases that would be regarded as illegal and obscene, and would receive swift justice in society today if discovered – i.e. obscene publications or images involving minors.

In the past, many literary writers have had their literary works banned due to claims the writing was obscene. The story we often receive is that the works in question were banned on strict grounds of what was considered immoral at the time. Yet on closer attention to detail, the story can be far more complicated. *Ulysses*, by James Joyce, was banned in Britain from 1922 to 1936.[19] Publicly, the UK's stand against *Ulysses* was that it included passages that put the moral well-being of the British people at risk. Yet of all the people who made these pronouncements, not one, it seemed, had read Joyce's novel in its entirety. In fact, most had barely read any of it at all. The official UK stand against the novel involved private and personal animus against Joyce within the British government and foreign service going back as far as 1918.[20]

The label 'obscene publication' was also given to D. H. Lawrence's *Lady Chatterley's Lover* and Henry Miller's *Tropic of Cancer*. Both works had to wait nearly

30 years before readers in the respective author's country of origin were able to buy copies.

In the US tradition of law on obscenity, the private use of material is usually protected. Regarding *Stanley v. Georgia (1969)*, Supreme Court Justice Thurgood Marshall wrote: 'If the First Amendment means anything, it means that a State has no business telling a man, sitting in his own house, what books he may read or what films he may watch'.[21] It can be unconstitutional to sell or distribute obscene materials, but it is not unconstitutional to possess and read them at home. This argument on private use is not extended to the practice of child pornography, whereby the protection of children is regarded as an overriding factor to otherwise normal rights granted by way of civil liberties. *New York v. Ferber (1982)* unanimously excluded child pornography from any protection, even if the pictures are not obscene under what is known as the Miller test. In *Miller v. California (1973)*, the Supreme Court, ruled in a five-to-four decision that to ban obscene material a three-part test had to be met:

- An average person, applying contemporary community standards, would find that the work, taken as a whole, appeals to the prurient interest [known as the Roth Test following *Roth v. United States (1957)*].

- The work depicts, in a patently offensive way, sexual conduct specifically defined by the applicable state law.

- The work, taken as a whole, lacks serious literary, artistic, political or scientific value.

# LIBEL AND LIBEL TOURISM

## LIBEL IN THE UNITED KINGDOM

In recent times the UK has become infamous for 'libel tourism', the place for the wealthy, from anywhere in the world to come in order to silence critics using UK libel law and courts to do it. From the point of view of libel lawyers, the UK's libel tradition is very good business.

Reacting to American use of the UK's jurisdiction to bring libel litigation, Congressman Steve Cohen of Tennessee in 2009 sponsored a bill in the US House of Representatives designed to block libel judgments brought against American writers in other jurisdictions:

'Libel tourism threatens to undermine the principles of free speech because foreign courts are not obliged to consider extensive First Amendment privileges in defamation cases,' said Congressman Cohen.[22]

Under 'Cohen's libel law', US courts would be able to protect a US citizen facing libel in a foreign jurisdiction if they do not account for the free speech provisions contained in the US Constitution's First Amendment.[23]

UK libel activists are also pressing for changes in UK libel laws. On 24 February 2010, the UK government's Culture, Media and Sport Committee released a report on *Press Standards, Privacy and Libel*. A month later, the UK's Lord Chancellor and Secretary of State for Justice bowed to mounting pressure from many groups and prominent individuals[24] and announced libel law reform. Among his proposals were:

- to limit the ease with which foreign libel claimants can be heard in the UK
- to establish **a single publication rule**[25]
- to protect publications that are in the public interest[26]
- to cut lawyers' 'success fees' in fee agreements (meeting resistance from lawyers)
- to 'consider' the creation of a statutory 'public interest' defence.

UK libel history numbers some very famous cases, from Oscar Wilde's unsuccessful libel suit against the Marquess of Queensberry in April 1895,[27] to far more recent cases, including *Jeffery Archer v. The Daily Star (1987)*, *Aldington v. Tolstoy (1989)*, *Jonathan Aitken v. The Guardian (1995)*, and *Galloway v. The Daily Telegraph (2004)*. Often libel involves the bad, unseemly, or even sleazy behaviour of people with reputations, and the reason why libel cases continue to fascinate the public. Libel is not, however, only about the lurid details of cases in which the 'mighty' are seen to 'misbehave' or worse, but can involve the 'persecution of the powerless' by those with enough money to use the law to silence critics.

---

### McLIBEL – McDONALD'S v. HELEN STEEL AND DAVID MORRIS

The 1990 case, known popularly as McLibel, became the longest trial in British history. Helen Steel, a part-time barmaid earning £65 a week, and David Morris, a single parent on income support, were sued for libel by the global fast-food company McDonald's for distributing pamphlets criticising McDonald's.

The action grew out of a London Greenpeace[28] campaign against McDonald's in 1985, and the subsequent distribution in 1986 of a leaflet listing a number of damning claims against the company. The leaflet, entitled 'What's Wrong with McDonald's?', accused McDonald's of 'exploiting children, cruelty to animals, destroying the rainforest, paying low wages and peddling unhealthy food'.[29]

McDonald's issued a writ against five individuals. The organisation, London Greenpeace, could not be sued for libel as it was an association of individuals, so McDonald's sued five helpers, demanding that the five retract the statements made against the company and provide full apologies. Advised by a lawyer on their legal position, three of the five decided to apologise. Only Steel and Morris would not agree to McDonald's demands.

The trial lasted 313 days. McDonald's employed a legal team headed by a £2,000-a-day libel Queen's Counsel and spent a reported £10 million on their case, while Morris and Steel defended themselves with £40,000 gathered from donations and free help and materials given to them. When they were denied legal aid by the UK government, as is the UK legal aid policy with libel, Keir Starmer, QC, offered the pair free legal advice.

The case was heard by Mr Justice Bell, who agreed with a petition made by McDonald's legal team that as a jury would not understand the legal complexities of the case, he should hear the case alone. This was a blow to Morris and Steel as it was widely thought that a jury would have been far more sympathetic to the pair than to a multinational corporation with millions available for its legal expenses.

In 1997, Justice Bell ruled that while many of the points made in the leaflet were true about McDonald's, the two defendants had failed to prove all the points. Therefore, they had libelled McDonald's. Steel and Morris were ordered to pay McDonald's £60,000 in damages. The pair refused to pay, Steel saying that McDonald's didn't deserve any money and in any case neither of them had any to give. McDonald's did not pursue damages.

Steel and Morris went to appeal to clear their names and be relieved of the judgment. The Court of Appeal, while sympathetic to the pair's case, and going much further than Mr Justice Bell's ruling in stating that more of the claims made by the pair against McDonald's were truthful, only reduced the damages by £20,000. Steel and Morris still had a judgment against them.

The pair then went to the House of Lords but were refused any further right of appeal. Their last resort was the European Court of Human Rights. On 15 February 2005, the European Court in Strasbourg unanimously sided with Steel and Morris, stating that the UK courts had breached their rights to freedom of expression and a fair trial. The Court awarded £13,750 to Ms Steel and £10,300 to Mr Morris. Their QC adviser, Keir Starmer, stated that before the case 'only the rich and famous have been able to defend themselves against libel writs. Now ordinary people can participate much more effectively in public debate without the fear that they will be bankrupted for doing so. This case is a milestone for free speech.'[30]

## LIBEL IN THE UNITED STATES

In 1969, Chicago-based attorney Elmer Gertz sued *American Opinion* for defamatory libel when it called him a 'Leninist and communist fronter', along with other 'communist fronters' Martin Luther King Jr, John F. Kennedy, Hubert Humphrey and John Foster Dulles. The defence Gertz used against *American Opinion* – the mouthpiece of the ultra-conservative John Birch Society – was that the statements were untrue and damaging to his reputation. The jury sided with Gertz and awarded him $50,000. When the presiding judge denied the damages, Gertz took his case to the Supreme Court. The highest US court agreed with Gertz and ordered a new trial. In the second hearing, the jury this time awarded Gertz $100,000 for actual injury and then $300,000 in punitive damages. The judgment was upheld in the Court of Appeal. In 1983 *American Opinion* asked the US Supreme Court to review the case, but it refused the request. So, finally, after 14 years, Gertz, a lawyer, won his case, forcing a major change in US defamation law.[31]

# COPYRIGHT INFRINGEMENT

Cases of infringement or plagiarism are not often brought to the public's attention. The reason is that very few infringement actions succeed in the courts. And charges of plagiarism are often dismissed as attacks by 'wannabes' with careerist motives.

In recent years, J. K. Rowling fought off a charge of infringement and plagiarism from an American author, Nancy Stouffer, who claimed in various media appearances that her self-published 'Larry Potter' children's 'activity books', written and sold from the mid-1980s, were the unrecognised source of the Harry Potter series.

Rowling, who began writing her Harry Potter books in the 1990s, was backed by her book and film publishers, Scholastic and Time Warner. In a legal move described by *The Washington Post* as 'pre-emptive', the author and the two companies launched a suit against Stouffer, arguing that the claims by the author of the Larry Potter books were baseless, even fraudulent.

The case, *Scholastic, Inc, J.K. Rowling, and Time Warner Entertainment Company v. Nancy Stouffer*, was heard in the US District Court for the southern district of New York in 2002. On 17 September 2002, the court ruled against Stouffer, ordering her to pay sanctions 'in the amount of $50,000 in damages' and 'to pay a portion of the plaintiff's attorney fees'. Stouffer's attorney, Thomas McNamara, said he and his client 'were surprised and disappointed with the decision', adding that they were 'particularly troubled by the court's determination that she [Stouffer] submitted falsified evidence', something her lawyer said Stouffer adamantly denied.[32]

There have been similar charges and tales of infringement, plagiarism and misuse of books. Hollywood, in particular, is no stranger to these charges, but infringement actions against producers and studios rarely succeed. Daphne du Maurier, who wrote *Rebecca* – the 1938 bestselling novel that catapulted her to fame and became a major Hollywood film – was accused of plagiarising a Brazilian novelist's work, although the charges were dropped.

Most claims of infringement are very difficult to prove. Some, if not many, of course, are probably false. For this reason any unsolicited book or screenplay of a book arriving at a major studio is immediately dealt with by the legal department. A letter will be sent back to the sender saying that the studio has not opened the material and will not even consider it. Robust legal defences are put up to protect companies from copyright suits.

In general, plagiarism is seen as an unethical practice rather than something that is unlawful. Literary or intellectual property, the financial and cultural capital contained in an author's writing, is also personally and commercially valuable. Reputation and careers are at stake on both sides of the equation – both for the victim and transgressor in an act of plagiarism. There are often mitigating circumstances or shades of grey, rather than any deliberate attempts to steal another's work. As a legal scholar, Stuart Green, argues: 'We all work within a cultural tradition, and to some degree, we all absorb those cultural traditions by copying.'[33]

---

## THE STRANGE STORY OF DR Y

In the early 1990s, Dr Y from the west coast of America, wrote and published a self-help book that I will rename here *How To Get Over Yourself*. Initially, he published it through his own company, which I will call The Very Small Press.[34] Two years after his first self-publication of the book, a fairly major US publishing house, Publisher A, acquired the work and published a new edition, selling on the UK rights to Publisher B based in London.

While preparing their UK edition, the UK Publisher B wrote to the American author asking if they could re-title the book, as they had discovered there was a book already out in the UK with the title *How To Get Over Yourself*, a book written by a writer X, who had been published by another UK house, Publisher C.

Intrigued, Dr Y asked a friend to mail him a copy of the book brought out by UK Publisher C. Reading it, Dr Y discovered that X's book had not only used the same title he had used, but had also followed his book's structure and substantial parts of his content. Author X had even copied quotes from Dr Y's interviews (without attribution). Checking his records, Dr Y realised that Publisher C had once asked him for a review copy, and he had mailed one off but heard nothing back. This had happened a few years before he had signed his contact with the US house A.

Dr Y was now convinced that the UK Publisher C had used the review copy he had mailed to them to initiate a blatant infringement. To pour salt in his wound, while other experts were acknowledged in the text, Dr Y's name was not even mentioned. To make it even worse for him, if that were possible, X's book carried a moral rights clause in the front: *The moral right of the author has been asserted*. As far as Dr Y was concerned, the UK Publisher C and Author X had not only infringed the copyright of his book, they had collaborated to allow X to masquerade as the book's true and actual creator as well.

Dr Y's US publisher, A, was just as outraged as Dr Y was. Publisher A wrote to Publisher C saying that X's book was a flagrant case of plagiarism and copyright infringement, a passing off and complete violation of Dr Y's rights. Particularly disturbing for the US house was Publisher C's role in the whole affair.

*(Continued)*

*(Continued)*

Publisher C wrote back immediately, agreeing that Dr Y's book had been plagiarised but saying that it wasn't the UK company's fault.[35] The lawyer given the task of replying for Publisher C wrote that the editor, attracted to Dr Y's book in the first place, felt it was 'too American' and needed a more British slant and approach. The lawyer implied that the editor had in good faith commissioned Author X (an experienced author, it seems) to write a self-help book for the UK market (not to plagiarise Dr Y's book at all), and that was the extent of Publisher C's involvement in the infringement.

To complicate matters, the lawyer explained, after commissioning the work, the editor in charge of the book at Publisher C had gone on maternity leave, leaving X's book in the care of other editors who had no knowledge of the book's 'history'. The lawyer added that the new editors trusted X, whom they imagined had read her own contract with Publisher C, meaning that X was alone responsible for any copyright infringement.

Publisher C recalled the remaining copies of the UK edition of *How To Get Over Yourself* and destroyed them. As a few thousand copies of X's book had been sold, earning several thousand pounds, Publisher C offered the US Publisher A a settlement of around the same amount. Negotiations over the actual figure went on for months. In the end the US Publisher A received about £1,000 more than initially offered.

Dr Y was not happy with this, but the US Publisher A told him that they had no intention of pursuing Publisher C further, as there was a transatlantic relationship between the two houses. When Dr Y would not accept this, the Publisher A withdrew from the case entirely.

Disappointed but determined to get justice, Dr Y decided to take on the case alone, only to find out that UK courts award *actual damages* only. Under UK law, there was no framework for deciding *punitive damages* for claimants in cases such as Dr Y's. So Dr Y instructed a London attorney to act for him. Fortunately she was able to negotiate a better settlement figure from Publisher C than previously offered to Publisher A.

The UK publisher paid up and agreed to publish an apology. A statement appeared the same year in *The Bookseller* (the UK equivalent of *Publishers Weekly*) with Publisher C and Author X named in a public expression of regret by Publisher C, stating that Dr Y's work had not been properly attributed and acknowledging Dr Y's moral right as the rightful author of the text.[36]

There is a history of infringement between the USA and the UK, but most of that was a long time ago. If this case had happened on US soil, it seems likely that substantial punitive damages would have flowed to the infringed author from any court judgment. As it was, the whole matter was paid for cheaply and more or less swept under a London carpet. Isolated as it probably is, this case is surely not the only case of its kind.

## MORAL RIGHT AND INTEGRITY

The rights of authors have existed in European jurisdictions since the 1800s. They were added to the original Berne Agreement. These include the right to be attributed as the sole author(s) of a literary work or text or creation under the Berne Agreement, whether published under a pseudonym or anonymously.

The tradition of the moral right (*droit moral*) entered UK law for the first time under the Copyright, Designs and Patents Act 1988, which provided for four statutory rights: *paternity*, *integrity*, *prevention of false attribution*, and the *right to privacy* (concerning photographs, film and video). The right of paternity – a statement that someone is the author – must be asserted and this will appear in the front matter of a book.

The right of integrity – the right to prevent misuse, mutilation, alteration or distortion of the work – is more contentious. Integrity as a concept has not found too much favour in anglophone editorial history. Anglophone publishers and editors believe they should have the right (usually stated in the author–publisher contract) to alter and change works.

Even if authors sell or contract away their commercial rights to a work, they retain the moral rights, the paternity and integrity associated with the work. In some jurisdictions an author can waive his or her moral rights. In the French jurisdiction, *droit de repentir* gives the author the right to withdraw the work even after it has been published. This not does apply in the UK or the USA.

In the USA only visual artists can claim moral rights under VARA (the Visual Artists Rights Act 1990). The United States became a signatory to Berne in 1989, but still does not include moral rights in US copyright law. In the UK, the law has never been weighted towards respecting authors' rights; it looks first to the author–publisher contract and whether or not it has been breached.[37]

## DIGITAL LAW

The Digital Millennium Copyright Act, signed into US law by President Clinton on 28 October 1998, set the benchmark and terms for the digital scenario. Considered the most significant piece of copyright legislation in the United States since the 1976 Copyright Act, the DMCA brought US copyright law into line with the copyright treaties of the World Intellectual Property Organisation (WIPO). Of particular relevance to publishing is what the DMCA prohibits under section 1201, 'the anti-piracy provision', which provides that: *No person shall circumvent a technological measure that effectively controls access to a work protected under this title.* The DMCA seems to give copyright owners the exclusive right to control any reproduction of works, including any form of private copying as well.[38]

An editor at ArsTechnica was scathing about the law: 'The DMCA, which outlaws the circumvention of copy protection mechanism, is widely recognized as one of the greatest frauds ever perpetrated on US consumers'.[39] Legal scholar, David Nimmer, claimed the Act was framed 'in a foreign language, a "paracopyright" ... protecting new avenues of exploiting as yet undefined objects', based on 'a case law vacuum'. Professor Jessica Litman of the University of Michigan Law School argued that traditional copyright law 'never gave copyright owners rights as expansive' as the DMCA now allows.

Legal scholars point out that the best copyright law has always sought a balance between protection and guarantees of freedoms of access and use. The overall verdict is that the DMCA does not reflect 'the balance of interests that copyright laws had slowly established over their half-millennia history'.[40]

The central dilemma of the DMCA can be found in conflict between control and access, coming down to the question: *is it possible to even view published material if I have not obtained permission?* (i.e. if viewing means making a copy, and in digital downloading it does). This raises serious fundamental issues relating to consumer freedoms over the use of published information in the digital environment. The DMCA implies that traditional copyright norms are not enough. The Electronic Frontier Foundation (EFF) objected strongly, particularly to copyright owners using technology to place locks on works.

Within two months of the DMCA being enacted, an open competition under the Secure Digital Music Initiative (SDMI), and backed by the large music corporations, was announced. The competition included a $10,000 prize. Entrants were required to design a technology that would overcome *unauthorised use of digitally recorded music*. The music corporations wanted to see if their 'watermarked' digital files could be 'cracked'.

Ed Felten, an associate professor at Princeton University, took up the challenge and with some colleagues successfully lifted the watermarks from the digital music files, without affecting the sound quality. Big Music and the SDMI were not amused. Felten, who had declined to sign a confidentiality agreement at the outset of the competition, thereby voluntarily forfeiting his chance at the prize, decided to write up his findings in a peer-reviewed article on his team's work. He intended to present his findings at a conference. Hearing of his plans, the RIAA and SDMI threatened legal action. After a period of internal pressure from his university and the music industry, Felten and his colleagues, backed by the EFF, decided to sue the RIAA, SDMI and the Attorney General, arguing that the DMCA was unconstitutional. Their petition was dismissed with the observation from the judge that the complainants were 'modern day Don Quixotes' tilting at windmills.[41]

## FAIR USE AND FIRST SALE IN THE DIGITAL AGE

Fair use and first sale are the two issues at stake in the digital scenario. Before the DMCA, both concepts were universally applied and accepted practices throughout the world of anglophone publishing.

*Fair use* allows for the legal reproduction and redistribution of works under copyright in certain circumstances and for specified purposes. Under the 1976 US Copyright Act these uses include '*criticism, comment, news reporting, teaching (including multiple copies for classroom use), scholarship, or research*'. In the UK, fair use is seen as a practice that the courts and the publishing industry more or less manage and adhere to following the US statutory precedent.

*First sale* is a practice that accepts that the price of purchase extends the 'exclusive right to distribute', that the rights of the seller has been exhausted by the sale. The buyer or new owner of a book is free to pass on the single copy, to sell it on or make a gift of it. Passing on a digital copy to anyone (unless authorised) is prevented by the new digital copyright law. Under digital legislation, *fair use* and *first sale* now are almost things of the past. Digital content controllers seem to want to set up a 'pay-per-view' system for every possible use of material.

The issue of copying, in principle, was tested in a US court over 20 years ago. The court found for the consumer's right to copy – in this case, with a video-cassette recorder. In *Sony Corporation v. Universal Studios 1984*, the court determined that if copying equipment was *used for legitimate, unobjectionable purposes, it was legal even if it would be capable of infringing uses*. Technology was judged to be free of guilt and incapable of infringement. The US court saw fair and private use as legal. What remained contentious and potentially illegal was the nature of the action, and its motivations and circumstances. It was this that would determine what constituted an infringement of copyright law or that which could not be defended under the fair use doctrine.

The DMCA reinvented the concept of 'technological guilt', serving the objectives of copyright holders over content consumers. The Act assumes that consumers cannot be trusted, that they must be regulated a priori regardless of the intention of any use of copyrighted material in digital form. The DMCA, as written, makes a reader, a borrower, a lender, a giver and a receiver all liable at law, even if there is no financial relationship or pecuniary motive in the action. The reason given for the strong measures are that they are necessary as a defence against digital piracy, even if piracy has long existed in the world of analogue publishing.

## FURTHER READING

Bettig, R. V., *Copyrighting Culture: The Political Economy of Intellectual Property*, Boulder, CO, Westview Press, 1996

Goldstein, P., *Copyright's Highway: From Gutenberg to the Celestial Jukebox*, Stanford, CA, Stanford University Press, 2003

Jones, H., *Publishing Law*, London, Routledge, 2006

Lessig, L., *Free Culture: How Big Media Uses Technology and the Law to Lock Down Culture and Control Creativity*, New York, Penguin Press, 2004

Litman, J., *Digital Copyright*, New York, Prometheus, 2001

Lutzker, A. P., 'Point/Counterpoint on the DMCA and CTEA: Copyright & Fair Use Stanford University Libraries, North America's Art Libraries Society annual conference'. http://fairuse.stanford.edu/commentary_and_analysis/2005_08_arlisna.html, 2003 [08/08/04]

Lutzker, A. P., 'What the Digital Millennium Copyright Act and the Copyright Term Extension Act Mean for the Library Community', Lutzker & Lutzker LLP Primer on the Digital Millennium, http://www.arl.org/info/frn/copy/primer.html, 2005

Patterson, L. R., *Copyright in Historical Perspective*, Nashville, TN, Vanderbilt University Press, 1968

Ploman, E. W. and Hamilton, L. C., *Copyright: Intellectual Property in the Information Age*, London, Routledge & Kegan Paul, 1980

# NOTES

1  M. Rose, 'The Claims of Copyright', in R. Rice, ed., *Media Ownership: Research and Regulation*, Cresskill, NJ, Hampton Press Inc., 2008.

2  William F. Patry, 'Copyright Law and Practice', Bureau of National Affairs, Washington, DC, 2000.

3  The Star Chamber was named after a star pattern on the ceiling in the room of Westminster Palace where meetings were held. With roots in medieval times, the Tudors expanded it to hear grievances, the court becoming separate from the King's Council in 1487. Its power grew under the Stuarts. In the time of Charles I the Star Chamber became a symbol of the abuse of power.

4  Cory Doctorow, 'Why the Digital Economy Act Simply Won't Work', *The Guardian*, 1 June 2010.

5  D. D. Kirkpatrick, 'Report to the Authors' Guild Midlist Books Study Committee', New York, Authors' Guild Midlist Books Study Committee, 2000.

6  D. D. Kirkpatrick, 'Another Format in the e-Book Field', *New York Times*, http://www.nytimes.com/2000/11/06/technology/06BOOK.html.

7  D. D. Kirkpatrick, '4 Publishers Agree to Sale of e-Books on Yahoo', *New York Times*, http://www.nytimes.com/2001/09/05/technology/ebusiness/05BOOK.html.

8  Ibid.

9  T. L. Tedford and D. A. Herbeck, *Freedom of Speech in the United States*, State College, PA, Strata, 2005, p. 352.

10  http://www.flickr.com/photos/petezab/4243266763/.

11  C. Doctorow, 'Copyright, Companies, Individuals and News: The Rules of the Road', *The Guardian*, 26 January 2010.

12  Tedford and Herbeck, op. cit., p. 348.

13  Tedford and Herbeck, op. cit.

14  Ruffhead, O., 'The Statutes at Large from Magna Charta to the End of the Last Parliament 1761', printed by Mark Basket, London, 1763.

15  Olasky, M., '"Whatever is, Is Wrong": Antinoniamism and the Teaching of Journalism History', *Academic Questions*, 3 (1), pp. 40–50.

16  T. B. Howell, *State Trials in the Reign of King Charles II. Vol. 6: A Complete Collection of State Trials*, 1816.

17  Tedford and Herbeck, *Freedom of Speech*, op. cit., p. 8.

18  A fundamental principle of contracts is that a contract must involve a monetary exchange. Hocking, B.A., *Liability for Negligent Words*, Sydney, The Federation Press, 1999.

19  In the USA in 1933, Judge John M. Woolsey allowed the importation of *Ulysses*. Immediately after the judge's decision, Random House began production of the book.

20  Alan Travis, *Bound and Gagged*, London, Profile Books, 2000, pp. 18–45.

21  From Congressman Steve Cohen's website, http://cohen.house.gov/index.php?option=content&task=view&id=634.

22  Stuckey, K. D., 'Internet and online law', *Law Journal Press*, New York, 1996, p. 17.

23  'House of Representatives passes US libel tourism bill', http://www.pressgazette.co.uk/story.asp?storycode=43805.

24  The organisations Index on Censorship, English Pen and Sense about Science all campaigned for libel reform as libel action can prevent publication of research in the public interest. Jo Glanville, 'A Victory for Libel Reform', *The Guardian*, 24 March 2010.

25 This freed libel law from a nineteenth–century precedent that holds that every new publication is potentially a new libel suit. This will help internet publications and any downloading of material.

26 This acknowledges that the protection of 'reputation' in the UK can negate freedom of expression.

27 When the Marquess of Queensberry left a calling card, with a written message on it, at a theatre door (making it public to a third party), addressing Wilde as a 'somdomite' (sic), Wilde decided to take libel action against the Marquess. The action failed and Wilde, having admitted to aspects of his private life in court, was charged by the Crown with gross indecency. He was found guilty and imprisoned for two years with hard labour, which he spent at Pentonville, Wandsworth and Reading prisons. The sentence destroyed Wilde's health and three years after his release from prison he died in Paris at 46 years of age.

28 Not the well-known Greenpeace International, but a much smaller UK group.

29 Clare Dyer, 'Libel Law Review over McDonald's Ruling', The Guardian, 16 February 2005.

30 Ibid.

31 Tedford and Herbeck, op. cit., p. 97.

32 Lexis 'US Dist. Lexis 1751', eyrie.org., www.eyrie.org/~robotech/stouffer.html, 2002; Italie, H., 'Harry Potter Prevails in Court', CBS News, www.cbs.news.com/stories/2002/09/19/print/main522563.html; Gomes, P., 'Harry and His Brother Larry', Associated Press, www.infosatellite.com/news/2002/09/p250902larrypotter.html; Weeks, L., 'Muggle vs. Wizard: Author Accuses Creator of Harry Potter of Lifting Characters' Names', Washington Post, www.detnews.com/2001/entertainment/0103/31/c03-205734.html.

33 Green, Stuart P., 'Plagiarism, Norms, and the Limits of Theft Law: Some Observations on the Use of Criminal Sanctions in Enforcing Intellectual Property Rights', Hastings Law Journal, 54 (1), 2002. Available at SSRN, http://ssrn.com/abstract=315562 or doi:10.2139/ssrn.315562.

34 As this case never went to court, the names of individuals and companies have been changed.

35 However, under the UK's Copyright, Designs and Patents Act 1988, it seems X's book was at least 'false attribution' on the part of the publisher UK.

36 In the USA, statutory 'punitive' damages can be awarded by the court without the plaintiff having to prove actual financial 'damage'. Damages go to a maximum of $100,000, repeated for every act of infringement.

37 Hugh Jones, Publishing Law, London, Routledge, 1996, p. 44.

38 UK measures are included in the 2001 EU Directive on Copyright & Related Rights in the Information Society 2001/29/EC, harmonising digital copyright law throughout the EU, and also implementing the WIPO Treaty of 1996. Article 6 of the EU Directive is considered even more restrictive than section 1201 in the DMCA.

39 Eric Bangeman, 'US Copyright Office Wants to Hear from You about the DMCA', ArsTechnica, 28 October 2005.

40 Loren, L. P., 'Technological Protections in Copyright Law: Is More Legal Protection Needed?', International Review of Law Computers and Technology, 16, 2002, pp. 133–148.

41 Goldstein, P., Copyright's Highway: From Gutenberg to the Celestial Jukebox, Stanford, CA, Stanford University Press, 2003, pp. 176–181.
'Muggle Versus Wizard'. The Washington Post. March 28, 2001. http://discuss.washingtonpost.com/zforum/01/author_stouffer032801.htm
Weeks, L. (2001) Muggle vs. Wizard: Author accuses creator of Harry Potter of lifting characters' names, from Washington Post, March 31, 2001.

# 6 RIGHTS AND CONTRACTS

The development of saleable publishing content starts with the buying and selling of primary and subsidiary intellectual property (IP) rights. The rights area represents a bundle of derivatives that come from a single property – the book or other copyrighted material. Rights can be extremely profitable because they involve little or no risk. Rights sales add directly to the bottom line and are therefore extremely important to publishers.

Publishers acquire non-perpetual, limited-term rights to publish when they contract writers. There are exceptions to the non-perpetuity rule in rights. For example, films financed and produced by a studio pay the artists and the production and post-production teams a flat fee or a flat fee plus a percentage of profits.

A primary right to publish describes the right to publish and distribute an English-language book in an anglophone territory(ies). The UK categories of primary book rights are:

- UK only
- UK and Commonwealth without Canada
- World rights without USA
- World rights with USA
- All Europe rights
- World rights in all languages.

The division of primary rights and subsidiary rights depends on each individual author–publisher contract, but as a general rule primary rights are those a publisher is able to exploit and subsidiary rights are those the author is free to exploit. Primary rights can include:

- first volume – hardcover, trade or mass-market paperback
- anthology, extract excerpt, quotation rights
- book club rights
- second serial rights

- microfilm, microfiche or other reproduction of text rights
- large print or visually impaired rights editions
- school edition rights
- photocopying rights
- direct mail rights
- special, review extract, business or promotion editions.

Subsidiary rights include:

- first serial rights and one shot serial rights
- foreign and translation rights (countries, geographical areas and languages)
- condensed book rights
- film, television and theatrical rights
- merchandising rights
- audio rights
- electronic book and publishing rights
- live TV, theatre or radio performance rights.[1]

Subsidiary rights are described by Thomas Woll (*Publishing for Profit*) as 'essential for the success' of a publishing company. Without subsidiary rights income 'most companies would barely break even'.[2]

When publishers contract books and authors they seek to exploit all the rights available in their contracts. If the primary publishing rights for titles also include foreign and/or translation rights, publishers will seek to sell exclusive foreign and/or translation copyright to foreign publishers. If an agreement is reached, the original and the foreign publishers will usually either form a co-edition or licensing arrangement for publication in the foreign territory or language.

---

## LICENSING

Licensing is based on a royalty agreement. A publisher from another territory will agree to pay an advance calculated on a projected print run (a sum multiplying the print run by the royalty to be paid on each copy). After the advance-based print run has been exhausted and more copies are printed, royalties on further sales will then be paid once or twice a year to the original publisher. Royalties usually range from 6% to 8% of the list price for paperback editions and from 10% to 15% for the hardcover.

The licensing agreement includes a copy of the original typesetting usually for a fee. The licencee publisher will then use this to produce copies in the language of the new territory.

Licensing can represent a good source of income, but to make the most of the arrangement publishers need to understand the market they are licensing into, to know how to adjust sales strategies accordingly. Some markets are very difficult to monitor. A projected 10,000 print run, on which an advance on royalties has been paid, may in fact turn out to be a much longer print run than that. For this reason sometimes a flat fee instead of a royalty fee is negotiated.

---

### CO-EDITIONS

A co-edition arrangement is a method of selling the rights to a title in another territory via a co-manufacturing arrangement – meaning the original publisher will print and provide copies (under instruction) at a per-copy price. The calculation of a fee for this is done either by:

- origination fee (including manufacturing cost, author royalty, etc.) plus non-manufacturing and transport, insurance costs loading (10–20%), or
- discounting on the retail price by around 65%, a standard industry method.

The original publisher prints all copies and ships them to the co-edition territory. This works particularly well for same-language territories, such as the UK and the USA. There may be requests for different cover art, a different title and prelims pages, etc. from the publisher buying the co-edition copies.

---

Co-editions concern consumer book publishing far more than any other sector. There is some trade in academic co-editions but in general, trade/consumer books sell far better across territories. Sellers and buyers of rights meet up to do business 'halfway', usually at the large international book fairs – Frankfurt, London and Bologna (for children's books) – sharing the costs of doing business between the international parties.

In a 2008 UK Publishers Association survey of rights and co-edition income, 25 participating UK publishers reported a total income of £116.6 million. This figure was down 8.7% on the £127.8 million earned from rights and co-edition sales in 2006. Yet, while co-edition income alone dropped from £61.6 million in 2006 to £43.6 million in 2008, rights income grew 10%, going from £66.2 million in 2006 to £72.7 million in 2008.[3]

## BOOK CLUB RIGHTS

Book clubs provide low-cost editions of titles to members only. By agreement, written into contracts with publishers, books clubs are precluded from selling on the open market. Reflecting the discounting practices by online retailers, superstores and supermarkets, in recent times, book clubs have seen declines in membership and market share. In four short years at the beginning of this century clubs went from nearly 23% of market share in 2000 to around 18% in 2004. The end of the Net Book Agreement (NBA) in the UK in 1997 also hugely affected clubs, the very time the online e-tailer, Amazon, was beginning to have an effect on the market. From the late 1990s onward, clubs have had to compete with standard trade outlets discounting prices. Prior to this, book clubs were the lowest priced book available and by a long way.

Book club members, in the main, read fiction and non-fiction trade/consumer titles, though reference books, encyclopedias and dictionaries are also in demand. Clubs still remain popular with many readers because of the lists and targeted special offers they make to members. The concept and operation of clubs are still very good for publishers, as members are dedicated readers who read many books.

Purchases by big book clubs follow two main paths: a publisher will sell stock to a club at an agreed (usually heavily discounted) price, or a publisher grants a reprint licence to a book club to produce special, low-cost editions for members.

Club member recruitment is carried out by mailings, often offering loss-leader priced books to encourage new membership.[4] Members receive regular catalogue mailings with new titles, and books are offered at around 30% off recommended retail prices. The main UK book clubs are:

- *Book Club Associates (BCA)*, controlling about 80% of the book club market, owned by Bertelsmann, a company with 25 million book club members worldwide. BCA's annual sales exceed £100 million.[5] BCA also owns Quality Paperbacks Direct.
- *Readers' Union* – photography, painting, history, once owned by Reader's Digest.
- *Scholastic* – children's books mainly for schools. Scholastic also owns *Red House*.
- *Letterbox Library* – children's books.
- *Folio Society* – illustrated, specially-bound classics.

Clubs operate one of three different methods of buying books from publishers:

- an overall contract based on purchase orders (POs) for each title
- purchase orders only, set for each individual title and each publisher
- a master contract with individual publishers, with individual POs for titles.

Title reprints are restricted so a book club's edition cannot compete with a publisher's first-volume edition. A book club contract will often require that the club does not release or license a lower-cost edition into the open market within 12 months of the date of publication of the trade edition, at least not without prior permission from the 'licensor publishing house'.

In the UK, the general agreement is overseen by the Publishers Association (PA), which requires clubs to inform the PA of coming titles four months in advance in order to allow trade publishers the chance to publish first if they so wish.

Reprint licences usually run for about three years with low royalty rates paid (5%) based on prices offered to members. Clubs like to produce their own editions and so care must be taken by the club to state inside the cover that they are providing exclusive or special editions.

## PAPERBACK RIGHTS

After a trade hardcover has been in print for one year – considered enough time to dispose of hardback copies – a paperback edition will usually be released. The hardcover publisher will either vertically integrate the softcover edition into hardcover/softcover programmes in-house, or auction or sell the rights to another publisher. The paperback house buying the rights will usually be a dedicated paperback house. A house may bypass the hardcover altogether, publishing only in softcover. More and more this is becoming standard practice.

Paperbacks come in three main sizes and formats:

- A Format, the smallest paperback, mass-market size, 110mm × 178mm (4.33″ × 7.01″)
- B Format 130mm x 198mm (5.12″ × 7.8″)
- C Format or UK trade paperback size, 135mm × 216mm (5.32″ × 8.51″) – US literary agents often refer to B format as 'trade paperback size'.

In the UK, hardcover publishers selling paperback rights generally do so on an agreed advance figure, plus a royalty per copy, based on a term of licensing set at about eight years. There will usually be a licence renewal option in the contract for a further five years. Royalties will be set at between 7.5% and 10% of RRP (recommended retail price) when a certain number of sales has been reached. Higher royalty rates of 15% plus can be set for name authors.

Trade book advances can range from low four-figure sums to high six-figure sums in the UK, and high four figures to seven-figure sums in the USA. Some *global* paperback publishers will ask for world rights, others will ask for UK, European markets and Commonwealth rights. For authors, royalties on sales of paperbacks depend on the market profile of the author. If the hardcover and softcover are kept within the same house, an author may get as high as 90% of the proceeds from the mass market paperback edition sales.

Whether paperback rights are sold by hardback publishers to specialist paperback houses or 'transferred vertically' down to an imprint within the same house, they create the most sales by volume, being exploited in every possible sales outlet, from traditional bookshops to supermarkets, airport bookshops, corner convenience stores and kiosks.

# TRANSLATION RIGHTS

Translation is an important area of anglophone publishing rights sales, as there are many territories to exploit. English-language translations dominate the overall translation market. Europe, where 30% of all books are translations, is a rich catchment area for anglophone publishers. By contrast, only 3% of books published in English are translations, though as the UK and the USA each publishes well over 100,000 books every year, 3% of the total means that several thousand new foreign language titles are released annually into the two leading anglophone book markets.

Apart from market knowledge in a particular language, the handling of a translation agreement requires cultural and historical awareness of the people, economics, social conditions and politics, and in particular very good knowledge of copyright law in that territory. Cultural leanings and tastes vary from country to country. A Chinese-styled exposé on a public figure is a vastly different publishing proposition from an English-language exposé published in the UK or the USA. Cultural, political and religious factors and sensitivities are involved in cross-territorial translation rights sales. For this reason, children's books travel more easily from culture to culture and language to language than any other sector. Literary fiction and some non-fiction can also travel well, if the books provide insights into the cultural life and living conditions of societies where they originate. Michael Moore's *Stupid White Men* sold over a million copies in Germany, around one-third of the book's global sales. Moore's view of America struck a chord with German readers.

In practical production terms, translations rights can be managed by employing co-edition printing. All this is handled by the original publisher, after consultation with the publisher in the foreign-language territory. For instance, a UK publisher arranging a co-edition with a German publisher will produce the same book in two languages, allowing for the differences in the extent (length) of the German text (usually longer) compared to the English text. Co-edition translations particularly suit illustrated books – cookbooks, how-to-books, graphic instruction manuals, children's books, coffee table and photographic books – where text volume is far lower than usual text-based books. The original English-language publisher makes an agreement with the foreign-language publisher on the print number, receipt and insertion of the translation text, unit cost and transport cost. An agreement is best negotiated early on when the house is still preparing the original text.

The second way is to license the foreign rights. This method is better for non-illustrated or text-only books. If a foreign-language publisher takes a license, it is usually based on an advance payment of royalties on an agreed first printing. The foreign-language publisher agrees to pay royalties to the original English-language publisher for further printings. Payment can be a straight agreed lump sum, which is useful when there is no possibility of monitoring the progress of reprints. Royalty percentages vary between kinds of books and territories. In Eastern Europe, book prices can change markedly between sellers. Children's books generally receive lower royalty payments (4–7%); academic books around 7% or lower, rising as the number printed goes up, although much of this depends on the work itself, its sales history in the original territory, and the market profile of the author.

The author's share of any translation deal will depend on who he or she is, but generally the publisher will split income with the writer from 50% upwards to as high as 80% for a major name author. High advances have been paid for foreign translation editions, but they are unusual. It is doubtful whether a Chinese publisher would pay a high advance for any work of fiction, but a Chinese house might pay a high sum for a book written by a famous entrepreneur, for instance. German publishers have paid large figures for exposés or critical portraits of American public figures, such as the over 1 million DM the German publishers Beck paid for the 'fictionalised' tale of Bill Clinton on his first run for the White House, *Primary Colors*.[6]

Selling a licence to a foreign-language publisher is a good arrangement as it is upfront money paid in exchange for the original text, layout and illustrations. There is no production to arrange for or carry out. Some foreign markets cannot be easily monitored by the original publisher. Royalty statements and size of print runs in the foreign market may not reflect the actual business being done. English-language publishers may lose revenue this way, but as it is an ancillary rights sale, requiring no investment, it may be easier simply to sell a licence and take the advance.

## EUROPA EDITIONS – MAKING THE MOST OF 3%

In 2005 a new small publishing company was created in the United States, Europa Editions. Its intention was to create a list from translations of contemporary European fiction. The idea for Europa originated in Italy with Sandro Ferri and Sandra Ozzola Ferri, owners and founders of Edizioni E/O, a Rome-based publishing house.

To carry the idea forward, the Ferris linked up with a veteran of New York publishing, Kent Carroll, formerly editorial chief at Grove Press and co-founder of Carroll & Graf, an imprint bought and discontinued by Perseus when it bought Avalon (Carroll & Graf's owner) in 2007. Carroll knew at the outset what he was up against. The US market was set in its ways – translations didn't sell easily.

Assisted by a part-time freelancer and two interns, he began a boutique operation in midtown Manhattan, running Europa from a tiny, two-roomed, shared office. Several years on, and many book sales later, Carroll still projects himself as someone focused on the business rather than someone trying to impress visitors with workplace luxuries. Farrar, Straus & Giroux's publishing chief, Jonathan Galassi's admiration for Carroll's approach contains an almost wistful lament for a lost way of doing things: 'Most of publishing was once that way. It wasn't about big money so much. He's sort of preserving the old values of it's-all-about-the-book and connecting the book with readers'.[7] Nostalgia aside, Europa has ambitions.[8] From the outset Carroll went after the market.

Following the European tradition of releasing only a trade paperback format, Europa began producing books with a distinctive European design flavour, including inside flaps, a single style of font on the book spines, and by displaying the company's stork logo together with the publisher's name on the front cover.

Europa's mission was to prove that the time had come for translated literature in the USA, in particular contemporary European fiction, which, except for some notable exceptions, the two large anglophone markets had largely avoided. Europa didn't set out to buy market share because it couldn't – the company rarely spends more than $10,000 on author advances. Carroll took the tried-and-tested route, attracting interest from major media outlets and booksellers.

When the *New York Times* published a positive article on the new venture, readers began responding well to Europa and its intentions. Independent booksellers were supportive. Carroll's approach combines the pragmatism of an industry veteran with values and publishing ethics from another era. 'There used to be a reason to get into publishing' and whether new publishing staff recognise 'it or not, they all want to be Maxwell Perkins. It's a kind of secondary immortality. They didn't flock to publishing because they want to publish Danielle Steel.'[9]

Europa Edition's first US publication was *Days of Abandonment* by Italian novelist, Elena Ferrante. The novel received positive reviews and began selling solidly through independent booksellers. Europa's sales were still only in the thousands though. Other titles followed. Then came the French novel, *The Elegance of the Hedgehog*, by Muriel Barbery. Released in the UK and the USA in the autumn of 2008, *Hedgehog* had already won the 2007 French Booksellers' Prize, the 2007 Brive-la-Gaillarde Reader's Prize and the Prix du Rotary International in France. A film adaptation was well into production. The book had European sales 'form' – over a million copies sold in France in hardback alone, 400,000 in Italy. Yet the initial reaction of anglophone 'publishing experts' was cool. Jonathan Ruppin, promotions buyer at independent bookshop Foyles, thought *Hedgehog* was in for a struggle. 'The British reading public are unduly wary of foreign fiction. And the plot is not the main aspect of this book – it's more subservient to philosophical and sociological observations, and I find with the UK market now the plot is what people want more than anything else. Something esoteric and tricksy is difficult to sell.'[10]

Writing in *The Guardian*, Alison Flood, a former news editor of the UK's *Bookseller*, implied the book wouldn't work in Britain. French literature was a touch too 'spiky' for British readers. Michael Sheringham, Marshal Foch Professor of French Literature at All Souls College in Oxford confirmed this impression. British readers often feel that French cinema and books can be akin to 'watching

*(Continued)*

(Continued)

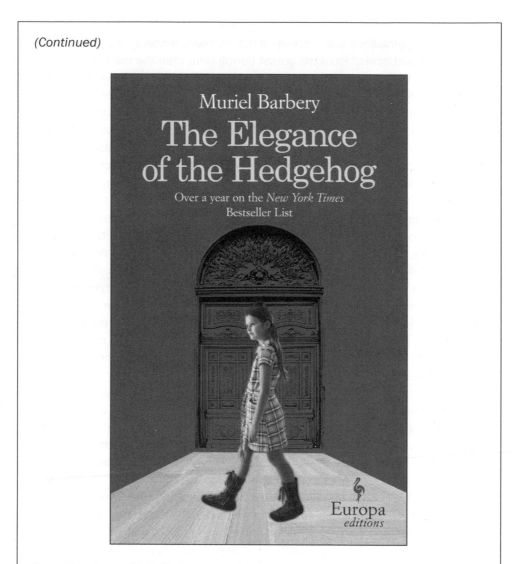

*Source*: Cover image with the kind permission of Europa Editions, New York

paint dry'. Alison Flood presented a bleak picture for translated fiction. 'Maybe it's the very structure of French novels, their introspective nature, their subtlety, which put off British readers. The self-referential device of the "author as character" recurs frequently in French fiction ... rare in British writing.'[11]

Flood had a solid point to make on British reader reactions. Add a vaguely post-modern theme and the mixture looked lethal. Barbery's postmodernist French novel would fail in the British market. The author herself was deeply unsure.

Will English and American people like [it]? Nobody can tell. ... taste: people will either like my characters, my style, or they won't.[12]

Against all predictions, US and UK sales of *Hedgehog* took off. By February 2010, the UK edition of *Hedgehog* had sold 37,000 hardcovers and 113,000 paperbacks. In the USA, Europa sales were close to 500,000. *Hedgehog* had been on the *New York Times* bestseller list for 55 weeks. Of the overall market 3% turned out to be good business. Flood's summing up of the UK market — '[F]iction in translation is not an easy sell to Brits, and French fiction is perhaps the hardest sell of all' — echoes William Goldman's famous words: 'Nobody knows anything.' When it comes to books in translation, perhaps nobody does.

# SERIAL RIGHTS

Serial rights sales are a win-win for all. They stimulate volume sales, raise awareness, increase circulation numbers of newspapers, etc., and bring in relatively easy revenue for the author and the publisher. There are three kinds of serial rights:

- first serial rights
- one-shot serial rights
- second serial rights.

*First serial rights* are excerpt rights sold to newspapers, magazines, journals and other periodicals prior to publication of a book. The publisher usually only has to provide a digital file of the literary work and the periodical does the rest.

First serial rights can earn six-figure payments for much sought-after material. Division of receipts ranges from between 80 or 90% for the author and 20 or 10% for the publisher. Giving a periodical first serial rights allows the newspaper or magazine to 'scoop' a book and its story to the world. If the book is controversial, politically timely, or involves details of the life or death of a major public figure, then a large payment for first serial rights is seen as justifiable by periodicals. Serialisation sales successes on the life and death of Princess Diana, for instance, occurred in many territories, not just in the UK.

*One-shot periodical rights* involve the publication of the entire book, usually spread over several editions, one day after another, or week by week.

From the first publication of Charles Dickens' *The Pickwick Papers* in 1836 by Edward Chapman and William Hall, one-shot serial rights deals represent a 'pot-of-gold' chance for publishers and authors alike. One-shot serial rights sales announce a work to a wide reading public while earning well for the author and publisher. They are a chance to earn twice from a book. Both one-shot and first serial rights sales increase book sales rather than cannibalise them. However, serial rights sales are not the sales opportunity they once were, especially in North America, where they are now known as the '"Skid Row" of American publishing'.[13] Newspapers and magazines are in circulation decline and are not snapping up serial rights deals for books in anything like the number they once did in the heydays of print journalism.

*Second serial rights* involve the publication of excerpts after the book has been published. Payments for these rights are much lower than first or one-shot periodical rights sales, but can be useful additions to the bottom line and are very valuable for ongoing publicity for a book, sometimes giving it a renewed public profile and leading to a resurgence of sales.

## TERRITORIAL RIGHTS

The main anglophone territories and markets are the United States, Canada, Australasia, Sub-Sahara Africa, India and Europe. Agreements may be made by anglophone publishers on a co-edition arrangement, the selling of licences or by the direct export of printed books into these markets. There is a major business in direct sales of rights between the world's two largest anglophone book markets, the UK and the USA. Co-editions are often used and can accommodate each territory's requirements, suiting all involved.

The concept of 'territories' is a hotly debated subject these days, due to the globalisation of markets. UK publishers argue that without the territorial exclusivity accorded in contracts there is little incentive to invest in titles, as another publisher could release exactly the same product into the same territory. Territorial rights operate on the doctrine of international exhaustion of rights, i.e. that a book must first sell out in its country of origin and then move on to be sold without territorial restriction in competing markets. The UK Publishers Association advises that the parallel importation and sale of the US edition of a book already selling in Britain is tantamount to copyright infringement. When confronted on this, Amazon and Bertelsmann's bol.com agreed to observe territoriality.[14]

As copyright is a form of monopoly an author enjoys and exploits, so territorial exclusivity is a quasi-monopoly a publisher exploits and enjoys. Publishers strive to sell rights into as many markets as possible. The concept of territories is crucial to this business idea and model. Every territory sale brings in more revenue. Authors also benefit from this because every sale into a new territory brings financial returns to them as well.

An assignment of world rights gives the rightsholder the freedom to publish a book anywhere in the world. Sale of territorial rights to local publishers, however, is considered advisable as they will know their own market better than a foreign publisher. One of the world's bestselling authors, J. K. Rowling, is signed to Scholastic in the United States, while her original publisher, Bloomsbury, releases her works in the UK. In the Australian market, her books are published and sold by Allen & Unwin. The general agreement is that all three publishers will not encroach into each other's territorial market, or compete against each other with the same title in each other's territory.

UK publishers, in particular, are against the idea of a global market, saying it contravenes international copyright law and agreements. But territoriality does not, did not ever, technically equate to copyright. Territoriality is a market division.

The current debate over *territorial* rights versus *world* rights brings Europe, Australia and India into play. US publishers are beginning to object to the UK's default position of 'owning' post-colonial markets. As one independent publisher Carolyn Savarese put it:

> Consumers in the global market, whether in Marburg or Mumbai, want what they want now. And with all due respect to the nation that gave us Shakespeare and the Beatles, the global market does not, I think, want to be restricted to the UK version of English language culture.[15]

# OTHER ANGLOPHONE MARKETS

## AUSTRALIA

With a population of 20 million, Australia has a publishing market worth A$2.5 billion annually, with book prices on average 30% higher than in other markets such as the UK.[16] In 2007, about 14,000 new titles were produced by around 4,000 publishers, with 130 million books bought by readers, making Australia's book market about 16% of the size of the UK's book market.[17]

Australia is the UK's fourth largest export market for books, accounting for 5.5% of all UK book exports. As in the UK, nearly 60% of the books sold in Australia are trade titles, of which UK titles account for about half. Of total market sales 30% are adult fiction (A$266m or £112m in 2004) with 66% of those titles produced by UK publishers. UK titles also make up 50% of children's fiction sales.

In terms of mass-market fiction, an Australian bestseller can sell around 200,000 copies. Names like Grisham, Cornwell, Smith and Clancy often sell 50,000 in hardcover. Literary novels also do well. *Life of Pi* scored 45,000 sales. DBC Pierre's *Vernon God Little* and Peter Carey's *My Life as a Fake* sold in excess of 30,000 copies each. Pamela Stephenson's autobiography *Bravemouth* went over 100,000 in sales. The biggest seller in recent years came in 2004 with *Harry Potter and the Order of the Phoenix* selling over 900,000 in hardcover sales alone. Australia is a market that for UK publishers is relatively easy to manage.

Australia's growing market and strong *per capita* reading habits make it one of the best anglophone book and magazine markets anywhere in the world. Countrywide there are 2,300 new and second-hand bookstores and around 2,000 public libraries.

In 2005, Angus & Robertson (A&R) owned or ran about 177 stores, including two up-market stores branded Reader's Feast, and had another five under the WH Smith banner. Independent bookshops are very strong, making up almost a quarter of the market. The Independent Collective has over 100 stores. Dymocks owns 81 stores (including stores in Hong Kong and New Zealand). A merger between Collins and Books City in 2007 brought together well over 60 stores under Collins management. The ABC has over 40 stores and outlets inside other stores. Borders has 11 shops in the major capital cities. Newslink (unlisted in Figure 6.1)

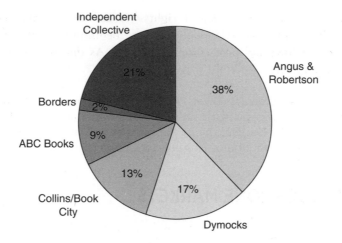

FIGURE 6.1  Overall guide to Australian bookseller market share

is prominent at airports and railway stations. Major department stores and super-markets also sell books.[18]

Amazon hasn't yet made the impact in Australia it has already made in the UK or USA, but an Australian online-selling version of Amazon, Fishpond, is developing internet sales. Internet booksellers thus far do not have to include the flat 10% Goods and Services Tax on sales, which bricks and mortar booksellers by law must include.[19]

Australia is not dominated by big distributors, such as Bertrams and Gardners in the UK. In recent years, Penguin, HarperCollins and Pan Macmillan have set up their own distribution operations. Being the sixth largest country on the planet, transport logistics and transport costs affect how distribution and wholesaleing is arranged.

As in the US and the UK, the main publishers are branches of the multinationals: *in trade*, Random House, Hachette, HarperCollins, Penguin and Macmillan; in *education*, Pearson, John Wiley & Sons, Cengage and Macmillan. A group of top ten publishers control around 70% of the total market. Local independent Australian publishers are also prominent in the markets, such as Allen & Unwin, Murdoch Books, Hinkler Books, Funtastic Books, Text, ABC Books, Scribe, University of Queensland Press, Fremantle Press, Black Inc., Hardie Grant, and more.

Around 60% of all books sold in Australia have some Australian factor or input, either as original Australian titles or 'buy-ins' published as Australian editions. Australian publishers overall earn around 14% of all income from exports.

The education sector is strong, with state-based text controls and provision in the main. In 2004 there were 3.3 million students attending 9,615 primary (to age 12 – 7,000 schools), secondary schools (to age 17 – 1,700 schools) and specialist schools. Seventy-two per cent of schools are government run and 28% are non-government owned and managed. In books published for primary education, Harcourt Education (Heinemann, Rigby, Reed), Horwitz Education (local), Macmillan, Oxford University Press (OUP), Pascal (local), Pearson (Longman) and Thomson Learning (Nelson) lead the way. In secondary education the main players are Cambridge University Press, Harcourt Education (Heinemann, Rigby, Reed), Jacaranda Wiley, Macmillan, McGraw-Hill, OUP, Pearson (Longman) and Thomson Learning (Nelson). Australian education publication exports in 2002–2003 went over A$60 million (£25.2m), with 'primary' texts accounting for $54 million (£22.7m).

The Australian ELT sector is small globally but is growing, catering in the main for students from Asian, European and South American origin, and generates annual sales of A$10 million (£4.2m).

The academic and professional market is much more open for foreign publishers than education. Of school leavers, 80% go on to a tertiary institution. With 42 universities and many other higher education institutions (TAFE and VET), the country has well over 2.5 million students enrolled in post-school education annually. The main and oldest universities, University of Sydney (45,000 students) and University of Melbourne (40,000) have the best academic traditions, but each state and territory has a range of well-attended institutions, many of which have achieved global recognition in recent years.[20]

Australian publishing and book retailing shows consistent growth in terms of both value and volume year on year, riding out the recent financial global financial crisis well. Local content and an independent industry are high on the wish-list of Australian publishers, authors and book consumers.

Up until 1991 Australia was more or less a UK publishing province, a suburb of London as one author described it. In 1977, an Australian judge commented that UK publishers were manipulating the Australian market. With the 1991 amendment to the Australian Copyright Act Australian book publishers bringing out foreign published works (or foreign companies operating in Australia or exporting into the Australian market) are now required to publish works in Australia within 30 days of first publication of a literary work/book in a foreign market, or face competition from overseas imports. This measure was introduced in 1991 to stop publishers bringing out an Australian edition when they chose to and hanging on to territorial rights at the expense of Australian readers. UK publishers still have a generous first strike at the market and they also have market knowledge and presence. When negotiating for UK and Commonwealth rights with US publishers, UK firms usually require that American companies cede the former colonies into an overall UK deal. UK publishers won't give up Commonwealth territories easily. Sales in Australia pay export royalties (half of home royalties) and sometimes UK publishers sell more than they do in the UK.[21] Australian publishers, when bidding for the Australian rights of American books face the reply that US publishers are waiting on a UK deal, with Australia part of that deal. This is changing and US publishers are now more prepared to make separate Australian territory deals. This UK negotiating position is seen by Australian publishers as an unfair business practice. They feel they can do a better job with US books in the Australian market. They also believe that the Australian book market is being used to shore up the balance sheets of UK houses. Rosenbloom sums up Australian publishing sentiment in his paper 'Territorial Rights and Wrongs': 'UK publishers are not entitled to Australia as a territory. It is our country, our market, and our industry.'[22] There is a decided lack of reciprocity in arrangements. Australian publishers of 'Australian originals' trying to sell the UK rights find that without any Australian rights UK publishers are not interested. Many Australian publishers believe that this is tantamount to market blackmail, stifling growth in Australian publishing.[23] It may only be a statistical coincidence, but in the post-1991 Copyright Act scenario, when UK publishers 'got serious' on the Australian market, US direct book exports to Australia declined significantly – down 33.5% from 1996 to 2004 (US$118.1m to $78.6m). During the same period US book exports to Singapore (a self-declared open market) went up by 61%, and US exports to the UK rose 28%.[24]

## INDIA

With a population of well over a billion, a democratic political system, a growing economy (6–8% annually), 343 public-funded universities, 15,000 colleges, well over 12 million undergraduates, English widely spoken among the educated and a book market worth well over a £1 billion annually, India is a natural home (and commercial target) for anglophone publishers. British publishers and their books are sought after in the Indian book market, in contrast to East Asia where US published books are more prized. India is important for both UK and US publishers. In 2006, India was eighteenth on the list of UK export sales (£21.1m) and tenth on the list for US book exports (£11.1m). The Indian book market is as intriguing and complex as the country itself. Overall, in terms of title output, it is sixth behind the USA, the UK, China, Germany and Russia, and third behind the USA and the UK in the number of English-language titles.

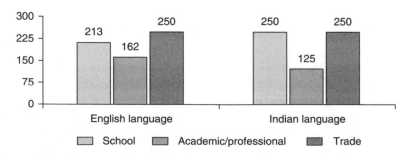

FIGURE 6.2   Indian book sales in 2007 (£m)

*Source of figures*: UK Publishers Association 2007, India Market Profile by Rob Francis

There are striking paradoxes in the Indian market. While it is a vibrant publishing market, with great support for reading and book culture throughout, it also generates *piracy*, *plagiarism* and *leakage* (illegal run-ons of books printed on top of customer orders). UK and US books are often illegally sold on Indian streets and online, often only days after original publication. Piracy and photocopying in educational institutions are estimated to account for losses of more than 20% of all sales. In some specific areas, losses run as high as 80%. From 2000 to 2007 Indian authorities arrested 328 people and prosecuted 107, and confiscated 620,000 copies of pirated books, 50 photocopiers and nine printing presses. Leakage is well established, with Indian distributors shipping illegal copies to the Middle East, Africa, Europe and the USA.

There are also structural anomalies in the way education and literacy has evolved. Many Indians are highly educated, a testimony and legacy of a strong belief in and support for higher education by leaders such as Jawaharlal Nehru. The country has a world-class IT sector, a direct result of a deliberate decision to concentrate on the sector from the 1950s onwards, instead of heavy manufacturing. India now supplies the USA with skilled professionals and China with IT teachers. Yet for all its love of books and success in education, a third of the Indian population is still illiterate. Neighbouring China, with a billion plus people, has 94% literacy. The 21 official Indian languages (not including English, which is not an official language) makes for a dispersed education system and book marketplace.

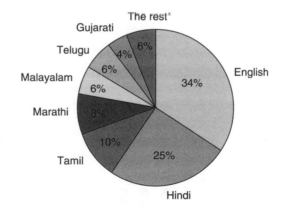

*The rest 6%: Kannada 2%; Bengali 1%; Oriya 1%; Punjabi 0.6%; Urdu 0.5%; Assamese 0.5%

FIGURE 6.3   Newspaper sales by language in 2006
*Source of figures*: UK Publishers Association 2007 India Market Profile

Newspaper sales are an indication of literacy, but a different picture emerges when looking at the number of Indian books published by language (Figure 6.4). Of the 82,537 book titles published in 2004, in contrast to newspaper sales, Hindi overtakes English, and languages such as Bengali and Urdu rise to greater prominence (Figure 6.3). While the Indian book market by volume is one of the largest in the world, per capita annual spending on books is very low – about £1 (compared to the USA $60, the UK £50, Taiwan £30, Russia £4 and China £2).

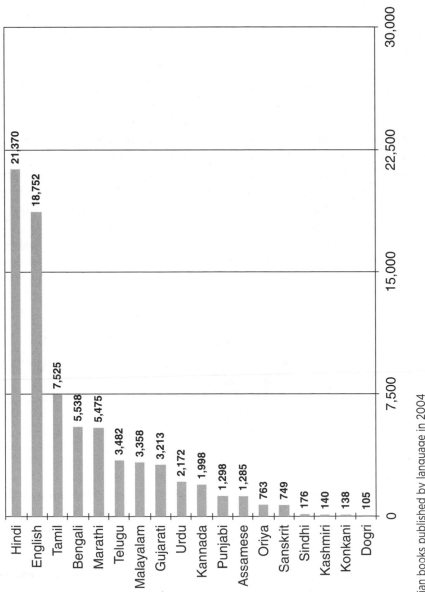

FIGURE 6.4  Indian books published by language in 2004

*Source of figures*: UK Publishers Association 2007, India Market Profile

There is a natural and steady move towards local production, with thousands of Indian publishers producing books in many languages. Foreign publishers produce and distribute books for India, but most books for the Indian market are printed locally. Trade titles in India can sell in the 30,000–50,000 copies range, and some as high as 200,000. Young, educated Indians like to read in their mother tongue but also in English.

The total annual trade market has a value of £500 million (R4,000 crores), with English-language books earning £300 million (R2,400 crores). The book trade is growing at 10% annually, which is above the average economic rate of growth. Growth of 12–30% for some new players is anticipated.

Indian investors have shown keen interest in retail bookselling chains and brands, such as Landmark, Reliance, Books & Beyond, and Shoppers Stop. The bookselling sector is predicted to grow by about a third in the coming years.

Of the global trade publishing names present in India, 'the usual suspects' – Penguin, Random House, Hachette and HarperCollins – lead the way. The largest local publisher is Rupa. The company began in Kolkata's College Street in 1936 and has been a joint venture with HarperCollins for many years. Other Indian publishers of note include: Parragon, India Research Press, Jaico Publishing House and Kali (for women).

The education market is strong, about 60% of the total market. The schoolbook market is worth £437 million (R3,500 crores). Oxford University Press and Macmillan are well established in India and lead the education market. Pearson Education and Cambridge University Press have made agreements with school boards in recent times. Others, like McGraw-Hill and Elsevier, are selling textbooks and library titles. Sage Publications established an Indian branch in 1981 and currently produces over 100 titles annually and 20 or so journals. Taylor & Francis has had an Indian company branch for several years and aims to produce upwards of 50 titles annually, mainly in the areas of humanities and social sciences.

Textbooks can sell 20,000–30,000 copies if adopted widely in educational institutions. English is widely used in private school and higher education, with 22% of all new education titles being published in English, many produced by the education sector of Indian publishing. Two hundred and twenty million pupils in state schools get free or very low price textbooks from their local state school boards. There is strong ELT potential, with 42 million students in 50,000 private schools studying in and learning English.

## SCANDINAVIA

With around 19 million people in total, Sweden (9.2m and growing in 2008's figures), Norway (4.8m) and Denmark (5.5m) have highly literate and educated populations (there is 99% literacy in Sweden). English is spoken widely (80–90%), and is the official 'language of business'. Scandinavia is an important anglophone publishing marketplace, especially for the UK, ranking third behind Germany and the Netherlands for UK book exports.

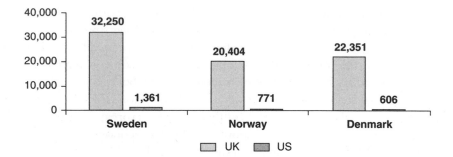

FIGURE 6.5   UK and US book exports to Scandinavia, 2003 (£m)

*Source of figures*: UK Publishers Association 2004, Scandinavia Market Profile by Paul Hawksworth

The UK and the USA account for 90% of all book exports to Scandinavia. The majority of anglophone books going to Scandinavia are academic textbooks and professional publications destined for university libraries and students. Anglophone fiction exports are also growing, although Scandinavia's imported books only account for about 10% of the total aggregated book sales for the three countries. Per capita, Scandinavians on average spend £3.96 on books in English (compared to Germany £1.06 and the Netherlands £4.38).

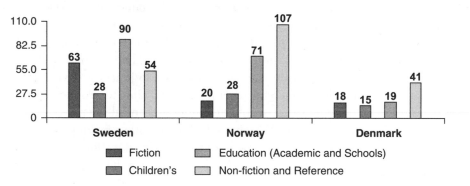

FIGURE 6.6   2003 Scandinavian print book sales (£m)

*Source of figures*: UK Publishers Association 2004, Scandinavia Market Profile

All three countries are signatories to the Berne Convention and the UCC (Universal Copyright Convention), and piracy is not an issue. In a 2002 EU Commission report on cultural habits, Swedes in particular score well on reading, topping the list of Europeans who read for pleasure at 71% (Finns 66%, the British 63%, Danes 55%, and Germans, French and Spanish at 40%): 28% of Swedes read more than 13 books a year; the EU average is 19%. In 2002 a bookseller survey found that 92% of Norwegians read at least one book a year. In a similar 2004 survey in Denmark, 30% of respondents indicated that they had read an English-language book in the previous year.

## CANADA

With a population of 34 million people, Canada supports book trades in two languages, English and French. Anglophones number 26.6 million and francophones 9.6 million (5.4m Canadians are bilingual); 59% of Canadians speak English as a first language, 23% French, with 18% speaking other languages. By sales and by revenue, the Canadian publishing industry is centred along a Toronto–Montreal axis. In 2003 the state of Ontario accounted for 47% of Canadian GDP and Québec 21%. The three largest publishing revenue-earning states/territories are Ontario (63%), Québec (28%), where 80% of the population speak French, and British Columbia (6%).

Canadian anglophone publishing has struggled to keep its identity alongside the US book industry. Of all Canadians, 85% live within 160km of the border with the United States. The USA is, by a huge margin, Canada's largest trading partner. In the 1950s and 1960s British publishing interests in Canada sold out to US companies.[25] Efforts have been made since the 1970s to promote home-grown Canadian writing and publishing. In 1972, Canada's arts funding agency, The Canada Council, started an Emerging Publisher Grants and Block Grant Program to promote and improve the position of Canadian authors. Observers point out how these funds were the cornerstone of a new generation of Canadian writers, and the basis for Canadian Studies programmes throughout the world. Canadian writers have developed a strong Canadian and international readership in recent years, for example Margaret Atwood, Alice Munro, William Gibson, and the Québec-born Nobel laureate for literature, Saul Bellow.

In 2002, Canada's total book market sales totalled C$2.1 billion, with the trade sector accounting for C$1.3 billion (62% of total books sales), with UK publishers shipping £30 million of books into Canada in 2003.[26]

Most big Canadian publishers are owned by US or US-based multinationals, with Nelson Canada, the exception, being a subsidiary of the Canadian-based ThomsonReuters Corporation. ThomsonReuters is a major international professional, legal, financial and educational house, ranked as the fourth largest publishing house in the world. Canada is also home to Torstar Corporation, proprietor of Harlequin, publisher of romance novels selling in 27 languages in over 100 countries.

Academic and professional publishing is worth nearly C$500 million annually, followed by science, technical and medical (STM) sales at C$149 million, with STM and social sciences offering the most opportunity for foreign publishing houses. The major publishers in the sector are BC Decker, Butterworth Canada (law), Canada Law Book Company, Carswell (legal, financial), CCH Canadian Ltd, Chenelière/McGraw-Hill, Elsevier Canada, Harcourt Canada, McGraw-Hill Ryerson, John Wiley & Sons Canada, Nelson Canada, and Pearson Education Canada. ELT publishing tied to distance e-learning is also on the rise.

In 2004 Education Canada calculated there were around 15,000 primary and secondary schools. Post-secondary institutions numbered 200 plus, including 75 recognised as universities. The education books market in 2002 was worth

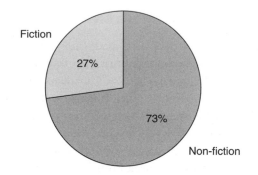

FIGURE 6.7   Total book sales in Canada in 2002

*Source of figures*: UK Publishers Association 2004, Canada Market Profile

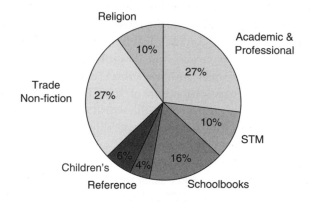

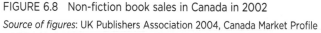

FIGURE 6.8   Non-fiction book sales in Canada in 2002

*Source of figures*: UK Publishers Association 2004, Canada Market Profile

C$243.6 million (£108.3m). Key educational publishers were, Nelson Canada, Pearson Education Canada, McGraw-Hill Ryerson, Chenelière/McGraw-Hill, Oxford University Press, Harcourt Education and John Wiley & Sons.

There are roughly double the number of anglophone publishers as francophone houses, which, given the population split, means a disproportionally large number of French-language publishers. Francophone publishers receive more public and private grants than their anglophone counterparts. Anglophone publishers make 4.5 times more revenue than francophone publishers and have an average profit margin of 10.9% compared to 8.7% achieved by francophone houses, supported by the simple fact that English is clearly the dominant language.

## SOUTH AFRICA

South Africa has a population of 50 million, of which only 1% regularly buy books. Twelve per cent of South Africans over the age of 16 buy three or more books a year.

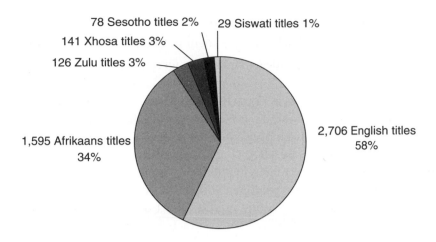

FIGURE 6.9   Publication of new titles in South Africa by language in 2003*
*Source of figures*: UK Publishers Association 2004, South Africa Market Profile – *and 10 Ndebele titles*

With the political changes of recent times, eleven official languages are now listed: isiZulu (22%), isiXhosa (17%), Afrikaans (15%), English (9%), Sepedi (9%), Setswana (8.5%), Sesotho (7%), Xitsonga (4%), isiNdebele (2%), siSwati, Tshivenda (2%). Publishing, especially in education, is in a time of expansion.

The total value of the South African book market in 2008 was £314 million: 14,678 local titles were published (5,091 new titles) with education accounting for 60% of the new titles. Overall, 52% of all sales were educational titles, trade following with 34% and academic with 6%. Of all trade books sold in 2008, 56% were imported from abroad. The average title output spread across sectors is 39% schools, 33% trade, 23% academic and professional, and 5% religious.

Foreign publishers such as Random House Struik, Pearson Southern Africa and Pan Macmillan South Africa are well established in the region. Macmillan South Africa, part of the Macmillan Boleswa Group, is a major textbook publisher. LexisNexis Butterworths (South Africa), and Kagiso Media Ltd, publish print and electronic law, tax, accounting and business titles, serving more than 350,000 sub-scribers with 800 titles. The company produces and distributes 75 million pages of legal, tax, accounting and business online documents every year.

Two main bookstore chains control most of the sales: CNA (180 stores) and Exclusive (51 stores), a specialist store with higher sales than CNA.[27] South Africa has a strong literary profile, with two Nobel prize winners in the last 20 years, J. M. Coetzee and Nadine Gordimer, as well as other writers of international renown, such as Athol Fugard, Alan Paton and André Brink.

## PUBLISHING CONTRACTS

Contracts are legally binding agreements that are enforceable at law. A contract is made between two or more parties and is founded on the following principles:

- An agreement has been reached on a specific matter.
- The parties intended to make an agreement or enter into a legal relationship.
- Both parties are legally entitled to make the agreement.

A contract can be quite simple in fact and in its operation. It can be written or made verbally, though usually it is written. It must be enforceable. Parties must be capable of making the agreement. Each party must be mentally competent and be of legal age (over 18 years of age in the UK).

The main common contract form in publishing is the author–publisher contract. Contracts written for or by a publisher will naturally reflect their interests more than an author's interests. Reflecting on this aspect of the publisher–author relationship, Coser, Kadushin and Powell saw contracts as symbolising the asymmetrical balance of power between the parties.[28]

If an author enters into a contract without full knowledge of the details and what they actually mean, it can lead to publisher–author conflict. Authors seeking publication may sometimes accept terms without a lawyer's review of terms. It is not in a publisher's interests, generally, for an author to be unhappy. A publisher needs a satisfied author. That said, many publishers (producers, agents and business managers) in the many spheres of publishing have taken advantage of creators. Wherever possible, an author should get legal advice before signing a contract, or at least read the document carefully.

The publisher and author may well share an identical vision of what is fair and just, but the most standard publishing contract allows a publisher to reject an author's work if the publisher is not happy with it. An author has no clause in a contract that states he or she can dispute the publisher's judgement on this, or reject or terminate the publishing house's hold over him or her.

Defending the publisher's side, a contract produced by a literary agent will represent an author's interests and may well not satisfy a publisher. This is why negotiations take place before any binding agreement is made, especially in the potentially lucrative trade sector. Contract scrutiny isn't as necessary in the less fractious, more 'stable' sectors, such as academic and professional publishing. That said, a contract is a contract is a contract, and signing one binds a party, making her or him liable according to its terms.

A contract engages a writer to write a book, paying him or her a large, medium-sized, small or even a token advance for licensing rights over the copyright ownership of a literary work. Publishers have the contracted right to see that the work they are paying for is in the condition they would want or expect. That is a natural function of the employer–employee relationship. But as with all things to do with creative work, publishing stands a little apart from most other work-related endeavours. An author is not strictly an employee, even if contracted to work for a publisher. The 'work' of the writer is contracted under licence and does not become the property of the publisher in perpetuity.

The creation of intellectual property is different from other work. A carpenter will build a room and when the work is done, he will be paid for the work and materials used. At that point the carpenter's relationship with that room ends. When a publisher contracts a writer and the contract terminates, the work returns to the writer, and is once more his or her intellectual property.

# CONTRACT CLAUSES

---

## SAMPLE ACADEMIC BOOK AGREEMENT BETWEEN AN AUTHOR AND PUBLISHER[29]

**Memorandum of Agreement**

Made this .... day of ........ between..........................., of........................................ (hereinafter called 'the Author' which expression shall, where the context admits, include the Author's executors, administrators and assigns or successors in business as the case may be) of the one part and...............of......................... (hereinafter called 'the Publishers', which expression shall, where the context admits, include any publishing imprint subsidiary to or associated with the Publishers, and the Publishers' executors, administrators and assigns or successors in business as the case may be) or the other part.

Whereby it is mutually agreed as follows concerning a work original to the Author and provisionally entitled .................................................................

hereinafter called 'the Work', the complete typescript of which shall not be more than ...............words in length where the non-text material (including all preliminary pages, tables, illustrations, notes, references, index, etc.) shall be deemed equivalent to words at the rate of....words per book page and pro rata for part pages and shall be delivered in duplicate to the Publishers together with illustrations and/or other material as agreed between the Author and the Publishers under the terms of this Agreement, not later than ...........................

---

## TIMETABLE OF DELIVERY

Should the author fail to deliver the work on time, the publisher will have the right not to publish it. Publishers tend to be lenient with authors on this, but in certain circumstances the author's failure to deliver on time can begin the process known in publishing houses as *slippage* – a publication slipping more than three months behind schedule – which can damage a publisher's commercial prospects. The delivery clause will also ensure that the work conforms with the terms laid out in the contract, usually stated in an appendix.

If for these or other reasons the author does not 'deliver', he or she can and sometimes will be required to refund all or part of the advance that has been paid within a set period.

Details on any return of an advance will depend on the contract, who drafted it (publisher or author's agent) and whether the author has the 'power' to set terms that suit him or her rather than the publisher. The author, though, is not at liberty to publish the work elsewhere until the publisher decides not to publish (equally, a publisher cannot 'sit' on a manuscript and do nothing with it — see *Publisher's Responsibility to Publish* below).

## COMPETING WORK

The publisher needs to be sure that there is no competing work, or that the author has not completed or is writing or has plans to write any other work that could prejudice sales for the contracted work. This can include abridgments. The extent of this clause must not be so wide as to prevent the writer using his knowledge and skills to reasonably earn a living.

## WARRANTIES AND INDEMNITIES

In this contractual clause the publisher seeks legal assurances that the work:

- is all the labour of the author and not the work of someone else
- does not infringe existing copyright
- has not been previously published
- contains no libellous or defamatory material
- contains statements in the text that are true
- contains no advice in the text that will be harmful to the reader.
- If damages are sought by any party because of the text, they are the author's responsibility.

    Here is an example of this last clause:

    The Author will indemnify and keep the Publisher indemnified against all actions, suits, proceedings, claims, demands, damages and costs (including any legal cost and disbursements paid by the Publishers on the advice of their legal advisers to compromise or settle any claim) occasioned to the Publishers in consequence of any breach of this warranty or arising out of any claim alleging that the work constitutes an infringement of copyright or contains libellous or defamatory matter.

## A PUBLISHER'S RESPONSIBILITY TO PUBLISH

Publishers agree to publish unless prevented by circumstances beyond their control. This is important to the author. As with authors who sometimes delay delivery of a work, publishers may have good reasons for delaying publication. Timing or releasing a work into a market is an important consideration for a publisher. Lawyers though will advise authors against a loose or general description of a publisher's right to decide the time of publication. Any publication delay should not be allowed to go much beyond half a year. After an extended delay an author should be allowed to reclaim copyright.

## PERMISSIONS

Permissions concern quotations or use of another's copyrighted material, illustrations, photos, graphics and diagrams, in a text. The use of any substantial amount of copyrighted text without permission is an automatic infringement. It is important to check the status of any material. The rule of thumb is: *if in doubt check with the source.*

Permissions are usually the author's responsibility to pursue, settle and pay for, if necessary. Under the Warranties and Indemnities clause publishers are usually protected from any legal action arising from an author's unauthorised use of copyrighted material, or problems that may arise from the author's failure to obtain proper written permission for use of copyrighted material.

For large, multi-author reference publications the process of obtaining permissions can be a major task. Some permissions may only be for one edition only. Care must be taken to check if they need to be renewed. Publishers advise early settlement of permissions for the use of copyrighted material as it can hold up publication. Ideally, the wording of a permission should be as strong as the author's own grant of rights to a publisher contained in the contract. Limited rights to use materials, in some territories but not others, presents a major problem and may lead to the exclusion of the 'permitted material' altogether from the text.

There are many misconceptions held by some authors about how permissions work. The absence of a copyright symbol or statement does not mean seeking permission is not necessary. Crediting the source is no defence against infringement. Fair use provisions and traditions may also not be enough to defend use without permission. The courts will consider the use, the particular section reproduced, the amount and commercial impact of the so-called fair use. Works that are in the public domain are not automatically permitted, as the use of trademarks and illustrations are not necessarily free from copyright, even if the text is. Other factors must be weighed in any use of material: out of print does not equate to out of copyright; the fact the copy is not attributed to anyone does not mean it is not protected.

One of the key factors is not the use of the material, but how the use might affect the commercial value of the original. Permissions are a thorn in the sides of authors and publishers. Marc Aronson wrote in *The New York Times* that 'permission costs are ... out of control ..., we have to fix a system that is broken'.[30] The permissions 'pay-up for everything' culture by big wealthy companies for even the smallest most trivial re-use is forcing authors to short-change readers by leaving material out of their books.

Small firms usually are far more generous than the large companies, perhaps for the reason that citing their company is good publicity. But in truth, the culture of small publishing is quite different from corporate publishing, and the way permissions are handled is an example of just how different small is from big.[31]

## PRODUCTION AND PROMOTION RESPONSIBILITY

Control over the publication is at the sole discretion of the publisher, as it concerns publication and includes choice of paper, printing, design, binding and jacket or cover, though some publishers are willing to involve the author in this. Promotion and advertising, what it consists of, where and how it takes place, the number and distribution of free copies for press purposes are all decisions the publisher generally makes. Authors are usually required to make themselves available for promotional works, signings, tours and interviews.

## CORRECTIONS AND PROOFING

All corrections that will be required from the author will be stated in most agreements, deliverable within a reasonable (usually a fortnight or three-week) period.

> The Author undertakes to read, check, and correct the proof and to return them to the publishers within twenty days of their receipt, failing which the Publishers may consider the proofs passed for press.

At proof stage, the cost of any alterations made by the author to the finished text and artwork beyond 10% of content will be borne by the author – charged per line. The sum is usually deducted from advances or royalties.

## GENERAL PROVISOS

Clauses in the contract will lay out terms of how free copies are dealt with and how copyright will be returned to the author, if after a certain period elapses, the book goes out of print and the publisher decides he or she cannot make further sales.

All contracts contain what are known to lawyers as 'boilerplate', setting out in what often seems to be arcane legal language over-used phrases stating terms and conditions, but inside many of these clauses are substantial details.

No royalties are paid on copies of the work given away to the author, for review copies, or on copies lost, stolen, damaged or destroyed in transit or otherwise. Any money received by the publishers for specimen or inspection copies (sent to teachers, etc.) or for publicity are regarded as expenses and are not accounted for as sales.

If after a period of say three years (for an academic title) after first publication, the work isn't selling, the publisher is usually allowed by contract to dispose of remaining copies via remainder shops or in an offer to the author to buy the stock left at 'best price' (including transport costs).

The author usually has a couple of weeks to reply to the offer and if he or she fails to do so, then the publisher can go ahead and dispose of the stock any way he or she sees fit. Author royalties on remaindered copies is usually pegged at about 10% of net receipts, which to all intents and purposes will be equivalent to nothing.

## ADVANCES, ROYALTIES AND FEES PAYABLE

The section on Advances, Royalties and Fees is the central substance of any contract – what an agent will often call the '*gimme clauses*'. Advances are paid on royalty receipt projections. A publisher in most cases will calculate a low estimate of sales and extrapolate an advance from that. For major authors, the terms of the advance will be negotiated between the author's literary agent and the publisher.

Difficulties for the first-time author may arise with phrases such as '10% of net receipts'. An author should seek the meaning of net receipts from the publisher. It may only mean sales receipts after discounts to the RRP have been subtracted.

A clause on advances will lay out the total amount payable and how the amount will be split up into a timetable of payments. Usually a commissioned author will receive a third of the money on signing the contract, a third on delivery of the manuscript (in the required form), and the remaining third upon publication. If the manuscript is not delivered, or finished, by the due date, the publisher reserves the right not to publish the work and to request the return of the portion of the advance already paid. The agreement is usually terminated at this point but the publisher often retains 'first refusal rights' when the manuscript is completed. The publisher usually reports on sales twice annually in a *royalty statement* to the author, with the author or her/his representative having the right to examine the *publisher's accounts*, though at the author's expense, unless errors are found of, say, more than £10, whereby the publisher will pay the costs.

# SUBSIDIARY RIGHTS IN CONTRACTS

After primary rights are a bundle of subsidiary or ancillary rights, the description of which varies from publishing sector to sector. In trade/consumer books, subsidiary rights are potentially an area for substantial revenues for a publisher and author, and are a growing area of activity. In academic and educational markets the chances for rights sales are far fewer.

Film and TV and serial rights can be very big business, or at least an ongoing area for the author via option agreements. An option lasts 12–18 months in general in return for a fee (anything from $1,000 to $50,000 depending on the work or author). It allows the option-holder to be the first to make a full deal within the stipulated time. In most trade book contracts, film and TV rights are retained by authors or their agents and eliminated from consumer/trade book publishing deals.

| **Subsidiary rights** | **Payment due to author** |
|---|---|
| **Quotation and extract rights** | 10% |
| **Anthology rights** | 10% |

Known generally as permissions to people in publishing, these rights cover the reproduction of text quotations or illustrations taken from existing publications. If a source is used or referred to consistently throughout the published book, a small royalty is a possible solution as a fee for every use.

**Digest journal/magazine rights      10%**

The right to publish an abridgement of 'the work' in a journal, periodical or newspaper.

**Digest book condensation rights      10%**

The right to publish a shortened form of 'the work' in volume form. It covers summarised works or work included in compendia. Reader's Digest was a major user of this kind of format, although the company is not the force in book publishing it once was.

| **Mechanical reproduction rights** | 10% |
|---|---|
| **Electronic rights** | 10% |

The right to produce or reproduce a work or to license its reproduction (or any part of it) by film micrography, reprographic reproduction, electronic reproduction, gramophone records, tape cassettes, film strips, or by means whether by sight or sound or a combination of both, whether now in existence or hereafter invented for the purposes of mechanical reproduction except in so far as reproduction is for use as part of or in conjunction with a commercial film.

*Electronic rights* involve the sale or transmission of a work or any adaptation of it in electronic form, whether by itself or together with or in combination with other materials including, but without limitation to, digital means to data storage, transmission and retrieval devices and systems of any kind, whether now in existence or hereafter invented.

| **Sound broadcasting rights** | 75% |
|---|---|
| **Television reading rights** | 75% |

This covers single-voice readings from the text or the showing of illustrations from the work. Single-voice reading rights deal with straight reading on radio or television, and can affect podcast downloads.

## Mechandising rights          50 %

These rights cover designs, characters, trademarks and story aspects that are transported into another medium. Beatrix Potter's *Peter Rabbit* is a registered trademark, renewed every ten years. In recent times the film franchise *Star Wars* has been a huge merchandising success for the director and producer, George Lucas, who was fortuitously allowed to keep them by Twentieth Century Fox before the release of the first *Star Wars* film. Children's books characters generate huge merchandising revenues. The Walt Disney Company is active in ensuring its storehouse of characters are not infringed upon – *Winnie the Pooh* alone now reputedly generates several billion dollars annually for Disney in licensing fees. As with film and TV rights, publishers usually have no control over merchandising rights. Most agents will retain them on behalf of their clients.

### Non-commercial rights for the disabled free of charge

Rights for the visually impaired are books in Braille or Moon (a tactile system of reading for visually impaired people), voice-activated systems or specialised, large-text versions.

**Audiobook rights** – Books that are recorded, read by an actor and sold as full or abridged versions of books. These rights are a relatively small (8% of overall book sales) but a good addition to the bottom line and an offshoot segment of book publishing.

**Reprint rights** – These rights may cover the acquisition of hardback rights to cater for *large-print versions* for the partially sighted, special orders such as specialised library markets, promotional editions and educational rights.

**Picturisation or cartoon rights** – Strip cartoon, drawings, photos with story told in speech captions.

**Infringement of copyright** – There will be a clause on what action to take if this occurs, stating that if the author 'refuses or neglects' to take proceedings on the infringement, the publisher is entitled to do so in the name of the author and publisher, giving the author 'sufficient and reasonable' indemnity against any liability of costs.

A clause will require that the publisher gives due *prominence to the author's name* and another states the number of *complimentary copies* to be offered to the author. The author will be required to provide or pay for an *index* (if applicable) for each new edition. There will be a clause on how matters will be dealt with upon *the death of an author*. A clause will detail how rights will revert to the author upon *non-compliance by publishers* to the terms of the agreement, or if the *publisher goes into liquidation*. Any and all legal disputes will be settled within a *stated jurisdiction*, governed by the laws of the particular state where the agreement was made. There is usually a *force majeure* clause covering circumstances beyond a publisher's control, such as war or disaster, which may prevent the fulfilment of the terms of a contract, and a clause on the *moral rights of an author*, and how and where these will be stated in the front matter to the text:

> The Author hereby asserts his/her right to be identified as the Author of the Work and the Publishers undertake: to print on every edition of the Work published by them the words: '[The Author] has asserted his/her right under the Copyright, Designs and Patents Act, 1988, to be identified as Author of this Work'; to use all reasonable endeavours to include in any contract for volume rights with any licensee concerning any edition of the Work to be published in the United Kingdom an undertaking that a notice of assertion in the same terms shall be printed in every edition published or further licensed by such licensee.
>
> SIGNED
> For the Publishers:  _ _ _ _ _ _ _ _ _ _ _ _ _ _ _ _ _
>
> The Author:  _ _ _ _ _ _ _ _ _ _ _ _ _ _ _ _ _
>
> Date

## OTHER RIGHTS

**Publisher's right** – This covers the publisher's text layout and general book design. If a licensee wants to produce a book using the original publisher's design and layout, then a separate fee may be charged.

**Public lending right (UK)** – Set up in 1979 after authors lobbied heavily for it, this right covers authors in the lending or loaning of their works by public libraries. The authors must register for it. Every time a book is borrowed from a UK library the author receives 5.26p per loan, up to a total of £6,600 for an author in any year. The payments come out of the UK government's Central Fund. In recent years payments have run to over £7 million. Ironically, though understandably, bestselling authors are the writers who receive most from the scheme.

## FURTHER READING

Clark, C. and Owen, L., Ed., *Clark's Publishing Agreements: A Book of Precedents*, London, Butterworths, 2002

Coser, L. A., Kadushin, C. and Powell, W. W., *Books: The Culture and Commerce of Publishing*, New York, Basic Books, 1982

Greco, A. N., *The Book Publishing Industry*, Mahwah, NJ, Lawrence Erlbaum Associates, 2005

Greco, A. N., Rodríguez, C. E. and Wharton, R. M., *The Culture and Commerce of Publishing in the 21st Century*, Stanford, CA, Stanford Business Books, 2007

Jones, H., *Publishing Law*, London, Routledge, 2006
Owen, L., *Selling Rights*, London, Routledge, 2006

## NOTES

1  Larsen, M., *How To Write a Book Proposal,* 3rd ed., Cincinnati OH, Writer's Digest Books, 2003, pp. 54–56.
2  Woll, Thomas, *Publishing for Profit*, London, Kogan Page, 1999, p. 215.
3  Rights survey carried out by the UK Publishers Association.
4  The loss leader is the sales of a product at an attractive price attracting custom, but whose costs are higher than the retail price.
5  Lynette Owen, *Selling Rights*, London, Routledge, 2005, p. 125.
6  Owen, op. cit.
7  Moto Rich, 'Europa Editions Finds Success Translating Literary Novels', *New York Times*, February 25, 2009.
8  Ibid.
9  Boris Kachka, 'The End', *New York Magazine*, 14 September 2008.
10  Alison Flood, 'Too Spiky for British Readers?', *The Guardian*, 11 September 2008.
11  Ibid.
12  Cited in Flood, op. cit.
13  Williams, Sam, 'Hillary, Harry and Serial Rights' (15 November 2003), cited in R. Lorimer, J. Maxwell, and J. G. Shoichet (eds), *Publishing Studies: Book Publishing 1,* Vancouver, CCSP Press, p. 52.
14  Owen, op. cit., p. 101.
15  Carolyn Savarese, 'English Language Rights in the Global Market: An American Perspective', *Pub Res Q* 23: 122–128.
16  Lenore Taylor, 'Labor Baulks at Book Reform', *The Australian*, 12 November 2009.
17  Tim Coronel, 'Australia', *Publisher Research Quarterly*, 24 (3), September 2008.
18  Colin Hayes, 'Australia: Publishing Market Profile', UK Publishers' Association, London, 2005.
19  Taylor, op. cit.
20  Hayes, op. cit.
21  Henry Rosenbloom, 'Territorial Rights and Wrongs', *Pub Res Q*, 24, 2008, pp. 175–177.
22  Ibid.
23  Ibid.
24  Greco, A. N., Rodríguez, C. E. and Wharton, R. M., *The Culture and Commerce of Publishing in the 21st Century*, Stanford, CA, Stanford Business Books, 2007, p. 54.
25  Jeff Boggs, 'An Overview of Canada's Contemporary Book Trade in Light of (Nearly) Four Decades of Policy Interventions', *Pub Res Q*, 26, 2010, pp. 24–25.
26  In 2003 £1 = C$2.29 or C$1 was 0.443 GBP.
27  From the UK Publishers Association Market Report on South Africa, 2010.
28  L. A. Coser, C. Kadushin and W. W. Powell, *Books: The Culture and Commerce of Publishing*, New York, Basic Books, 1982, pp. 229–230.
29  This example of an academic book contract is reproduced with the kind permission of Sage Publications UK.

30  Marc Aronson, 'Permissions – The End of History (Books)', *New York Times*, 2 April 2010, http://www.nytimes.com/2010/04/03/opinion/03aronson.html

31  All the small companies that I approached generously allowed me to use their covers inside this text gratis. By contrast, the one large publishing corporation that I approached wanted me to pay for the use of a cover image on a book that was published 75 years ago.

# 7  MARKETING, PROMOTION AND BOOKSELLING

The answer to the question *How to sell books?* will decide whether the vast majority of publishers survive or not. The age-old, tested and standard form of book marketing is still the most widely used – providing information on the text in a timely way to wholesalers, distributors, big chain sales outlets, buyers and readers.

Whether the set up is business to business or business to consumer, the process begins many months prior to publication. Good commentary, reviews from respected sources, and positive word-of-mouth from readers have always been the best methods for promoting a book. Critical commentary and negative word-of-mouth can also work in a book's favour – *anything* almost to get books into the public eye and discussed.

A publisher often strives to create an aura around a title, seeking to capture the attention and imagination of readers – many books are voyages, holidays for the mind. If a book is able to 'stand out', it follows naturally it will have a better chance of selling in its specific market. But saying this, with a book published every four minutes (in the two major anglophone markets), is like saying it's a good thing the sun rises every day. Nielsen recorded 604,768 English-language publications in 2009 throughout the anglophone world.[1] With a total like that, the competition is not just fierce, it's absurd. A lot of the aptitude for selling books or related products is common sense attached to a certain marketing vision and some courage. When Stanley Bond decided to invest Butterworth's time and capital in publications on English law early in the twentieth century, he went about the task with a single-minded zeal that paid off very well in the coming years. Bond saw a market opportunity and went after it.[2] With many sectors, categories and sub-categories, each subject area of publishing occupies its own field, has its own experts, followers, readers and associated spheres of interest. A huge number of books is quickly divided by areas, categories and specialised reader groups. Some very select journal publications are so knowledge-specific that only a handful of people in the world can actually comprehend them.

Many books are practical necessities, so in a sense they sell themselves, for instance, books with information for a career or studies. No magic stimulation of the psychic centres of consciousness is necessary for every book to find sales. The right book, with the right information, should be there in the market at the right time. School and academic years start in September/October. Teachers and lecturers need new texts well in advance of new academic years to be able to decide whether they fulfil their teaching needs.

Books and authors develop market auras or auras develop around them for odd reasons. Some books need a long time arc to sell themselves, but then generate a 'title brand' or 'author brand' that lasts for generations or, as in Shakespeare's case, centuries. Developed 'brands' have marketing power, although nothing beats a friend, a peer, a respected source saying: 'You *must* read this book.'

# THE MARKETING JIGSAW

The cover of a book is not the only, or even the main, jigsaw piece in a marketing puzzle, but it is the first thing a browsing buyer will see. With serendipity playing a huge part in many book purchases, first impressions, especially in trade, count a great deal — though far more in fiction and trade non-fiction than any other categories. *Cover art, the title, the name of the author, the publisher brand, testimonials, shoutlines* and *price* all help readers decide. In those crucial first seconds, any of these elements can speak to a buyer in that special way, turning her or him from browser to buyer: '... so much of a book's fate [is] dependent on everything but what is between its covers'.[3]

Seeing a book for the first time, if intrigued by the cover art, a reader will probably turn to a blurb on the back, then go to page one with fiction, or the contents page with non-fiction. In those seconds a sale can be made. But for it to happen quickly, it seems logical that elements of design and content must work in concert to convince the browser. Which single factor it is, though, that moves a reader to buy a book is still largely a mystery. It would probably help buyers in any decision to buy a collection of stories by Lucia Berlin (see opposite), to know that the book and author won a Before Columbus Foundation/American Book Award in 1991. A shoutline telling us this positive news should influence readers, but in truth no one knows enough to say for sure that it would make the sale.

## UNIQUE SELLING POINTS (USP)

Books sell by sector and categories, and buyers are 'trained' by promotion, experience and developed tastes to respond to what they can recognise. Consumers overall seem to favour things they readily understand, so anything that is unique requires careful thought and strategies. Being unique, of course, can represent a shift of a few small degrees from the norm.

When Allen Lane started selling the first Penguins, the paperback was not new. Hundreds of years of cheap paper books had preceded the 1935 Penguin Books

Black Sparrow Press cover, with the kind permission of John Martin & David R. Godine Publishers, Boston

experiment and venture. What was unique was Lane's market timing. In 1935 a repackaged idea (though to many it looked entirely new), tagged with the right price, sailed into bookshops at just the right time for household economies still blighted by The Great Depression. Perfect binding technology enabled Lane to create a portable, 'short-life' paperback to strike just the right chord with British book buyers at just the right price, at just the right moment. Or you could say, that is all bunk, and the high street discount store, Woolworth, with its mid-1930s sales call of 'nothing more than 6d', was the true unique selling point (USP) in Penguin's rise. Without Woolworth's prices, a penguin might still only be a flightless bird.

Whatever the USP turns out to be, a good selling product will usually have one. When Apple created its range of personal computers in the late 1980s, its graphic user interface caught on right away. When John Grisham was tagged as the creator of the 'legal thriller', bookstore shelves were emptied of his books. Google's advertising-based free-to-user service model, revolutionised the online search scenario.

# SALES TIMELINE AND TECHNIQUES

When a publishing house decides to publish a title, a timeline towards publication is set up. It is of crucial importance that this process, once begun, is not held up. First, the author should deliver the required text to the house as agreed in order that other aspects of production and promotion are also carried out on time.

Around four months or so before publication, staff are often hard at work preparing copy for titles with Advance Information Sheets (AIS). An AIS is sent out to inform sales reps, wholesalers, overseas contacts and agents that the title is on its way. The more information the better; the better-informed the market is, the more chance there will be that word-of-mouth will develop and travel. This is often crucial for a title's market chances. What the bookselling and buying market does not know it may not trust. What it doesn't understand it won't support. Well-written, well-structured and well-timed releases of information are vital aspects of marketing.

Each company will have its own style in making up an AIS, adding images and copy as it sees necessary, but an AIS sheet has standard requirements, including the contact details of the editor, the language of the title, binding details, and the intended readership (Figure 7.1).

*Company name details & logo*

**Advance Information Sheet**

---

**Title and subtitle**

**Author**

**ISBN**                                    **Extent**
                                            **Format**

**Publication date**                        **Illustrations (colour/b-w)**

**Price**

**Category**

---

**Description**

---

**Selling points**

---

**Marketing and PR programmes**

FIGURE 7.1  Example of an Advance Information Sheet (AIS)

We don't want to tell you too much about this book. It is a truly special story and we don't want to spoil it.

Nevertheless, you need to know enough to buy it so we will just say this:

**This is the story of two women.**

**Their lives collide one fateful day, and one of them has to make a terrible choice.**

**Two years later, they meet again – the story starts there ...**

Once you have read it, you'll want to tell your friends about it. When you do, please don't tell them what happens either. The magic is in how it unfolds.

FIGURE 7.2   Example of a striking blurb from Chris Cleave's *The Other Hand* (Sceptre, 2009)

## THE BLURB

The blurb was invented in the USA at the beginning of the twentieth century. It now appears in many forms – on an AIS, on the back of a book or in spring and autumn catalogues listing coming titles. However, the most important role of the blurb is in the brief back-cover description of a book's content.

There are two main inherent 'industrial problems' with blurbs: its status is low as editorial assistants generally write them; and copy can quickly become stale – *AIS copy* becomes *catalogue copy* becomes *cover copy*.

Blurbs are written to turn a potential buyer into a book purchaser. They are also publishing's unheralded 'art form'. We will always know who a novelist is, but the blurb writer remains anonymous. Any writer would agree that the hardest thing to do is to be effective in a few words. Blurbs have to get their message across to book buyers in only a few lines of prose. The example in Figure 7.2 is what I would call a *meta-blurb*, referencing the process of writing a blurb in the blurb, an aspect that Sceptre's Marketing Director, James Spackman, admits he didn't like initially: 'I had a right old cringe at the notion of "we", The Publisher, addressing the reader. 300,000 sales later ... I might have revised my stance a tad.'[4]

Cover copy and how it is placed is a design choice. For *The Other Hand*, it is spaced out over a picture of a sunrise/sunset scene of the ocean, using the surf-line to divide back-cover blurb copy from review *testimonials*. On the front, it is in reverse position, divided from the title/author (Figure 7.3).

Whatever the copy writer's intention, a blurb should not dissuade a 'decided' reader. Whether copy succeeds in making up (or changing a mind) is a complex emotional and intellectual question that happens usually in a matter of seconds. It might involve a reader's attitudes, beliefs, tastes, and stand quite apart from any book needs and wants at the time.

We don't want to tell you what happens in
this book. It is a truly special story and we
don't want to spoil it.

Nevertheless, you need to know enough to
buy it so we will just say this:

This is the story of two women.

Their lives collide one fateful day, and one of
them has to make a terrible choice.

Two years later, they meet again
– the story starts there...

Once you have read it, you'll want to tell your
friends about it. When you do, please don't
tell them what happens either. The magic is
in how it unfolds.

the other hand

chris cleave

Shortlisted for the 2008 **COSTA** Novel Award

'A powerful piece of art...
shocking, exciting and deeply affecting'
*Independent*

'Searingly eloquent'
*Daily Mail*

'Ambitious and fearless'
*Guardian*

'Totally believable'
*Daily Express*

'It would be hard not to romp through it'
*Financial Times*

'Impresses as a feat of literary engineering...
the plot exerts a fearsome grip'
*Daily Telegraph*

the other hand
chris cleave
Author of *Incendiary*

ISBN 978-0-340-06342-5

Fiction      £6.99

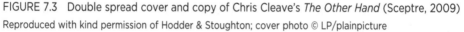

FIGURE 7.3   Double spread cover and copy of Chris Cleave's *The Other Hand* (Sceptre, 2009)
Reproduced with kind permission of Hodder & Stoughton; cover photo © LP/plainpicture

We don't, as an industry, spend that much on research, and what we do
spend probably isn't too closely focused on the role of copy. It happens, but
it's not exactly common. So we don't know enough about what works.[5]

Publishers don't engage sophisticated marketing theories or commission major
research. Most marketing ideas are rooted in everyday practices that have grown up
in the trade over centuries. It might just be time for publishers 'to read the business
books they publish'.[6]

## BUSINESS TO CONSUMER (B2C)

So much of established book marketing, promotion and sales techniques have been
based on what is known these days as B2B – business to business operations. The
publisher informs the distributor and wholesaler, who informs the sales reps, who
travel the country informing bookstore sales outlets of new book products. After
orders are placed, the publisher sends books to distributors, who sends them to
bookshops. Publishers inform periodical media, which spread the word via
reviewers to readers.

With Amazon's huge success in business-to-consumer (B2C) selling, old practices are beginning to change, or at least major changes are being considered. However, to be successful at B2C, publishers now need to know more than they currently do about consumer likes, tastes and needs directly. They need to know as much about reader and book buyer preferences as Amazon, Google and Facebook now know about their worldwide service users and members. The 'intelligence' role was once carried out by the local independent bookshop, informing sales reps who informed publishers. Bookstores still advise and still know clients and are still selling books, but the statistical decline in bricks and mortar stores points to more changes to bookselling in the future. 'We have to change from being a b2b company to b2c over the coming years,' says Random House's CEO, Markus Dohle.[7] Publishers must now learn how to compete successfully or collaborate seamlessly with online retailers such as Amazon.[8]

Direct selling is not new, of course. Publishers have used it for special sales. Book clubs use it to both service and recruit clients. However, direct mail is not the power it once was. It now competes with online direct selling. Anecdotal evidence also tells us that many householders resent the unsolicited 'junk mail' they receive – witness the stickers on many front doors 'No Junk Mail' and the same goes for unsolicited junk email. One writer said that research contradicts this 'popular notion', pointing to research in the late 1990s on junk mail – 77% opened it, 59% read the contents.[9] There are problems with client-dependent market research companies carrying out surveys for firms who want to hear good news. In the early days of the e-book at the turn of this century, misleading research was not just occasional, it was rife (see the section on *E-books* in Chapter 8, p. 210). If publishers are serious about selling direct, rather than using the usual B2B methods, they will need to accumulate their own data, or obtain intelligence on buyers and their preferences from sources that can produce impartial research.

## PRIZES AND SALES

The UK's most prominent literary award for fiction is the Man Booker Prize. Sponsored by the Man Group since 2002, the Booker is now worth £50,000 in prize money to the winning author and millions of pounds in increased sales to the publisher.

After the UK's Net Book Agreement was abolished in 1997, Booker sales boomed. Apart from earlier isolated huge successes in the 1980s – *Midnight's Children*, *Schindler's Ark* (1982), and *The Remains of the Day* – post-1997 Booker winners now regularly earn over £1 million. Sales for the 2002 winner, *Life of Pi*, went well over £9 million.

Each Man Booker Prize year is judged by an entirely new panel, led by a new chairperson. Together the judges tackle an entirely new array of fiction in their own way, according to their interests and tastes. The Booker judging panel in 2010 was chaired by Sir Andrew Motion, former Poet Laureate. In 2009, BBC broadcaster, James Naughtie, took on the role. In 2008, the chair was former Conservative party cabinet minister, Michael Portillo. Each year the choice of book and author is quite different in style and content to another year. In his speech on the 2009 award night, James Naughtie said 'the prize was about one thing, quality'.[10] Naughtie made a point of dismissing any other influence or purpose (economic, or even political) in Booker Prize choices.

The Booker has three main phases: nomination for the long list; nomination for the short list; and the announcement of the winner. Sales for books nominated for the long and short lists can often be quite modest, whereas winning the prize usually has a dramatic effect on the selected book's market fortunes.

Overall, the six shortlisted books in 2010 sold 8,228 copies in the week after the announcement of their inclusion in the shortlist. Emma Donoghue's 'Josef Fritzl inspired' *Room* sold 3,451, Howard Jacobson's novel *The Finkler Question*, 1,382 copies. Peter Carey's *Parrot and Olivier* went from 95 copies sold the week before to 1,088 copies sold the week after the shortlist was released (an increase in sales of more than 1,045%). Tom McCarthy's *C* sales grew 523% to 845 copies. Damon Galgut's *In a Strange Room* sold 760 copies and *The Long Song* by Andrea Levy sold 702 copies in the week after they were included in the shortlist.[11] The week after *The Finkler Question* won the prize on 12 October the book's sales shot up from 3,505 copies to 12,649 copies, the largest percentage margin week-after sales increase ever recorded – 1,920%.[12] By June 2011, Jacobson's novel had recorded sales of around 400,000 (hardcover, paperback and 30,000 e-book downloads).

Part of understanding the commercial effect of literary prizes is knowing how figures are collected, how accurate they are – what territories, areas and formats they cover – before any true comparison can be made book to book, year to year, prize to prize.

Winning any literary prize – the Man Booker, Pulitzer, National Book Award, or the most prestigious and global of all, the Nobel Prize for Literature – is life-changing for authors and publishers. After Richard Russo's *Empire Falls* won the Pulitzer Prize in 2002, US sales rose 6,500% to 99,000 copies. In 2003, the Pulitzer Prize winner for fiction, Jeffrey Eugenides, for his novel *Middlesex* about an adolescent Greek-American hermaphrodite, saw a 200% jump in sales. In the same year, the 2003 Booker winner, DBC Pierre, for his debut novel about another 'troubled' adolescent, *Vernon God Little*, registered a 677% boost in US sales (the book had only sold 1,000 US copies before winning the prize).[13] The success with the *Life of Pi* in the 2002 Booker was a huge event for the Edinburgh-based independent publisher, Jamie Byng, who said at the time: 'This to me is absolute validation of what we are thinking we can do at Canongate.'[14]

However, big prizes don't always produce huge sales. In the year following Herta Müller's 2009 Nobel Prize for Literature, her translated novel, *The Appointment*, sold 20,000 paperbacks in the USA.[15] Considering the brand image of the Nobel prize, this is a modest result, though prior to winning Müller was unknown to many, and her novels, originally in German, detailed bleak conditions for an immigrant in Romania under the Ceauşescu regime.

The business challenge for literary publishers is to replicate the author-brand sales successes that commercial fiction publishers have long achieved (J. K. Rowling, Dan Brown, John Grisham, Stephen King and Stephenie Meyer). In 2009, after only five days on sale in the UK, 550,946 copies were sold of Dan Brown's *The Lost Symbol*, bringing in nearly £4.6 million in revenue. Prizes are *the brand* for some books, even if literary fiction sales will always fade against retail results for commercial fiction.

## BOOKSELLING PRACTICE

When Tom Clancy first came out, the reason he sold a ton was because President Reagan had a friend who worked at the US Naval College at Annapolis who knew Clancy personally and had a manuscript. He passed it along and at one point President Reagan held it up at a press conference and said this is the greatest book, all you people have to read it. ... If that had not happened, we might never have heard of Tom Clancy. Nobody knows who the markets are. (Paul Hilts, publishing consultant)[16]

The most important marketing message for any book is the aura it can develop around it. There is no evidence to show that booksellers understand how to create that aura 'on demand', even if corporate selling techniques have lifted sales over the last half century. The last widespread boom period for book publishing in the USA was 1982–1989, when per annum sales for hardcovers grew 12.4% and paperbacks 6.4%.[17] In 1989 Simon & Schuster announced a 15% reduction in title output and Macmillan began a three-year cutback, trimming its list by 25%.[18] Thereafter, print book sales increases continued to grow year on year but increases progressively diminished, up and until the twenty-first century when growth almost flatlined.

The corporate reformation of publishing from the mid-twentieth century onwards brought with it aggressive promotion, marketing and sell-through techniques,

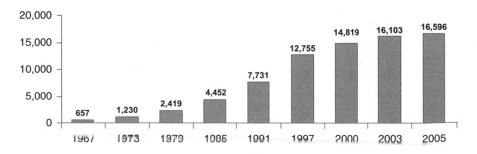

FIGURE 7.4   Book sales in US bookstores, 1967–2005 (in $m)

described by one observer as the 'barbarians with M.B.A.s' taking over.[19] Executives, recruited from other industries, newspapers and technology companies, now run publishing, marketing and bookselling operations. Ted Solotaroff coined a name for this process – 'The Literary-Industrial Complex'.[20] The biggest casualty in this process has been backlist books, as more commercially-minded publishers and bookshops sought to reduce inventory in search of the quick, sure sale.

In 2006 there were 22,321 shops or similar venues selling books in the USA, a number that fell from 25,137 shops in 2002 and 28,510 shops and outlets in 1995. In 2005, the three leading US bookstore chains were Barnes & Noble, Borders and Books a Million (Table 7.1).

TABLE 7.1  Three leading bookstores in the USA, 2005

| Bookseller | Number of stores | Earnings |
| --- | --- | --- |
| Barnes & Noble | 820 (673 superstores, no international stores) | $4.45 billion |
| Borders | 1,167 (464 superstores, 80 international stores) | $3.88 billion |
| Books a Million | 207 | $475 million |

Over the last 40 years, the expansion of book chains, the appearance of super bookstores, the entrance of discount bookselling in supermarkets and the advent of internet bookselling has reconfigured the way books are sold – but has not grown the practice of reading.

In the UK in the early 1970s independent stores were dominant in the market, accounting for nearly 60% of sales. By 2002 the independent bookstore market share had fallen to 15% (Table 7.2). More and more commercial books seem to suit the supermarket model these days. Most commercial books are perishables, meaning not that they will decay like foodstuffs, but that they have a limited amount of time in the market to make a mark. The average trade hardback or softcover is given six to twelve months to sell, and if it fails to reach certain sales either it will not be reprinted, it will be remaindered, or it will be withdrawn from the market and copies pulped.

TABLE 7.2  UK bookselling by market share

| Year | Independents (%) | Chains (%) | Non-traditional methods (%) |
| --- | --- | --- | --- |
| 1972 | 58 | 11 | 31 |
| 1983 | 44 | 18 | 38 |
| 1994 | 19 | 27 | 54 |
| 2002 | 15 | 23 | 55* |

*Book clubs 20%; internet 8%; wholesale price clubs 7%; mass merchandisers 6%; mail order 6%; food and drugstores 3%; discount stores 3%; used bookstores 2%.

Yet, for all the decline in business, the tradition of independent book stores goes on, just as famous independent names such as the Harvard Book Store in Boston, the

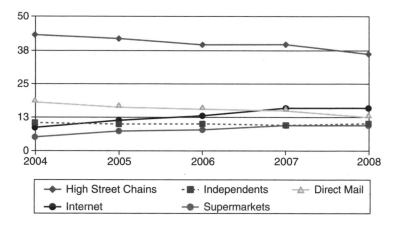

FIGURE 7.5 Percentage share of bookselling market in the UK, 2004-2008 (by value)

Tattered Cover Book Store in Denver, and The Strand Book Store in lower Manhattan, all continue to exist.

Independent booksellers in all locations and of all kinds have been the coal face for bookselling down through the centuries, and they are still the point where many readers go to be inspired and personally catered for. So even though independents throughout the *anglosphere* of books face the threat from big booksellers, and niche bookstores they still exist, catering for local or unusual areas and differing tastes.

The main UK book retail outlets are still the traditionally-styled bricks and mortar bookshops, though internet bookselling and supermarkets are gaining market share year on year. The main high street book chains (Waterstones, Ottakers, WH Smith, etc.) lost 7.2% market share by value from 2004 to 2008. Over the same period, supermarkets grew their books sales revenue share by 4.3% (+ 5.7% by volume) and internet booksellers grew their share by 7.2% by value (6.8% by volume). UK independent bookshops lost relatively little ground over the same period – 0.3% by value and 1.1% by volume. The big loser was direct mail, dropping 5.6% by value and 4.9% by volume. As a direct result of mail order woes, early in 2010, Reader's Digest, the UK's biggest mail order bookseller, went into administration (Figure 7.5).

## HOW AND WHY BOOKS SELL

Good reviews, industry and reader word-of-mouth, the status and publishing history of the author, the image or brand of the publisher and book awards combine to create a positive marketing image and sales results. Pre-publication marketing and promotion efforts begin months before publication day, informing the marketplace of the coming book and aiming to convince booksellers and book reps of the title's qualities. Factors that will help this include:

- confidence in the book and the author within the house
- the sales force getting behind marketing efforts
- the spread of positive information on the book in the community and media
- favourable reviews
- selection by clubs
- a film or television rights deal
- author tours
- bookshop pre-orders.

In general, books sell for key reasons that work in concert:

- author brand
- cover art
- price
- reviews
- personal recommendation
- advertisements
- prominent display in bookstores
- interviews on major media outlets (TV or radio)
- media celebrity endorsement.

Each category of title forms its own yardstick with different sales hopes and trajectories attached to books. Commercial fiction usually has a short shelf life. An academic title might sell well in moderate numbers for many years. An independent niche novel can gather sales pace over months or years as word-of-mouth develops. An unknown novelist could win an award out of the blue and suddenly be in demand.

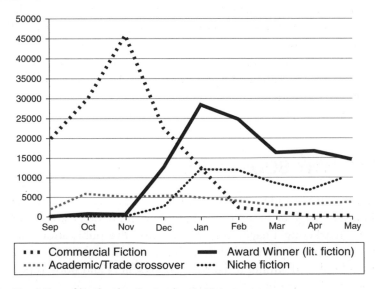

FIGURE 7.6   Simulation of book sales, September to May

## THE LONG TAIL

> The average Barnes & Noble carries 130,000 titles. Yet more than half of Amazon's book sales come from outside its top 130,000 titles. Consider the implications: If the Amazon statistics are any guide, the market for books that are not even sold in the average bookstore is larger than the market for those that are. In other words, the potential book market may be twice as big as it appears to be, if only we can get over the economics of scarcity.[21]

Publishing's 'long tail' is a sales concept that books can and do sell from 'an endless' distribution base. The short sales 'windows' used by the bestseller or even moderately selling sales model is the real anomaly. The long tail confirms that the book business is in truth about backlist sales. With digitised files, books are potentially available for sale 'forever', with print on demand (POD) and Google editions styled solutions.

The term 'long tail' was popularised by Chris Anderson of Wired.com, defining its main benefits as unlimited availability combined with unlimited selection. 'You can find everything out there on the Long Tail. There's the back catalog ... new ones ... niches by the thousands, genre within genre within genre ...'[22]

Digital file availability potentially regenerates lost titles, stretching potential sales over time to the marketing horizon, no matter how small the number.

> One of the amazing curiosities about publishing is that, barring miracles, the fate of a book is set long before it is printed and makes its way to bookstores. It is sealed at a sales conference, months before publication date, when publishers try to guesstimate just how many potential book buyers there are out there and try to determine how to catch their attention. (Arthur T. Vanderbilt)[23]

## REVIEWS

Publishers send out galleys to pre-press review publications and independent bookshops sometimes up to eight months prior to publication date. A staggered mailing-out programme is then set for review publications that like to receive the printed book, again as long before publication date as possible – two to three months if practicable.

Industry professionals believe reviews in major newspaper, magazine or specialist review journals will sell books. Yet only a fraction of the books published get selected for review. The ratio of the number of books published every week to those reviewed is about 100 to 1. Dedicated book sections in newspapers and book clubs on television shows, such as *Oprah* and the UK's Richard and Judy Book Club, have proven to be important ways of achieving book promotion, but again only for a fraction of books published.

Between 1996 and 2005 Oprah chose 58 books for her club. Many were already classics and some were published over 50 years earlier. Titles such as Faulkner's *As I*

*Lay Dying, The Sound and the Fury* and *A Light in August, Anna Karenina* by Leo Tolstoy, *The Good Earth* by Pearl Buck, Alan Paton's *Cry, the Beloved Country*, John Steinbeck's *East of Eden*, and the more recent novels by Nobel laureate Toni Morrison, all made Oprah's list. There were also some contemporary titles on Oprah's list. One in particular, *A Million Little Pieces* by James Frey, went to number one on Amazon and the *New York Times* bestseller lists (and stayed there for 15 weeks in 2005), catching a second wave of interest when the story broke that Oprah had been hoodwinked by the author.

Frey's book was found to be fiction passing off as fact, yet the novel went on to sell 3.5 million copies in the USA, and was translated into many other languages.[24] The Oprah effect on sales is huge. Many chosen books exceeded 1 million, sometimes 2 million, sales.[25] Negative publicity in the Frey case only increased the Oprah effect. Overall, though, Oprah's title selection was and is tiny in number and usually historic in nature.

In the UK, Richard and Judy began a book club on their daily TV show, following Oprah's model, though they chose newly released titles. From 2004 to about 2007 the show and club had a huge effect on the UK's book sales. *The Bookseller* reported that the show effectively sold 30.8 million books worth £183.3 million.[26] In 2006, Dorothy Koomson's first two books *The Cupid Effect* and *The Chocolate Run* sold less than 5,000 copies in the UK. When her third, *My Best Friend's Girl*, was chosen as a Richard and Judy 'summer read', it sold 545,000 copies. Her next, *Marshmallows for Breakfast*, sold 230,000 copies. When re-released, *The Chocolate Run*, went on to sell 120,000 copies.[27]

Online, many new reviewers are generating followings, although columns in traditional newspapers and magazines and TV air time are still by far the best way to promote titles. Reviews should cost a publisher nothing. The results can travel widely in syndicated form. A good review, of course, is better than bad commentary, but the general rule of thumb is 'no publicity is bad publicity'. That said, readers are still swayed by the nature of the commentary.[28] The tendency for celebrities to review each other is rife and to an extent has diminished how reviews work on the public, though not enough to have a major effect.

## ADVERTISING AND PUBLICITY

Advertising is expensive, especially for small publishers. Big publishers often include clauses promising full-page advertisements in contracts with major authors, mainly because agents or authors demand it.

For a big publisher, media coverage is the point, not the advertisement itself or its cost. Whatever keeps a book (or any product) in the mind of the consumer is valuable advertising. Do prominent media ads work in themselves though? No one can say with any surety.

Publicity, on the other hand, often costs nothing and it comes in many forms. Media outlets need content, and books, authors and writing provides good copy and material for book and culture programmes. Small publishers often fail to take advantage of this, or don't know how to exploit it, while big publishers have departments dedicated to chasing down every promotional opportunity. It is also true that small publishers can often be overlooked by the media outlets.

## WORD OF MOUTH

The best book sales method is based on peer-to-peer, friend-to-friend, contact-to-contact recommendations, and these still form the most vital factor in book sales, forming a cascade from reader to reader. Personal recommendation has a very strong effect on book sales, as it does with all media, but is also highly unpredictable. Muriel Barbery's *The Elegance of the Hedgehog* has done very well as a result of word-of-mouth recommendations in English-language markets, even if initially the reaction from 'market experts' was mixed.

## BOOK SIGNINGS AND TALKS

Some writers relish face-to-face contact with readers. Some authors don't mind travelling. Others hate to travel and don't like meeting readers, feeling awkward appearing in public. Book promotion can be hard work even for those who thrive on it.

Author events do not always go as planned. Andy Warhol had his blond, glued-on wig snatched off his head by a girl while he was signing books in a New York bookstore. A stoic by choice or nature, Warhol kept on signing, later describing the moment as perhaps the most humiliating experience of his life.[29]

G. P. Taylor, a bestselling young teen author, spends months on the road giving talks to classes of young readers in UK schools. Taylor enjoys the process, finding he can promote himself well to his reader group – early teen readers. While it's a good way to boost sales, the value of reading and signing sessions often depends on the author's capacity for self-promotion.

# DISCOUNTS, SALE AND RETURN

Wall Street and London City investors and businessmen from other industries have consistently been put off by the scale of discounting in the book sales model. They are also perplexed by the practice of *sale and return* as well. Brought in during the Great Depression in order to keep stores open, sale and return enabled booksellers to return books for full credit within a three-month period. The percentage of returns can be startling. In 2005 in the United States, return rates were strong across several sectors and formats were:

| | |
|---|---|
| Hardcovers | 35% |
| Trade paperbacks | 22% |
| Mass-market paperbacks | 47% |
| Young Adult hardcovers | 13% |
| Young Adult paperbacks | 18% |
| Religious | 18% |
| College books | 26% |
| Academic press hardcovers | 17% |
| Academic press paperbacks | 15% |
| Professional books | 20% |

Over the years publishers have tried to reduce returns with a variety of techniques, among them:

- increasing discounts
- refusing returns
- penalising wholesalers with high returns rates
- printing fewer copies
- cutting back on new titles
- dispensing with the midlist
- convincing retailers to rationalise ordering
- not over-hyping new titles.[30]

Half a century ago, just before the conglomerates began to take control of publishing, sales reps regularly spent their days travelling by car, talking-up books to storeowners, while publishers sat in their small offices guesstimating print runs. 'The best way to make a bestseller is to have fifty thousand copies in the store.'[31] A book was good if a bookstore was overflowing with copies. The reps were motivated to push wares, selling for the most part what there was most of in the warehouse, and buyers were impressed by book tables overflowing with the same title.

The logic of the guesstimate was brought to heel in the 1970s by publishing's new managers — former accountants, lawyers and sales people from other consumer industries — who saw overprinting as a major weakness in the book chain. It confirmed what they had long believed — the book business was poorly managed.[32] Yet, without guesstimation and the sale and return policy, there would have been far fewer books and far fewer stores. When the 1930s saw a devastating collapse of business — the number of printed books in the USA fell from 214 million in 1929 down to 11 million in 1933[33] — it required a good deal to keep bookstores open. Sale and return saved the industry, at least once.

Bookstores now would not even consider taking on the risk of stocking a huge number of books without the possibility of sending books back. Equally, discounting continues as an indelible part of bookselling culture. Book buyers are attracted to the deals and discounts booksellers offer — a pound/dollar or two off the retail price, two for one or three for two offers, half-price sales, and so on. But are these policies enough to save bookstores in the digital age?

The UK trade gave away £573.5 million in discounts in 2009, beating the total 2008 'discount record' by £37.3 million. Yet in 2009, 1.14 million fewer books were sold. The average retail price of books fell for the sixth year in a row, down to £7.44. Borders went into administration in 2009. The major UK high street bookstore chain Waterstones posted bad sales and its chief executive was removed. The only bookselling winners in recent times have been Amazon and the supermarkets, both of which are capable of and practise 'brutal' discounting to lift sales, with Amazon in particular hitting the fortunes of independent booksellers.

## WINDOW BLOCKING

Big publishers are prepared to spend large sums to 'buy sales', paying for prominent window or book table placement in most major bookshops and chains.[34] The practice poses cultural and moral issues. As Harvard Professor Michael Sandel points out, it is a bribe if a small publisher pays a bookstore chain owner to put her or his 'unimportant' book in a store front window, but is it somehow less of a bribe when it is done to 'boost sales of really important authors, like O. J. Simpson or Newt Gingrich?'[35]

Sandel sees 'window blocking' as part of the continuing commodification of books, which in turn is leading to a breakdown in cultural values. He compares the practice to the privatisation of prisons and the branding and marketing of symbols and artefacts once part of a nation's cultural identity.[36]

Independent store owners pick and choose what books to display, decorating windows and shops according to themes and special dates to attract passing trade. Display techniques are both creatively satisfying and commercially necessary, with an independent book shop free to express personal or store preferences. Independents are not organised into marketing cartels as the chains and superstores are, not yet at least.

### CONVERSATION WITH AN INDEPENDENT BOOKSELLER

*On the trade*: Christmas is the busiest, followed by late June/early July. That's because people are going on holidays and they buy three, four or five books to take on holiday with them. February's pretty grim. Everyone's got their credit card bills. January's alright until the bills start coming in. So February, March are a bit hellish, and then it picks up again around Easter. The rest is pretty even, really.

Q: How do you deal with returns? Do you send them back after three months?

No, I don't send them back after three months (*laughs*). Life's too short. To be honest I'm not terribly organised about it. Returns are not my favourite thing to

*(Continued)*

*(Continued)*

do. I don't do them if I can possibly avoid it. I do send back a certain amount, but I certainly don't say: those books have been here three, four months, they're going back now. If there's a massive pile that hasn't sold at all, then I'll bring them down here and toss them on the shelf [in the storeroom] and I do returns about two or three times a year, and I find them completely unproductive. You know, you have to get rid of the old editions, the hardbacks, damaged stock, and the stuff that hasn't sold, but it's not an element I find terribly interesting. It's like me packing up all my mistakes in a box.

*On payments to publishers*: Every invoice that comes in dated March gets paid at the end of April. That's how everyone does it in the business. If you are going to send books back in three to four months is irrelevant. You pay for a book when it comes in.

Q: So it's not really a credit industry. Publishers are not really giving you credit?

Well, they do give us credit when we send it back. It would be very hard to buy the new stuff on a firm sales basis. You couldn't. You'd never take a risk on anything. If some Rep comes in and says this is a fantastic new author but he's completely unknown. He's never done anything before. You'd say: Forget it, I'll wait until I get asked for it. But if you know you can return it, that the return facility is there, then you'll take a punt on it. You say: OK send us a copy and we'll see what we can do with it.

Q: So how do you budget?

It's all worked out in months. I know whatever I buy in March has to be paid for at the end of April, so we look at last year's April figures and we can see how much there is coming in. So we say less the rates, staff etc., that's how much we can spend.

Q: Do you think independents like you are disappearing?

Depends who you listen to really. Some people say, Oh the independents are the only really successful bit of the industry left and other people say the independents are dropping like flies. On the whole the not very good independents are dropping like flies and the reasonably good independents are doing OK. But I don't think any of us feel we are doing any better than OK, because it is a struggle – this year particularly [2009–2010], just the last few months.

Q: As an independent, what do you think you bring to the business that the big chains like Waterstones can't?

The personal touch. It has to be that. We don't do big discounts. We don't do ridiculous deals that bust Borders and sent them bankrupt.

*(Continued)*

*(Continued)*

Q: You don't do deals and things like that?

We do some deals, a half price thing in January that lasts a couple of months. We do a big 3 for 2 in summer, which works quite well. But I don't have deals going all the time. We just decided to take £2 off all the hardbacks over 15 quid. I just decided to do that this morning *(laughs)*. I just came in and decided right that's what I'll do today. You know that's kind of how it is, you can just come in and just go, that's how it's going to be.

Q: 3 for 2, how does that work?

You get three and pay for two.

Q: My maths isn't very good, how do you end up getting a good cut out of that? How does it work? You just sell more, is that how it is?

Actually ... *[pause]* ... well, we have two bargain shops with an enormous amount of the stock that I buy very carefully, and the 3 for 2 comes from my bargain shops, so I don't pay anything approaching like full margin on it, but on the other hand, I select incredibly carefully and it fits the shop, so it's not bargain rubbish I'm buying. It's decent titles I would sell at full price at normal everyday business in the shop anyway. But if you know the right suppliers, there's stuff out there to be bought at bargain prices, so I do a mixture of my 3 for 2 from the stuff that I buy for my big new summer titles that I'll do quite well at. I get 50–55% discount on those but I couldn't do a promotion on that basis because you really wouldn't be making any money. But if it's topped up with books that I'm paying £1, £1.50 for, from the remainder dealers, and the customers can't tell the difference because it's absolutely pristine stock, the sort of stock they would be expecting to be seeing here, then I can make the margins on it. That's not a piece of information that I share with my customers on the whole because I don't want them to feel that they're being sold a ... you know what I mean.

Q: They are buying the title, anyway, really.

Everybody's happy, really. I get my margin and they're getting a free book.

Q: Why do you think Borders failed?

I think they gave away too much money. They were doing ridiculous offers. I mean you have to make a profit. You have to cover your costs. I mean it's all very well producing massive turnover but if you aren't making any money out of the turnover it all falls apart. I don't know, it's two and a half years since I walked into Borders. I thought they were mad. They bought Books etc to enable them to

*(Continued)*

*(Continued)*

get into the UK, and I don't think they ever really appreciated Books etc for what it was, which was really fantastic niche marketing, a nice little London bookselling chain that I don't think they ever understood.

Q: They didn't care?

No, I don't think they cared at all. Books etc were quite successful. I'm not privy to what happened at Borders, but I always assumed they were going for the turnover and forgetting about the profit, which is a dangerous game to play, frankly.

Q: Would you say Foyles was a good shop?

Well, if you own your own building it makes a huge difference. I wish we'd been able to afford to buy this, but never mind.

Q: What do you think is going to happen? Are we going to lose the book? Are we going to end up with e-books? Are you going to come in one day and say it's all Kindle from now on?

I don't know. The demise of the book has been long prophesied, frankly, and they're still here. They were talking about 'Oh, the book is over' fifteen, twenty years ago. They said there won't be any more books. It'll all be computers. I cannot get my head around the e-book and everything at the moment. Somebody said the other day, why weren't we selling e-books. I just said I don't even know how you do that (*laughs*). As an independent bookshop I'm not sure how you would do that. You'll have to do it through a website of some kind because it's a downloadable file, so I'm having a lot of trouble getting my head round the whole e-book business. And also I think the e-book's strange, because they're really expensive, because they're pretty much the price of a book which I think is quite odd considering it's an e-book, because when you look at apps for iPhones you're paying 59p or £1.79 for an app. And those are pretty involved programs. They're not potty little programs you're buying for at £1.79, so the idea of actually having to pay, I don't know, £7.99, £5.99, for an e-book doesn't sound somehow that it's going to be fantastically popular when people are used to paying a couple of quid for a file that you can play some incredibly long and involved game on, which'll keep you occupied for longer than a book.

Q: So who's your big competitor, the killer whale?

Amazon.

Q: So they really are, you can really feel ... [their influence]?

Ohh... They are a nightmare as far I'm concerned. Amazon is just a real problem. It's just too easy. I have to confess I buy my CDs on Amazon because there is nowhere

*(Continued)*

*(Continued)*

else to buy CDs from. And it's quite difficult buying other than Tesco's selections CDs, which is not necessarily what I am looking for and I guess the same applies for books. I mean I don't buy books from Amazon but I can see why people do. You do it in the middle of the night. You can browse around. They're cheap.

Q: And they come to the door.

Well, coming to the door around here is not so good because it doesn't always get delivered. The postman tries to deliver it and won't leave it. Actually, that's the one thing that is bad for them. But we've had problems recently. Several times we've had people coming in here spending half an hour talking to one of my staff, trying to get advice about which book, if this book is in print, if it's available, for half an hour and at the end of it, they say I think I can get it cheaper on Amazon. You just think: actually you *&!!!? You have just spent half an hour with my expertise, my knowledge, my advice or my staff's, whichever one of us it happens to be. We've spent half an hour finding you the information that you want and now you are going to buy it cheaper on Amazon. Of course it's cheaper on Amazon. They haven't spent half an hour helping you out with the information that you want that has taken 22 years to learn, you know what I mean. That's why it's cheaper. They've got a drone in a warehouse sticking an item in a box. They don't care what it is. They don't have to advise you, help you find the right edition. It's all on the computer. I mean they do have to do all the programming and everything ... you can tell I'm ranting ... and then they stand there in front of you and say I think I'll get it cheaper on Amazon. Which actually is just rude! I mean, think that in your head, but don't say it out loud!

Q: Maybe they think you'll drop your price.

You can't drop your price. Half the time I can't buy it for what Amazon are selling it for. Because I'm paying high street rent, high street rates, and I'm training staff who can advise and recommend and Amazon aren't. They're in the middle of nowhere, somewhere in a warehouse.

Q: What about small publishers coming in?

Not my favourite really. The problem with small publishers, and I've always had this kind of problem, is it's just the logistics. It's the messing around with one or two books and messing around with discount, and trying to remember who to return them to. And you never can, so you always end up selling the things off at half price. They're no more likely to sell than the stuff that comes in from Penguin and the logistics are much more of a hassle. So unless a small publisher produces something that I'm more likely to sell, not just another novel, because I can sell a novel, but I can sell a novel that comes from Random House or

*(Continued)*

*(Continued)*

Penguin or HarperCollins without the hassle. You know what I mean. And that's so brutal. It's pure business. It's pure simplicity. … Britain has had a tradition of small publishers but I think I am very, I do have to say, I have a personal laziness over small publishers. I can't be fiddled with trying. And it is that mental attitude, this book isn't any better than anything I can get from anywhere else. Why would I want to involve myself in more hassle in getting it from a small publisher?

Q: But if you have a book on local history?

If it's about the local area. If it's either a novel set in the local area or it's about the local area, that's a whole different ball-game. Previous comments don't apply. Local history and stuff is fantastic. There's a bloke named Gavin, and he's just written a history of the cinemas around here and he's published it himself and he doesn't even have a flipping barcode and he drives me absolutely mad because I don't spot the fact I've run out of it because it's not going through the computer when I sell it. And someone goes: 'where's that book on the cinemas around here?' and I realise I've run out again. I mean it's a dreadful production and it's a funny little book, but it's actually selling really well (*laughs*) because it's local and people say, yeah I'll take that …

Q: It's obviously a profitable business.

Well, it is at the moment but it's getting tougher and tougher. This last year has not been amusing [2009–2010].

## FURTHER READING

Epstein, J., *Book Business*, New York, W. W. Norton, 2001

Greco, A. N., *The Book Publishing Industry*, Mahwah, NJ, Lawrence Erlbaum Associates, 2005

Greco, A. N., Rodríguez, C. E. and Wharton, R. M., *The Culture and Commerce of Publishing in the 21st Century*, Stanford, CA, Stanford Business Books, 2007

Powell, W. A., *Getting into Print: The Decision-making Process in Scholarly Publishing*, Chicago and London, University of Chicago Press, 1985

Tebbel, J., *A History of Book Publishing in the United States*, 4 vols, New York, R. R. Bowker 1972–1981

Vanderbilt, A. T., *The Making of a Bestseller: From Author to Reader*, Jefferson, NC, McFarland & Co., 1999

## NOTES

1   Catherine Neilan, 'UK Publishes More Books than ever in 2009', *The Bookseller*, 26 January 2010.

2   Gordon Graham, *From Trust to Takeover (Butterworths 1938–1967)*, London, WS&H, 2006.

3    Vanderbilt, A. T., *The Making of a Bestseller: From Author to Reader*, Jefferson, NC, McFarland & Co., 1999, p. 91.

4    James Spackman, *The Back of the Book*, The Lounge (blog), http://hodder.co.uk/lounge/blogpost.aspx?BlogPostID=20

5    Ibid.

6    A. N. Greco, *The Book Publishing Industry*, Mahwah, NJ, Lawrence Erlbaum Associates, 2005, p. 40.

7    Mike Shatzkin, 'Publishers, Brands, and the Change to B2C', 6 September 2010, http://www.idealog.com/blog/publishers-brands-and-the-change-to-b2c.

8    Amazon and Google, and all online merchants, are collecting data daily on consumer use.

9    Baverstock, A., *How to Market Books*, London, Kogan Page, 2000, p. 113.

10   James Naughtie's speech at the Man Booker dinner, The Booker Prize Foundation, 2009 http://www.themanbookerprize.com/perspective/articles/1294.

11   Philip Stone, '*Room* Leads Booker Sales Race, but *The Slap* Sells More', *The Bookseller*, 22 September 2010.

12   Philip Stone and Charlotte Williams, 'Random House makes Jacobson a Vintage Classic', *The Bookseller*, 20 October 2010. In 2008, sales for the virtually unknown Aravind Adiga and his *The White Tiger* shot up by 1,650% in the post-award week.

13   Miriam Datskovsky, 'Winner Does Not Take All', Portfolio.com (bizjournals), 17 March 2008.

14   http://edinburghnews.scotsman.com/bookerprize/Booker-for-Canongate.2371714.jp.

15   J.A. Trachtenberg, J. Decórdoba and R. Kozak, 'Peruvian Writer Wins Nobel Prize', WSJ, 8 October 2010.

16   J. Besek and J. C. Ginsburg, 'The Future of Electronic Publishing: A Panel Discussion', *Columbia Journal of Law and the Arts*, 25 (2/3), 2002: 91–118. There is research, of course, but do publishers use it? US research carried out in 2005 shows that around 55% of book purchases are planned, not impulse buying, with 58% of books bought by readers over the age of 45. The best anglophone book buyers, buying more than the average number of books per capita, are in the Pacific Rim region of the world.

17   Vanderbilt, op. cit., p.184.

18   Ibid., p. 193.

19   A. N. Greco, op. cit., p. 200

20   Ted Solotaroff, 'The Literary-Industrial Complex', *New Republic*, 8 June 1987, p. 28.

21   C. Anderson, *The Long Tail: How Endless Choice is Creating Unlimited Demand*, New York, Random House Business Books, 2007.

22   Chris Anderson, The Long Tail, *Wired.com*, Issue 12, 10 October 2004, http://www.wired.com/wired/archive/12.10/tail.html?pg=2&topic=tail&topic_set=.

23   Vanderbilt, op. cit., p. 89.

24   David Carr, 'How Oprahness Trumped Truthiness', *New York Times*, 30 January 2006.

25   A. N. Greco, C. E. Rodriguez and R. M. Wharton, *The Culture and Commerce of Publishing in the 21st Century*, Stanford, CA, Stanford Business Books, 2007, p. 51

26   Finlo Rohrer, 'How Richard and Judy Changed What We Read', *BBC News Magazine*, 1 July 2009.

27   In 2008, Richard and Judy's TV ratings began to fall, and by 2009 the influence of the show as a TV book club simply died. The club is now back online, this time linked with WH Smith.

28   Greco, Rodriguez, Wharton. op. cit., p. 49.

29  Andy Warhol, *The Andy Warhol Diaries*, Ed. Pat Hackett, London and New York, Simon & Schuster, 1989.

30  Greco, op. cit., p. 40.

31  Walter Goodman, 'The Truth about the Bestseller List', *McCalls*, November, 1966, p. 66, cited in Vanderbilt, op. cit. p. 90.

32  Banker J. P. Morgan thought as much when he bought into Harpers in the early twentieth century, selling out as soon as he could. Vanderbilt, op. cit., p. 179.

33  Ibid., p. 184.

34  '… tens of thousands of dollars for placement of their books in windows or other prominent places.' Cited in M. J. Sandel, 'What Money Can't Buy: The Moral Limits of Markets', *The Tanner Lectures on Human Values*, Brasenose College, Oxford, 11 & 12 May 1998, p. 90.

35  Ibid., p. 91.

36  Ibid., p. 92.

# 8  THE ERA OF DIGITAL PUBLISHING

In 1997, Alan Stone, in *How America Got Online*, foresaw a twenty-first century 'emergence of hypercommunications groups embracing local-loop service, international long distance, national long distance, cable television, Internet provision, satellite, wireless (cellular, PCS and other technologies)'.[1] For Stone, the real power was in the connection not in the content. Almost half a century earlier, information scientist, Norbert Wiener, theorized a fundamental power in the act of information transference.[2]

To a large extent they were and are still both right. Digital delivery of content is in the hands of the telecommunications companies, which in the 1990s already had annual sales far larger than either of the world's leading content providers at the time, Disney or Time Warner.[3] The growth in telecommunications underpins the growth of new media. The proliferation of email, text and phone messaging, and social networking has long supported the idea that the power is in the messaging process itself.

The communications sector over the last 150 years has spent more on connectivity, standard point-to-point communications than on broadcast media or distributed content. The US postal system of 1832 carried newspapers which 'weighed about 20 times as much as letters' with 'newspaper "content" ... delivering at least a hundred times as much information as letters,' though ordinary letters brought in '85% of the money needed to run the postal system'.[4] And to further cement the point, newspaper delivery was heavily subsidised by the US government.

In the early 2000s the revenue of the US phone industry combined with the US postal service was already higher 'than [US] military spending, and almost three times higher than the revenues of the airline industry',[5] with spending on phone services higher than all advertising outlays. Ten years on, continuing broadband and internet expansion confirms that content is no longer king, if it ever was. Connectivity is of paramount importance to 70% of people in the UK, who have indicated a broadband connection is as essential to them as electricity or water supplies.

In *The Rise of the Network Society*, Castells described a 'cultural change around the emergence of the grand multimedia fusion'. We were experiencing a convergence, 'an integration of all messages in a common cognitive pattern', where media, information, education, and entertainment blur into a 'culture of real virtuality ... in which reality itself is captured, fully immersed in a virtual image setting, in the world of make believe'.[6] If you're not in the virtual system, effectively you cease to exist.[7]

At the beginning of the twenty-first century, one time e-book and e-reader pioneer, and founder of Gemstar, Henry Yuen had a vision of the future: 'In a few years our leisure time will be spent either surfing, shopping, or chatting on interactive, Web-enabled television sets and reading novels, newspapers, or magazines on electronic books.'[8]

Digitisation now underlies the whole process of publishing, whatever the end product, and has done for nearly two decades. Published texts are produced and stored digitally, with title output potentially available in paper, digital or computer-generated audio books. As well as the rapidly growing digital storehouse in recently published titles, there is the scanning and digital conversion by Google and others of neglected and out of print books written and compiled before the world went digital. When this project is finally complete, a huge array of textual materials, multimedia content and books will be online and available for digital distribution. Much is already available now, a great deal of it represented in the long tail of choice. The changes to publishing brought about by digitisation have altered the way editors and publishing firms develop, produce and sell intellectual property (IP). These days IP can be packaged for separate needs and sold in parts not as whole texts catering for diverse consumption and needs. A flexible, decentralised, multi-use global internet, both as a publishing platform and library for all media, is no longer just a wild dream of digital enthusiasts writing on the web in the 1990s.

Except for an emphasis on televisions as the hardware carrier, Yuen's vision has proven accurate. Yuen and Gemstar have disappeared. Gemstar's attempt to promote the e-book and e-readers on a mass scale can be compared to the Albatross paperback. Both have spiralled into closed loops in media history, but Albatross inspired Penguin, and Gemstar prefigured Sony, Kindle and iPad's exploration of electronic reading markets.

## THE INTERNET

The internet is a catch-all term, a series of gateways and nodes, computer networks, a sum of processes that signify a vast amount of diverse digital network activity. Perhaps the best metaphor is still the first that was made popular – *the information superhighway*. The marriage of hypertext to the internet led to the breakthrough of the World Wide Web. Bits of data sent from one computer to another using a TCP/IP (Transmission Control Protocol/Internet Protocol) format suddenly could be used by anyone.

Using different web browsers to seek information via search engine portals, the world began to browse virtual spaces, searching and discovering a multitude of sites and webpages. Internet Service Providers (ISPs) or Internet Access Providers (IAPs) helped us connect to URLs (uniform resource locators). Using these site locators, we began to visit online merchants such as Amazon. Traditional media content providers such as *The Guardian* and *The New York Times* built websites and grew their international readership.[9]

The internet owes its existence to the ARPANET (Advanced Research Projects Agency Network), a research and development project that underpins the whole online scenario today. It began in 1969 using 'packet switching', a digital communications method and network for transmitting data. ARPA, a United States Defense Department project, started in collaboration with researchers at the Stanford Research Institute, University of California Santa Barbara, University of California Los Angeles, and the University of Utah. ARPA was renamed DARPA in 1973 (Defense Advanced Research Projects Agency). In 1983, MILNET (military network), part of the original project, separated from ARPANET and expanded to become the Defense Data Network (DDN).

Digital publishing developed from the 1970s onwards, with researchers using email, circulating digital documents, leading to the appearance of CD-ROMs for storage and hypertext for interconnecting digitised information. When Tim Berners-Lee (now Professor of Engineering at MIT) unveiled the World Wide Web in 1991, early digital publishing began to have wider impact beyond the computer, digital networks and the scientific research community. Web and browser technology and general internet use spread, growing at a phenomenal rate. One estimate puts internet and web expansion at over 300,000% annually in its earliest years. Websites went from 130 in 1993 to over 600,000 in 1997. By 2009 there were more webpages than humans on the planet.

The developed world has only been connected for two decades, commercially for about one decade, but already our browsing activities cover wide aspects of work and leisure. Nearly 70% of the population in the USA now have access to computers and the internet at home. Almost any data, even complete films, no matter how large are streamed at the highest quality to home-based computers, now a 24/7 convergence site for all media.

Internet activities globally have leapt forward, not only in North America and Europe. In 2000, Asia already led the world in online activities, and is still growing fast, with Africa, the Middle East and Latin America also increasing their internet use rapidly. At the beginning of the twenty-first century, North America represented nearly 30% of the total world internet activity. In nine years, North America's share of the total global internet activity halved.

Yet, even as its global internet share is diminishing, over the last 12 years inside the United States computer use has almost doubled, internet use has quadrupled, and broadband use has expanded 16 times. By 2009, 69% of US homes had internet access and 64% were connected to broadband, although 90 million Americans still did not have home access to internet services.

In the UK, in 2008, 56% of all households had a broadband connection and 86% of households connected to the internet were using broadband. That still left 8 million – 35% of all households – without any internet connection at all.[10] It seems likely that of those who do not have an internet connection, a good proportion are not simply resisting or ignoring computer, internet or broadband use. Many 'withouters' are elderly, and are increasingly excluded from digital developments and services. This group will be even more marginalised and disadvantaged in the future, it seems, as the digital scenario continues to expand.

## OPEN SOURCE CULTURE

Open source was born in the late 1990s among technologists, who began 'freely' sharing computer codes in order to develop what they hoped would be the best software possible. The movement advocated:

> ... commitment to total and free access to computers and information, belief in the immense powers of computers to improve people's lives and create art and beauty, mistrust of centralized authority, a disdain for obstacles erected against free access to computing.[11]

Open source now underpins a vast, largely non-commercial, online culture of sharing and collaboration among disparate groups and individuals. Open source culture operates according to a different publishing ethos from standard commercial publishing activities. One early example is the *Project Gutenberg* (PG), which now offers over 100,000 digitised books online free. Project Gutenberg was started in 1971 by Michael Hart, who was given $100,000 worth of computer time on a mainframe to kickstart the project. He began by scanning a book a month. By 1996 it was a book a week. With the help of volunteers, by 2008 PG was adding 400 books a month.

Project Gutenberg provides a unique solution for the maintenance of the integrity of book content on the Web and internet, as copies of scanned books are distributed to countless public websites and and private computers all around the globe.

> No single disaster can destroy them; no single government can suppress them. Long after we're all dead and gone, when the very concept of an ISP is as quaint as gas streetlamps, when HTML reads like Middle English, those texts will still be safe, copied, and available to our descendants.[12]

Open source culture now numbers collaborative sites such as Wikipedia, and movements and facilities such as Creative Commons, as part of its reach. The popularity of open source across all its activities is a testimony to a worldwide appetite for a democratised internet.

*Crowdsourcing* is another web concept and practice that has grown up recently, but it should not be confused with open source. Crowdsourcing can involve companies asking individuals to collaborate online on projects for little or no pay, with the project originator benefiting and retaining copyrights to all developments. Open source is quite different. It promotes and advocates a realignment of technology and web publishing cultures. Instead of the media corporations and the traditional publishing industry controlling creation, production and distribution, open source culture encourages:

- direct contact between creators and readers, listeners, viewers and consumers
- the widespread democratisation of publishing practices and cultures
- the scaling back of copyright traditions.

Critics say open source culture will destroy the content industries – the reasoning being that content must be paid for if the content industries are to survive. Supporters of open source culture reply that the main powers in the copyright industries are corporations operating draconian, undemocratic intellectual property regimes, which are unhelpful to the progress of the arts and sciences.

Open source culture criticises the current copyright scenario, saying that it has grown into an exclusive club engineered and controlled by corporate owners and conglomerate-led media industries, with a single aim: *to create and exploit cultural scarcity in order to produce higher profits.* Lawrence Lessig wrote in *Free Culture* that 'culture' has never been more 'owned' than it is now, with 'the concentration of power to control the uses of culture' more generally accepted than ever before.[13] Open source culture supports and encourages a climate and culture of oppositional new media, its new mood characterised by small-scale, interventionist, subcultural literacy, ironic comment, perishable content, collaborative initiatives and hetero-topic existences.[14]

Open source proposes an internet full of cultural difference, not a commercial marketplace for the sale of intellectual goods. Open source seeks to promote a culture of free speech and self-expression, rather than societies that are spoken for and dictated to. The open source movement wants a better, more open digital technology culture, saying that the countless bloggers, websurfers, downloaders and file and source code sharers, 'voting' daily with their keyboards, are proof of its widespread support.

## SOCIAL NETWORKING

Social Networking sites present a chance to 'speak' as well as to be spoken to and for, and interest in them in recent years has soared. The social network site leader, Facebook, which first appeared out of a Harvard dorm in 2005, became the most popular US site on 13 March 2010, accounting for 7.07% of website hits. The previous 'site hits leader' was Google (second with 7.03%).

Facebook has grown its web hits by over 200% annually against Google's main site growth of 9% per annum (without factoring in the Google-owned YouTube, Google Maps or Gmail). Three years ago Facebook had 50 million users, 81% of them under 24 years of age. In 2010 there were 500 million Facebookers all around the globe, with 45% of them over 35 years of age.[15] Around the same time a cautionary Hollywood film called *The Social Network* was released in 2010 – deconstructing the myth surrounding Facebook's founder, Mark Zuckerberg. The social network site at the beginning of 2011 was valued at $50 billion. Facebook's power of reach makes it significant.

*How long does it take for an author to reach 50 million people?*

Radio:              38 years.
Television:         13 years.
Internet:           4 years.
iPod:               3 years.
Facebook:           3 months.[16]

Word-of-mouth has become world-of-mouth. The two major brands online are now Facebook and Google. They provide different services and therefore are not in direct competition, but recent trends highlight the attraction that online socialising seems to have over research for specific information. The main attraction of the social networking trend is the expanded, personalised, creative, two-way communication.

Most web-based services are linear, one-way providers of information. Facebook and others have taken this idea laterally, providing several levels in the two-way exchanges. Recognising the desire for social interaction, Google has set up its own social networking site, Google Buzz, but so far without major success. Facebook's success has to be tempered by the fact that the site has yet to generate revenues to match its market value or its global reach. By contrast, Google earned $23 billion in 2009.

The online socialising trend now includes Twitter.com (interactive messaging site); Zimbio.com (an interactive online magazine); Multiply.com (an interactive family-oriented site); and Wikia.com (an interactive, collaborative web document tool). These sites are also growing very fast. The attraction to 'something new' seems to be a factor. While Facebook grew hits by 228% in 2008–2009, Twitter grew by 1,382% over the same period.[17]

Each one of these sites has different groups of followers and offers diverse tools, but the collective theme is 'interaction'. Facebookers, Twitterers, Zimbio and Wikia users are not only communicating, interacting, sharing, informing, chatting, they are also redirecting and coaxing people to other smaller websites.

## BROADCASTING V. NETWORKING

Broadcasting, one-to-many 'Big Media', which grew up in the twentieth century, is now head to head with one-to-one 'Little Media' in the twenty-first century. A competitive antagonism has developed in recent times between the two, but those expecting a revolution in media distribution and culture may be disappointed – if history is any guide (Table 8.1).

When little media radio broadcasting first began to proliferate in the 1920s, the field was perhaps, given the times, reach of technology and population, as wide open as the internet and World Wide Web are today. Individual ham radio operators and small radio broadcasters sprang up all over the United States and growth continued for nearly a decade. But consolidation of the industry began to take effect when Radio Corporation of America (created in 1919) took control ten years into the boom.

TABLE 8.1  Networking v. broadcasting[18]

| Networking or netcasting – one-to-one | Broadcasting – one-to-many |
|---|---|
| Open-style and source, complex, freely distributed, discursive, anarchic, free, literary | Paid-for channels, simplified, publicly proposed information and entertainment, commercial |
| Horizontal, symmetrical, decentralised, egalitarian, democratised | Vertical, asymmetrical, centralised, hierarchical, politically organised |
| Access is open, easy, often free, usually cheap | Access is restricted, paid for, often expensive |
| Informal, global distribution, participant generated uncontrolled content, unregulated | Formal, territorially defined, centrally controlled commissioned content, regulated |
| Letters, telegraph, ham radio, telephone, email, peer-to-peer sharing, blogs, individual webpages, social networks | Books, newspapers, magazines, films, radio & TV broadcasts, podcasts, spam, direct mail, company webpages |
| Heterogeneous, the personal made public | Homogeneous, the public made personal |
| Ethics on privacy of information and behaviour | Law of copyright, plagiarism |
| The ecology of communication | The institution of standards |

Throughout history, media provision and participation has generated many corporate versus individual struggles. The struggle today over the internet is about who will eventually control it for all media publishing.

The question of who should have control and who has the right to make public pronouncements on the internet goes to the heart of free speech.

# MEDIA REGULATION

Media regulation is central to the maintenance of the interests of the public good and free expression. Good regulation has worked in media history (1710 Statute of Anne and the US First Amendment attest to this). So how can governments best manage media – by doing a little or by doing a lot?

Professor Robert McChesney argues that recent US media exploitation and deregulation has led us to a crisis of hypercommercialism. Media consumers in the United States (and other anglophone markets) are increasingly colonised subjects. In the past, books have not been readily identified with media controls. The book trade is largely self-regulating. But the book (and all media), throughout the anglophone world and markets, is part of a commercial culture where content is mined for revenue and profit. Globalised anglophone media and culture corporations have spread the commercialisation of media through all cultures and across all territories. In the mix of world media, only organisations such as the BBC seem to represent a line of defence against this tendency. The BBC is constantly under attack from owners of major commercial media, such as the Murdoch-owned Sky TV, which wants to dismantle what the Murdoch empire describes as the BBC's 'privileged position'.

The key to a mutually beneficial media future seems to be in how to balance the interests of the public good with the desire for profit. Fond as he was of money (and power), Henry VIII rejected the first petition by the Stationers' Company in 1542 to become *de facto* commercial controllers of English printing and books. Did Henry VIII know something of drawing media lines in the sand that could help current legislators?

Unbridled commercialisation of media does not seem to have ever been in the public interest. Henry Tudor and Robert McChesney might agree on that. McChesney argues that the idea for deregulation is built on *five mythical discourses*:[19]

- The media system is based on free market principles.
- The media was intended to be a free enterprise.
- Professional and editorial standards will protect us.
- The media gives people what they want.
- Technology will set us free.

Governments in the past have helped private as well as public media organisations. The US postal system of subsidies for cheap distribution of newspapers represented a huge government subsidy for US newspaper proprietors. Grants of radio and TV licences, cable and satellite franchises have effectively provided big companies with monopolies.

McChesney believes that it is pointless to oppose protective policies and subsidies because they are 'unavoidable'. It would be better to recognise that the market is not free and that intervention is in every one's interest.[20] The only question is what sort of intervention should there be? With the internet evolving around us, the kinds of media regulation that is drawn up and enacted is of prime importance for all our futures.

## ADVERTISING

The enduring economics of the book business model – revenue from unit sales – means that book publishers miss out on advertising revenue tagged to digital delivery and the internet. There still seems to be no industry appetite for including advertising in books. So far books have been a cultural story free from it. Books in the early twentieth century did use end papers in the back of books to advertise coming titles, but the industry resisted direct advertising as a means of earning revenue. Could digital books force a reassessment?

As the 'odd medium out' in modern media, book publishing is commercially vulnerable. The US book industry generated impressive revenues of $25 billion in 2007, but this result is dwarfed by the collective ad-funded media revenue

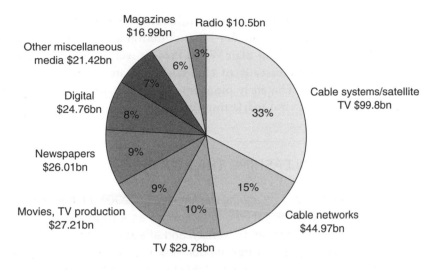

FIGURE 8.1   US Media earnings from advertising in 2008
*Source of figures:* AdAge US

results – businesses such as Cable and Satellite TV and networks. Ad-funded big media have raced ahead of books in getting involved with the digital age (Figure 8.1). The advertising model has smoothed the way. Sectors such as Journals and Reference have employed digital methodologies but don't widely use advertising, encamped as they currently are inside the still lucrative subscription model. With 'knowable' lists of clients, institutions and individual readers, advertising is not (yet) needed.

The lowering of e-book prices, which seems inevitable – regardless of the current policy in consumer books to use *the agency model* – could drive print book prices down to a point where they cannot go lower, threatening the entire business model of books. Feeding advertising into the mix, e-books could change the whole way books are sold as well as read.

# GUERILLA MARKETING

Guerilla marketing – a concept credited to Jay Conrad Levinson – is based on low-cost advertising techniques that work on people and consumers spreading *the word* about a service, a product or an idea, rather than a company or an individual paying (often heavily) for traditional methods of disseminating marketing information.

Guerilla marketing can be very effective, with successful campaigns such as *The Blair Witch Project* to prove what can be done. Made on a production budget of US$50,000 *The Blair Witch Project* grossed over $100 million in the USA alone (US$248 million worldwide). After its screening at the Sundance Film Festival, the film was bought for $1.1 million by the company, Artisan. Using the film's mockumentary style as a guide, Artisan spent $1.5m on Web promotion, distributing promotional material online that further blurred fiction and fact lines in the plot of the film. As a result, the official Blair Witch Project website spawned countless other websites, generating a cascade of chat room debate, as web users passed around stories on the film. The early pioneers of word-of-mouth online created the benchmark for guerilla viral marketing campaigns.

---

### UNLEASHING THE IDEAVIRUS

When Seth Godin published *Unleashing the Ideavirus* in 2001, he created a web-wide run on his text by offering it free-for-download as a free e-book. Godin, a marketing graduate from Stanford University, and already a veteran of advertising, initially gave away 200,000 free e-book downloads before his book was printed and released by Hyperion. It sold 26,000 copies in hard cover alone. In the book the author defines his internet concept as 'sneezers' spreading ideas like a virus on the World Wide Web.

Nearly a decade later, Godin's website reports that more than 2 million people have downloaded the e-book of *Unleashing the Ideavirus*, making it, Godin claims, 'the most popular ebook ever written'.[21] Godin succeeded with a technique that many try with their own websites.

Much of Godin's work is dedicated to exposing the failure and myth of traditional marketing methods, offering his own targeted, lower-cost solutions. One of Godin's earliest marketing techniques, first conceived in the mid-1980s, was 'permission marketing', asking consumers whether they would like to receive information about a product, and proceeding to inform them further only if a 'yes' is received.

Godin went out on his own in the mid-1980s, starting a book packaging company. Later, with a partner, he created Yoyodyne, which attracted venture capital investment in the mid-1990s. The company was sold to Yahoo for $30 million in 1998, with Godin becoming a vice-president of Yahoo for two years. He then left the company to write and market his own books. Godin's first three books almost tell the evolution of his marketing story and technique in the titles alone – *eMarketing: Reaping Profits on the Information Highway* (1995), *Permission Marketing: Turning Strangers into Friends, and Friends into Customers* (1999), and *Unleashing the Ideavirus* (2001).

---

## PIRACY AND DIGITAL MUSIC

Music producers were the first to experience commercial difficulties and the full effects of digital markets. As peer-to-peer (P2P) file swapping exploded among online devotees early this century, Big Music (Universal, Sony/BMG, Warner and EMI) saw P2P as a continuing dilemma and a major threat. Sales for the big four music companies dropped 20% from 1999 to 2003, and Big Music blamed internet piracy for all of it. Yet, in 2002, music producers earned $33 billion worldwide,[22] and the respected periodical, *The Economist*, reported that between 66% and 75% of the fall in American sales 'had nothing to do with internet piracy'. Actual reasons oscillated from 'rising physical CD piracy, shrinking retail space, competition from other media, and the quality of the music itself '.[23]

Big Music kept up with their claims that P2P music lovers had taken fair use into their own hands and were responsible for the music industry's decline. The line between piracy and fair use, once clear in the analogue world, became blurred, almost beyond recognition, in the digital world. Online file-swappers began enjoying freedoms they could never have dreamed of in the past – and many music artists supported them in this quest.

The big Music corporations went after transgressors, in effect using the confusion of the actual size and nature of threat in the process to make a 'land grab' for the online music scene and P2P was successfully labelled 'deviant behaviour'. The US courts supported Big Music's draconian crack down. Organised P2P elements were absorbed (Napster bought out)[24] and the rest, largely powerless (many bewildered) individuals, were litigated into oblivion.

> In September 2003, the RIAA [Recording Industry Association of America] sued 261 individuals – including a twelve-year-old girl living in public housing and a seventy-year-old man who had no idea what file sharing was. As these scapegoats discovered, it will always cost more to defend against these suits than it would cost to simply settle (the twelve year old, for example ... paid her life savings of $2,000 to settle the case).[25]

The RIAA even threatened four students with 'a $98 billion lawsuit for building search engines that permitted songs to be copied. This at a time when World.Com – which defrauded investors of $11 billion, with a loss to investors of over $200 billion – received a fine of a mere $750 million.'[26]

A NPD group survey[27] 'estimated that 43 million citizens used file-sharing networks to exchange content in May 2003'.[28] Vaidhyanathan identified the trend that the music industry truly most feared – the growth of 'an ideology of file sharing'.[29] Consumers and copyright owners were in a piracy war.[30]

The US Institute for Policy Innovation (IPI) concluded in a 2007 report that piracy created annual music losses of $12.5 billion every year. The RIAA's website described the report as a 'credible analysis'. The RIAA, representing big music as it does, is an interested party and the IPI is an ultra-conservative Texas-based 'think tank', One man's *piracy* is another's *fair use*. Is that all this is about – a semantic quibble? Unfortunately not.

As head of the Motion Picture Association of America (MPAA), the film industry's indefatigable advocate for rights holders, Jack Valenti, argued before the US

Congress in 1982: 'Creative property owners must be accorded the same rights and protection resident in all other property owners in the nation.'[31] Author of *Free Culture,* Professor Lawrence Lessig, described this sort of analysis as 'property talk … a closed rhetorical system, a specific cultural instrument that extends a specific agenda or value … shutting down "conversation." You can't argue against theft.'[32] Lessig points out that intellectual property has never been considered ordinary common law property. This principle, underpinning the entire copyright system, was written into the 1710 Statute of Anne and supported by a Law Lords decision in 1774.

Copyright, though, is often a contradictory process, touching 'directly on conflicting cultural, economic, and political values – the desire for art and literature; a commitment to free markets; traditions of free speech … John Milton in the *Aereopagitica*, excoriating *censorship but supporting copyright*'.[33] The realities of copyright can be seen in 80 million users joining in Napster's P2P file sharing at the peak of its online experiment as well as in the actions of 'a federal district court' putting a lid on it.[34] Consumer freedoms have always been at odds with the legal rights of copyright holders. It seems that until 'piracy' is fully tested in the courts, or until the law is redefined to re-establish old *first sale* and *fair use* provisions, new media consumers growing up in the digital age will not know what fair use actually means.

## PRINT ON DEMAND (POD)

Book publishers are extremely wary of walking into a similar experience as the music industry. The Print On Demand model provides flexibility and addresses some of their fears. With POD, print runs can be made according to *the market's actual needs*, just-in-time, rather than on a traditional projection of just-in-case, based on what *the market might accommodate*. The POD model of short digital printing runs combines digital storage and e-copy distribution functions with the printed book. POD allows a viable short-order printing of books. From one copy to about 600 copies POD is a viable alternative to traditional methods.

POD is still 'small potatoes' for big publishers, it is useful only for uncorrected proof review copies and for short special orders. Traditional litho printing is still used for main 'long' printing – 1,000 copies and above.

*A 2010 cost projection for a POD print run could look like this:*
10 copies of a 300-page book 197 × 132mm paperback     **£96 – £9.6 unit cost**
100 copies of a 300-page book 197 × 132mm paperback     **£370 – £3.7 unit cost**
200 copies of a 300-page book 197 × 132mm paperback     **£660 – £3.3 unit cost**

In this example POD savings show up best at the 100–200 copies mark, a number which only suits short orders or small publishers – or larger publishers planning very short print runs of some limited academic titles. POD isn't a viable option for long printing. The quality of the POD cannot yet be compared to books printed using traditional printing methods. The quality difference between the two options, however, will continue to narrow.

One way POD could take off on a mass-market level is via a consumer operated ready-to-use, ATM-styled machine, connected to digitally stored book files in online databases. An example of this is the *Espresso Machine* (Espresso Machine EBM 2.0), a desk-top photocopier-sized device designed to print and bind paperbacks while a customer waits. Designed to sit in libraries, book or photocopying stores, public facilities or even in the entrance halls to apartment blocks, the Espresso operates in a similar way to other coin or cash operated goods dispensing machines.

Veteran publisher Jason Epstein teamed up with the inventor of the Espresso, former CIA officer Jeff Marshall, to develop and market the Espresso. One machine was bought by the World Bank's InfoShop in 2006 to handle its internal publishing. Another was placed on trial in the New York public library system in 2007. The UK publisher and bookseller Blackwells bought an EBM 2.0 in 2009 and placed it in its central London store.[35]

Espresso has now made an agreement with Xerox, which announced plans in 2010 to market the machine (Figure 8.2). The solution is an important print development for backlist books, giving publishers (large and small), as well as booksellers and educational institutions, the option of producing many more titles using a short order title production and sales model.

Jason Epstein has been a longtime supporter of emerging digital technologies, but he believes strenuously that print books must be maintained. In a 2004 interview he was scathing on current electronic reading solutions:

> ... you can't read those things. People who do that don't know anything about books. They've never read one. ... These people understand technology and fundraising and all that sort of thing, but they don't know anything about books, or what people actually do with them. They think a book is a best seller. They don't see that it's an entirely separate business to book publishing. Book publishing is creating backlist.[36]

From a traditional publisher's point of view, POD is not disruptive. Managed POD production fits well into existing production processes, even if it will alter the overall business model somewhat. But publishers would welcome this kind of change to a sell and produce model. Significantly, the Espresso approach means that digital files of texts are not openly distributed, remaining in secure online systems, as secure as credit card machines. This way, POD is not just a tool that publishers use in the production and promotion process, it is also an adaptive, mobile, boutique-styled, just-in-time sales model. It could develop a mass market, in particular during any interim period between a shift from print books to e-books — if e-books do in fact become the next paradigm, which is still not certain.

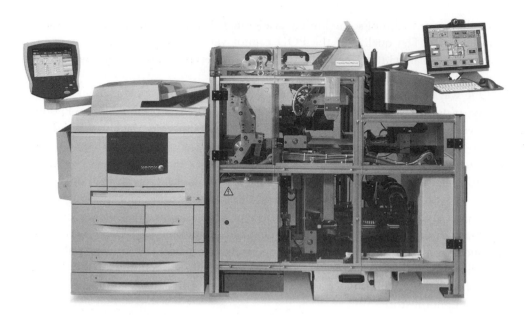

FIGURE 8.2   The Espresso, EBM Version 2-2.2 (Xerox Phase II - Xerox 4112™ Printer) courtesy of On Demand Books, LLC

POD Espresso-style does not threaten traditional printing operations either as it is more a way of dealing with small orders, which litho printing was never designed for and has never been good at servicing.

## GOOGLE BOOKS

Google Book Search came into being 17 November 2005, after its predecessor Google Print was sued by the Association of American Publishers (AAP) and Authors Guild. Both organisations claimed Google Print wanted to control other people's content. Google replied that the programme was only intended to make many millions of backlist, out-of-print and under-marketed books findable, something they argued would benefit readers and authors.

Google began its project with five research libraries and a few publishers on board, arguing that its plan was consistent with established practices of fair use. As an internet search and information distribution platform, Google is without peer, and its interest in book content spread fear within established publishing circles. Publishers believed that once their content was on the Google Books database it would be out of their control. Google has insisted throughout that copyright ownership remains with authors and rights holders. The main general objection of publishers is that the Google Book Settlement seems to reverse copyright law, giving Google a blanket licence over works and relieving it of the responsibility of tracing individual rights holders and negotiating licensing deals one by one.

In October 2008, after trying to convince publishers of their good intentions, Google decided to settle the court battle brought against them in 2005 by the Authors Guild and the Association of American Publishers. Google offered authors and publishers a deal worth $125 million, with $34.5 million earmarked for setting up a book rights registry to manage a collection and distribution system of payments for authors and publishers – to be managed by the Guild and the AAP.

The main issue at stake (and in litigation) is whether Google should be allowed to scan in copyright books in order to make content snippets available online for online researchers via Google Book Search. As part of its settlement offer, Google offered $60 for every book the company had already scanned.[37] The three main areas of books that are both in contention or that interest Google are:

### In-copyright and in-print books
Books publishers own and which Google wants to place online with authors and publishers able to 'turn on the "preview" and "purchase" models that make their titles more easily available through Book Search'.

### In-copyright but out-of-print books
An agreement that allows for digitised previews and purchases, unless the author or publisher wants to "turn off" that title'.

### Out-of-copyright books
Books already in the public domain and therefore free for Google to place online for preview, and sale.[38]

In Google's own description of the current Amended Settlement, rights holders would authorise Google on a non-exclusive basis to:

- continue to digitise books and inserts
- sell subscriptions to an electronic books database to institutions
- sell online access to individual books
- sell advertising on pages from books
- display portions of a book in a 'preview' format to encourage sales
- display snippets from books
- display bibliographic information from books.

Google's plan is to create a sales system so that readers and researchers are able to purchase a digitised book from Google Editions – with a split of receipts according to an 'agency model', i.e. 63% payment for authors and publishers, and 37% commission for Google.

As for the service itself, universities and colleges will pay for full access to Google Books, while public libraries will have it for free. Book consumers going online to search from home would get limited excerpts and would be able to buy the complete work. Google has accepted book publishing's central argument – that information should not be free.

> *The NO case* – Google is inverting copyright law, asking rights holders *to opt out, rather than opt in,* making Google the controller of published content by default, with no other competitor likely to be in a position to challenge that control. Google is not interested in the millions it might earn from books, but the potential billions it could generate from advertising.

Critics of the programme say that Google's real intention is to destroy the 'payment for content' model that books sales have been based upon for centuries, replacing it with an advertising model.

> *The YES case* – readers, researchers for the first time will be able to choose from millions of books, with authors benefiting, all based on the much vaunted 'long tail' of sales model, with obscure and rarely sold books, in particular, getting online exposure.

On 19 November 2009, Judge Denny Chin gave preliminary approval of the amended settlement, then in late March 2011 halted the entire project, saying the arrangement 'granted Google a defacto monopoly'.[39]

# E-BOOKS

Commercial e-books and e-reading devices appeared in the late 1990s, at a time when the consumer book trade was facing 'stark sales figures, a fickle and price sensitive consumer base, the "rise" of chains and superstores and price clubs and the concomitant "decline" of independent bookstores'.[40] Personal computers were revolutionising workplaces and home life. The World Wide Web and the internet had just arrived. Together, and connected to internet developments, early e-book proponents claimed they would make the creation, production, storage and distribution of information and leisure texts easier, cheaper and more relevant to the age. For pro-digitalists such as Nicholas Negroponte, the e-book was a 'no-brainer':

> What weighs less than one millionth of an ounce, consumes less than a millionth of a cubic inch, holds 4 million bits, and costs less than US$2? What weighs more than 1 pound, is larger than 50 cubic inches, contains less than 4 million bits, and costs more than $20? The same thing: *Being Digital* stored on an integrated circuit and *Being Digital* published as a hardcover book. [41]

Some people believe e-books can positively transform information and leisure book provision. Others were and are still not convinced. New media usability expert, Harold Henke has argued that people have been trained 'since childhood, to read books, not chunks of information'.[42] To follow his argument to its logical end, print books will continue to be used, at least while children encouraged to read print books are still alive.

The print book has so far resisted the e-book. It has survived the rise of the personal computer, the internet, the World Wide Web and video games, as it survived challenges from the radio and film industries in the twentieth century. Nearly 15 years since the first commercial e-book began circulating, many trade publishers, who first saw e-books as dangerous intruders, seem to be changing their minds about the technology. The e-book still represents a threat to the paper book trade publishing infrastructure – the copyright, book and paper production, printing and book distribution systems – but, commercially, e-books now present a potential source of revenues.

Sectors such as journals, law, education and reference publishing have had a lot to do with this change of heart, continuing to move forward successfully with their own electronic solutions. Trade book publishers have been slow in taking to the e-book, but from a publisher's point of view there have been several good reasons for this:

- Print books are a continuing love story for readers.
- Knowledge preservation and the library systems are still dependent on paper books.
- Digital data and information storage is not yet safe or permanent.
- The book trade copyright model is uncomfortable, if not incompatible, with electronic books.
- Digital piracy is still a huge risk.

The print book still remains a cultural force with mature age brackets, but, the Harry Potter phenomenon aside, books do not inspire young readers as they once did. Video games, mobile telephony and online web activities are absorbing their attention. Forty years ago it was 'cool' for a university-age student to carry a book around. Now it is 'cool' to use electronic devices. Reading is far from dead as a cultural activity, but the nature of reading is changing fast. Most readers still seem unsure and perhaps a little confused by e-books. Many factors still stand in the way of a wholesale change in attitudes and reading practices. While digital software and hardware technologies are everywhere, the cost of e-books and e-reading devices remain high. At the outset of the e-book's commercial rise ten years ago, small publishers and authors saw an opportunity to reorganise publishing. Observers imagined the e-book evolving into an author-friendly, democratised system. Time has disabused almost everyone of this notion. The commerce of e-books is now the main preoccupation.

No one can see the future, but almost anyone can see the potential for e-books at the end of the first decade of this new century. Even if the owners of the more than 7 million iPads sold in 2010 only buy ten e-books, that is already 70 million e-book sales.

TABLE 8.2   E-book v. Hardcover in 2010: costs and profit breakdown

| Costs & profits 2010 | E-books $14.00* | % | Hardcover $26.00 ** | % |
|---|---|---|---|---|
| Marketing | $1.00 | 7% | $1.00 | 4% |
| Design, edit, type | $0.44 | 3% | $0.80 | 3% |
| Printing, storage, distribution | | | $3.20 | 12% |
| Seller's profit | $3.90 | 28% | $12.00 | 46% |
| Author's royalties | $2.28 | 16% | $3.90 | 15% |
| Publisher's profit | $6.38 | 46% | $5.10 | 20% |

*E-books sold via the agency model; ** Hardcovers sold by traditional sell-through discount model

Publishers continue to defend hardcover sales wherever they can, acting not only for themselves but also in the interests of traditional booksellers, which make their best profits from hardcover sales. The major trade publishers have also insisted on the application of the agency model for e-book sales from Amazon's site, currently the largest distributor/vendor of commercial e-books in the anglosphere. Amazon still wants to discount e-books in order to stimulate the market, but have bowed to the pressure from the major publishing houses which insisted on setting their own prices for their own e-books. While this arrangement continues, book and e-book publishing profits are safe-guarded in the way publishers currently wish them to be.

## THE HISTORY OF E-BOOKS

In the early days there was a wave of enthusiasm for e-books. In 1998, Rick Lockridge wrote: 'Electronic books have finally arrived. Portable, versatile and easy to use, they represent a challenge to the paper and ink we've relied on for 1,500 years.'[43] G. J. E. Rawlins, from Department of Computer Science, Indiana University, provided an 'economic argument':

> A 500-page textbook typically costs $50 retail, or 10 cents a page. Second-hand it costs $25, or 5 cents a page. On a large copier it costs $15, or 3 cents a page. On a large printer it costs $5, or 1 cent a page. If it were distributed electronically, it would cost about $1 to send it to any phone in the world, at a cost of 0.2 cents a page. And whether it is an excellent or a terrible book doesn't change the cost. [44]

The public was intrigued. Long before 2010's sales rush, set off by iPads and Kindles, 2000 was the e-book's 'first *annus mirabilis*'. In March 2000, Stephen King had the wires zinging with the first of his two experiments for the year, a 66-page novella e-publishing experiment, *Riding the Bullet*. Managed by his print publisher, Simon & Schuster, 400,000 copies were downloaded in 24 hours, a figure to match the total sales of all fiction e-book titles combined up to the time. Librarians began referring to 'before and after *Riding the Bullet*'.[45]

Simon & Schuster and other publishers were watching developments closely. The company's CEO, Carolyn Reidy, was bluntly realistic: 'You get a proven author like Stephen King, who's pretty good and has written so many books he probably knows how to do some editing. He could take his works right to the Internet.'[46] In June 2000, King announced that he planned to self-publish an e-book of an old novel, *The Plant*, one reportedly he had discarded in the early 1980s. The author appealed to readers on his website: 'Dear Constant Reader,' he wrote, 'Can I trust people to pay?'[47] His fans emailed him back to say they would. King went ahead with the publication: 41,000 fans downloaded the first chapter within the first 15 hours. King's two e-book experiments exercised the imagination of the publishing industry. In October 2000, at a New York publishing event attended by all the chiefs of all the major trade houses, Henry Yuen, the founder and CEO of the rising new media company, Gemstar, announced his e-book strategy to the world. He predicted his company would sell 500,000 of Gemstar's new dedicated e-readers in six months. E-book sales would quickly rise to 3 million annually.[48] Gemstar's RCA manufactured REB 1100 and RCA REB 1200 e-readers would be the electronic reading device no reader could do without. The CEO of PenguinPuttnam, Phyllis Grann, seemed convinced: 'We're security minded, and we are confident that this system will protect our authors'.[49]

Yuen promised to lower the price of the cheaper of the two Gemstars, the REB 1100, from $299 to $100 before the end of 2001. Many observers felt it was too little. The e-readers were way too expensive to reach a broad enough audience quickly enough – 'setting up a chicken-and-egg scenario where the demand may never arrive'.[50] Yeun, however, was optimistic that Gemstar could grow the e-book and e-readers markets, even at luxury prices. Gemstar, which in 1999 had merged with TV-Guide, owned by News Corporation, seemed to excite the market. Gemstar's e-readers permitted internet connection, allowed readers to browse titles onscreen and to purchase e-books, all for immediate download to PCs, laptops and/or dedicated e-readers. Gemstar's secure servers would control and oversee the sale, preventing piracy, Yuen said. His company's business model made e-book buying 'easy for consumers and secure for publishers'.[51]

The future of the e-book in October 2000 looked very bright. In November the skies darkened. Out of the blue King suddenly cancelled his self-published e-book experiment. Fans were bitterly disappointed, though King had earlier warned everyone that he would do this if people did not pay. Chapters one and two (5,000–7,000 word instalments) had been posted in good faith, but after that, the author had warned, if downloaders didn't pay up he would stop the process. In a Q and A on his website King made his position abundantly clear.[52]

Fans were so enthusiastic that King continued on with instalments of *The Plant* well after posting episode three. But when wayward fans continued to download and not pay King decided enough was enough. Honest and dishonest fans were penalised alike. Many readers had paid several dollars for a novel without an end. One fan offered to pay for those who hadn't, but King was adamant; his digital self-publishing days were over.

Yet, by any objective assessment the experiment had been a startling success. The author took in well over $700,000 and made a self-declared profit of over $400,000.[53] While online sales for *The Plant* were not anywhere nearly as huge as King's print sales standards, the author had earned an extraordinary 60% royalty on his first self-published e-book experiment. King's experiments indicated what a brand author could do with e-books. King had cut out the middle man, the trade publishing houses, showing others following him just how to do it. Traditional publishing had watched King's experiments in trepidation, terrified a Napster-style experience, that had all but melted the profits of Big Music, was awaiting them as well. A wealthy author like King could do as he pleased, whether he published in print or electronic form. He had the power to call the shots. King's decision to stop with his e-books was pivotal. It sent shock waves through the electronic book world at the time, and gave book publishers what they desperately sought, some breathing space. From then on, newspaper columnists researching the e-book and e-reader revolution began to produce increasingly critical copy. Now the new media technology could do nothing right. The e-book was now a pointless creation of technology geeks who knew nothing about reading and nothing about books.

In 2001 e-books and the dot.com revolution began to stall. Analysts spoke of inflated expectations, bad technology and poor business models. Professor Terje Hillesund concluded that it was quite natural that there would have been 'resistance' to e-books 'since publishers ... built their businesses and fortunes on the production of traditional books'.[54] By the end of the year, Random House's AtRandom, AOL Time Warner's iPublish and BN.com's MightyWords were all out of business.[55] John Feldcamp, CEO of Xlibris.com, summed up the year:

> 2001 has not been about innovation, but about general devastation and retrenchment. In this new and very Darwinian world, the first crop of new publishing-related companies has been massively selected for extinction and most real innovation will need to wait for a few more years.[56]

In 2002 nails could almost be heard going into the lid on the e-book's coffin. David Cardof of Jupiter Media Metrix wasn't in mourning: 'E-books were a dumb idea. I am very negative on this market.'[57] A senior executive at a large US textbook firm claimed: 'e-books were a non-event. We had 500 textbooks that you could pay for and download online. We sold 2,300 units. That's nothing.'[58] Even the journalists and academics reporting on or researching the subject began to lose interest. In a search I carried out in the British Library, on articles and papers written on e-books, the rise in interest from 1998 to 2001, and equally the fall off in interest from 2002 to 2004, is dramatic (Figure 8.3).

Yet, even as the e-book's image darkened, sales kept rising. In 2002 Adobe reported that 20,000 titles had already been published using its software.[59] Critics discounted

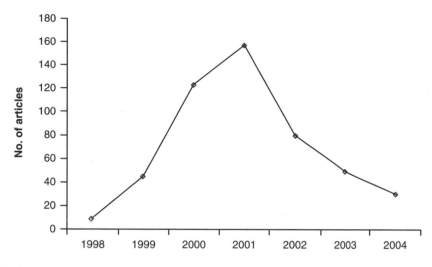

FIGURE 8.3   Articles on e-books in the British Library, 1998-2004

the new reading technology's marketability and usability. The leading e-book/e-reader company, Gemstar, went into irreversible decline, leaving users stranded.[60]

For all the gloom, though, the Association of American Publishers reported that e-book sales rose from $211,000 in January 2002 to over $3.3 million in January 2003. In the same month, US print hardcover sales fell 13.7%, paperback sales dropped 15.4%, and the trade mass market fell 10.1%.[61] Oddly, as e-book sales rose, the media's disenchantment also grew. A 2003 UK Joint Information Systems Committee report hinted at why: 'The e-book industry is currently dominated by the big players of the print-on-paper book industry: publishers, particularly international conglomerates.'[62]

Between 2003 and 2007 the e-book scene was relatively quiet. The main development was the Sony Librié, an e-reader that Sony released and did little to promote outside Japan. Licensing the highly regarded new E-ink black-and-white screen text technology,[63] Sony had produced a thinner, lighter, better e-reader with longer-life batteries. But without colour, something e-readers already had in 2000, and no wireless connection, the Librié seemed destined not to excite the anglophone market. Four years after the furore over Stephen King's *Riding the Bullet*, e-books still barely registered in overall book sales.

By its own yardstick, though, the e-book was doing very well. Sales from 13–15 reporting publishers grew from $6 million in 2002 to $165 million in 2009. Annual sales gains were something print publishers could only envy, with compound growth from 2002 to 2007 outstripping all other sectors/formats and products by a big margin (Table 8.3).

In 2007 Amazon released the Kindle e-reader, and digital books began to generate a buzz not seen since 2000. The big increase in e-book sales, December 2008 to December 2009, caught many by surprise. Apple's release of the iPad (a multi-use

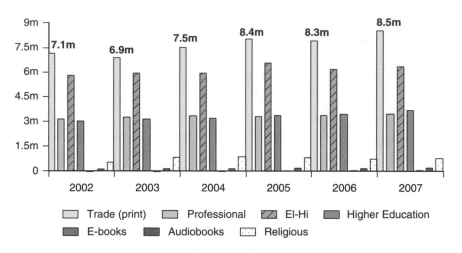

FIGURE 8.4   US book and consumer e-book sales, 2002–2007 (in $m)

*Source of figures*: Association of American Publishers

tablet and e-reader) in April 2010 inspired digital enthusiasts enough for them to camp outside American stores to buy it. Kobo, Barnes & Noble's Nook and Amazon's Kindle 2 all dropped prices.[64] E-reader sales now seemed to be driving e-book sales – e-readers required content.

During May 2010, e-book sales were reported as reaching 55% of the paperback mass market.[65] By October, conservative estimates calculated iPad sales at around 7.5 million units, with over 4 million iPads sold in the quarter ending in September alone.[66] The success of the Apple iPad seemed to spur the competition into action. In November 2010, Amazon reported that it had sold three times as many e-books in the first nine months of 2010 than for the same period in 2009. The company said its Kindle sales were also up significantly, though it did not provide figures.[67] Amazon's most interesting statement was that digital book sales were 2 to 1 over print, though when Publishers Weekly analysed Amazon's ten bestselling books (hardcovers) over 'a 30-day sales window' in 2010, the figures Amazon provided were in reverse of Amazon's stated trend (Table 8.4). The majority of Amazon's e-book sales seem to be coming from the long tail outside the bestseller list.

The rate in the rise of e-book sales (even though it showed some signs of slowing in 2010) made 2009–2010 a huge growth period, an exponential leap forward for the whole e-book market. Together with iPad's market success, the future seems not to be whether e-reader and e-book sales will drive publishing's future, but rather by *just how much*.

## WHITHER THE E-BOOK?

We no longer ride around in *horseless carriages*, listening to the *wireless*, on our way home to read our *codices*. We don't communicate on the *talking telegraph* or sit at

TABLE 8.3  Sales gains by sector, format or product, 2002–2007

| Sector, format or product | Percentage gain 2002–2007 |
|---|---|
| E-books | 55 |
| Audio books | 8.8 |
| Religious | 7.1 |
| Higher Education | 4.0 |
| Trade | 3.6 |
| Professional & Journals | 1.9 |
| El-Hi/Schools | 1.4 |

TABLE 8.4  30-day sales window on Amazon's bestsellers in 2010

| No. | Title | Author and Publisher | % print | % digital |
|---|---|---|---|---|
| 1 | The Girl Who Kicked the Hornet's Nest | Stieg Larsson Knopf (May 2010) | 67 | 33 |
| 2 | The Girl with the Dragon Tattoo | Stieg Larsson Knopf (Sep. 2008) | 82 | 18 |
| 3 | Freedom | Jonathan Franzen FS&G (Aug. 2010) | 70–75 | 20–25 |
| 4 | The Girl Who Played with Fire | Stieg Larsson Knopf (July 2009) | 82 | 18 |
| 5 | Fall of Giants | Ken Follet Dutton (Sep. 2010)* | – | – |
| 6 | Obama's War | Bob Woodward Simon & Schuster (Sep. 2010) | 00 | 20 |
| 7 | American Assassin | Vince Flynn Atria (Oct. 2010) | 67 | 33 |
| 8 | The Lost Hero | Rick Riordan Disney (Oct. 2010) | 80 | 20 |
| 9 | The Reversal | Michael Connelly Little, Brown (Oct. 2010) | 74 | 26 |
| 10 | Safe Haven | Nicholas Sparks Grand Central (Sep. 2010) | 85 | 15 |

*Penguin reports digital sales of many titles ranging from 12% to 30%.
Figures reproduced with the kind permission of Publishers Weekly[68]

night in front of our *radios with pictures*.[69] Inventions such as the car, radio, book, telephone and television evolved and found clear identities for themselves. The term *e-book*, on the other hand, carries an implicit message of dependence, labelling it as surrogate and subordinate to the print book. That, together with the tendency to view print and e-books as an *either/or* proposition, rather than the possibility of having both formats, seems to limit the e-book's potential.

The e-book is currently a digital copy of the original print version (in truth, the print book is a copy of the original digitised text). The e-book could be an interpretative medium in the way a film is a cinematic interpretation of a book. It could merge the graphic novel, animation, music and film into a new format, becoming a creative mix of multimedia rather than a cannibalistic competitor for sales with the original paradigm – the print book.

The e-book has overcome the earlier resistance shown towards the format. The consulting firm Forrester predicts that 2010 sales of e-books will hit $966 million, 'easily' reaching $3 billion by 2015.[70] The single biggest problem with these sorts of predictions is that e-book consultants have been so wrong in the past. In 2000, Andersen Consulting (later Accenture) forecast that by 2005 28 million people would be using e-readers and that the total market for consumer e-books would reach $2.3 billion. By 2005, 10% of the trade book market would be in electronic form and formats. None of Accenture's predictions came even close to materialising.

Forrester predicted that, by 2005, digital delivery of on-demand-printed books, textbooks and e-books would account for $7.8 billion, 17.5% of publishing industry revenue. Forrester was not as positive on e-books or e-reading devices, which they predicted would be only a small part of the total figure, with dedicated e-reading devices generating only $251 million. Forrester was sure, however, that by 2005 digital textbook sales would account for about one quarter of all textbook sales, selling about 147 million units, earning $3.2 billion, with trade e-book and e-readers selling 73 million units and netting $674 million. This did not prove to be true. Jupiter Communications was more sober in its predictions. Considering that US e-reading sales in 2000 had only reached 50,000, Jupiter determined that the pre-dicted estimate of 1.9 million sales for dedicated e-readers by the end of 2005 was still far too small to alter how most publishers thought about, planned and delivered books. This perception did turn out to be true.

While it seems likely, on current trends, that e-books will keep growing strongly for some time yet, they could settle at a quarter, a third or a half of the total book market. No one knows yet. No one can say how the e-book will mature technologi-cally beyond its current form, let alone predict sales in two or three years' time. And digitisation, of course, does not mean a market only for and of e-books. A storehouse of e-files online supports a just-in-time print on demand market for print books just as readily, with texts and titles in all languages delivered to a decentralised outlet, shop or POD machine in a public place. Readers will be able to choose what they want from an almost infinite array of titles on a screen menu, paying for and printing out a copy while they wait minutes for the machine to complete the task.

E-books and e-readers, however, due to the sudden recent growth (2009–2011) in tablet readers such as the iPad, Kindle, Nook have captured the market's imagination. E-books and tablet e-readers are the 'star' growing niche market. Sales of consumer e-books alone hovered at the end of 2010 at 10% of consumer book sales – in the most advanced market, the United States. This of course still left 90% or so of the US book market left to conquer, even more in the rest of the world. Whether the format remains a solid niche or eventually becomes a dominant market product seems to depend, at least in the near term, on what publishers are prepared to do with e-book prices. Apart from the online retailer Amazon, no big publishers seem willing to drop e-book prices. Certainly, no publishers have yet shown any readiness to take an Allen Lane leap in the dark – which, relative to Penguin's paperback pricing in 1935, means that e-books would now be selling at around $2 each.[72]

After ten years of commercial life no one yet knows the true long-term consumer and reader appetite for the e-book. In 2008, the educational electronic publisher, Ebrary,carried out a survey, one of the few on electronic use, with 6,492 university students from 400 higher education institutions in 75 countries taking part. Ebrary asked the students to indicate how they used digital or online facilities, including e-books. This survey was carried out before the 2009/2010 e-book and e-reader boom, but still, half of the participants – 3,132 students – had never used e-books in libraries. Of that number, 1,790 did not even know where to find them and 1,420 said they still preferred print books. There is still no clarity yet on the actual prefer-ence for or use of e-books. The only thing that seems clear is that digital alternatives, hand-held tablets, e-book sales and online usage is all on the rise. Even Stephen King, who has shown more than the average interest in e-readers and e-books in the past, is cautious on the digital book's future.

> Here's the thing  –  people tire of the new toys quickly. ... Let's just hope there won't be a terrorist EMP [electromagnetic pulse] that'll wipe them all out. They are ephemeral. In a very real sense, not books at all. Of course, books themselves are hardly indestructible.[72]

E-books *are* ephemeral. However, contrary to statements by ardent book lovers, print books are not a perfect technology either. If the price of paper were to escalate dramatically, book production would wither and die. There are envi-ronmental issues with both media. Both media satisfy different cultural and practical needs, but as long as there is no clear evidence that e-books can actu-ally replace what the print book currently provides, the print book tradition will go on.

The future should not be decided by *either* an e-book *or* a print book proposi-tion. With a clear separate identity, and publishers firmly behind them, electronic books could expand, technologically and commercially, in ways not yet widely imagined, let alone practised. Judging from the histories of other technologies, e-books almost certainly will go their own way eventually, adding many uses to this as yet underdeveloped format. But just how far and how soon it will all happen is still anyone's guess.

# FURTHER READING

Castells, M., *The Rise of the Network Society*, Oxford, Blackwell Publishers, 1996

Kellner, D., *Media Spectacle*, London, Routledge, 2003

Kuhn, T., *The Structure of Scientific Revolutions*, Chicago, University of Chicago Press, 1962

Lessig, L., *Free Culture: How Big Media Uses Technology and the Law to Lock Down Culture and Control Creativity*, New York, Penguin Press, 2004

Rice, R., Ed., *Media Ownership: Research and Regulation*, Cresskill, NJ, Hampton Press, 2008

Vaidhyanathan, S., *The Anarchist in the Library*, New York, Basic Books, 2004

# NOTES

1   Alan Stone, *How America Got On-line: Politics, Markets, and the Revolution in Telecommunications*, Armonk, NY, M.E. Sharpe, 1997, p. 200.

2   Wiener, N., *The Human Use of Human Beings*, London, Eyre & Spottiswoode, 1954, pp. 9–12.

3   Herman, E. S. and McChesney, R. W., *The Global Media*, London, Cassell, 1997, p. 114.

4   Odlyzko, A., 'Content is Not King', *First Monday*, 6 (2), February 2001, http://firstmonday.org/issues/issue6_2/odlyzko/index.html.

5   Ibid.

6   Castells, M., *The Rise of the Network Society*, Oxford, Blackwell, 1996, p. 373.

7   Hersmondhalgh, D., *The Cultural Industries*, London, Sage, 2002, p. 235.

8   Stone, A., 'Will Gemstar Be Our Guide to the Future?', *Businessweek Online*, http://www.businessweek.com/bwdaily/dnflash/may2000/sw00524.htm.

9   There are other services that don't use URLs, such as email, VOIP (voice over internet protocols) and FTP (file transfer protocol). There are multiple methods of connections – standard dial-up narrowband connections, DSL (Digital Subscriber Line) or ADSL (Asymmetric Digital Subscriber Line), broadband wireless, cable modem, fibre to premises (FTTH), and Integrated Services Digital Network (ISDN).

10  US Office of National Statistics.

11  Nissenbaum, H., 'Hackers and the Contested Ontology of Cyberspace', *New Media Society*, 6, 2004, DOI: 10.1177/1461444804041445, p. 197.

12  Project Gutenberg, quoted by Jack Schofied in 'Peruse the World's Best Public Library', *The Guardian*, 14 January 2008.

13  Lessig, L., *Free Culture: How Big Media Uses Technology and the Law to Lock Down Culture and Control Creativity*, New York, Penguin Press, 2004, p. 12.

14  Leah A., Lievrouw, 'Oppositional New Media, Ownership, and Access', in R. Rice, Ed., *Media Ownership: Research and Regulation*, Cresskill, NJ, Hampton Press, 2008, p. 398–399.

15  George F. Will, 'Robert Weissenstein's Exhilaration', *Newsweek*, 5 November 2010, http://www.newsweek.com/2010/11/05/robert-weissenstein-looks-to-the-future.html#.

16  http://socialnomics.net/tag/social-media/, citing: United Nations Cyberschoolbus Document.

17  Nielsen NetView Ratings 2009.

18  Extrapolated from William B. Warner, 'Networking and Broadcasting in Crisis', in R. Rice, Ed., *Media Ownership*, op. cit., p. 79–80.

19  Robert McChesney, 'Media and Politics in the United States Today', in Rice, op. cit., pp. 29–49.

20  Ibid.

21  http://www.sethgodin.com/sg/bio.asp.

22  Vaidhyanathan, S., *The Anarchist in the Library*, New York, Basic Books, 2004, p. 43.

23  'Music's Brighter Future', *The Economist*, October 28, 2004.

24  Napster was created by Shawn Fanning in 1999, a free peer-to-peer online music sharing service. Sued in 2000 by A&M Records and the RIAA, Napster went into liquidation in 2002. Napster 'amassed over 10 million users within [the first] nine months. After eighteen months, there were close to 80 million registered users of the system.' The

courts 'quickly shut Napster down, but other services emerged to take its place' with a
new P2P service, Kazaa, soon boasting 'over 100 million members' Lessig, op. cit., p. 67.

25  Lessig, op. cit., p. 200.

26  Ibid. p. 185.

27  Created in 1967, known then as the National Purchase Diary, NPD is a leading market
    research company in the USA.

28  Lessig, op. cit. p. 67.

29  Vaidhyanathan, op. cit. p. 18.

30  Lessig, op. cit., p. 17. May, C., 'Digital Rights Management and the Breakdown of Social
    Norms', *First Monday: Journal of the Internet*, 11 (8), 2003, http://firstmonday.org/issues/
    issue8_11/may/index.html.

31  'Extending copyright terms pays big for rightsholders' (Lessig, op. cit., p. 216). The 1998
    Sony Bono Term Extension Act in the United States gave copyright holders an extra
    20 years on copyright (life plus 70 years) bringing US law in line with other copyright
    law in the western world. In the lobbying that led to the passage of the Bill through
    Congress '[t]en of the thirteen original sponsors of the Act in the House received the
    maximum contribution from Disney's political action committee; in the Senate, eight
    of the twelve sponsors received contributions. The RIAA and the MPAA are estimated
    to have spent over $1.5 million lobbying in the 1998 election cycle' paying out 'more
    than $200,000 in campaign contributions' with Disney 'estimated to have contributed
    more than $800,000 to reelection campaigns in 1998' (Lessig, op. cit., pp. 215–217).

32  Lessig, op. cit., p. 117–118; Vaidhyanathan, op. cit., p. 22.

33  Goldstein, P., *Copyright's Highway: From Gutenberg to the Celestial Jukebox*, Stanford, CA,
    Stanford University Press, 2003, p. 30.

34  Vaidhyanathan, op. cit., p. 34.

35  Alison Flood, 'Revolutionary Espresso Book Machine Launches in London', *The
    Guardian*, 24 April 2009.

36  Interview with Jason Epstein, New York, December 2004.

37  Pamela Samuelson, 'Should the Google Book Settlement be Approved?', *Communications
    of the ACM*, 53 (7), 2010, pp. 32–34.

38  http://books.google.com/googlebooks/agreement/#1.

39  http://books.google.com/googlebooks/agreement/#1 and Miguel Helft, 'Judge Rejects
    Google's Deal to Digitize Books', *New York Times*, 22 March 2011. Judge Chin said the
    settlement was not fair, adequate and reasonable and urged parties to renegotiate.

40  Greco, A. N., *The Book Publishing Industry*, Mahwah, NJ, Lawrence Erlbaum Associates
    2005, p. xv.

41  Negroponte, N., 'The future of the book', *Wired.com*, Feb. 1996, http://www.wired.
    com/wired/archive/4.02/negroponte.html.

42  Henke, H., 'Consumer Survey on Electronic Books', *Open eBook Forum*, http://www.
    openebook.org/doc_library/ surveys/consumer/consumerresults.asp, 2003, p. 2.

43  Lockridge, R., 'E-books Change the Face of Reading', *CNN*, 1998, http://www.cnn.
    com/TECH/computing/9812/17/t_t/e.books/.

44  Rawlins, G. J. E., 'The New Electronic Book Technology', Computer Science
    Department, Indiana University, http://www.roxie.org, Department of Computer
    Science, Indiana University, 1998.

45  Rose, M. J. (2000) *The King of E-Books*, Spark-Online. http://www.sparkonline.com/
    april00/trends/rose.html and Schneider, K. (2000) *A Funny Thing Happened on the Way to the*

*E-Book*, American Libraries. http://www.ala.org/ala/alonline/inetlibrarian/2000columns/may2000funny.htm.

46   Offman, C. (2000) *The Future of the Book – Brave new e-books*, Salon. http://www.salon.com/books/special/2000/03/29/future/.

47   From Stephen King's official website www.stephenking.com [accessed 2001].

48   Kafka, P., 'Horror Story', *Forbes Magazine*, 21 August 2000.

49   Reid, C., 'Publishers Embrace Gemstar's E-book Devices', *Publishers Weekly,* 16 October 2000.

50   Rose, M. J., 'At What Cost, E-Books?', Wired.com, 2000, http://www.wired.com/news/culture/0.1284.39471.00.html.

51   Ibid.

52   From www.stephenking.com accessed in 2001:
     Q:  I am worried that people won't pay, can I pay a little extra?
     A:   Though we aren't asking you to do this, we have seen that many of you in your comments have asked if you can pay extra to help cover the costs of the dishonest people who will download The Plant and not pay. You should be applauded for this desire to pay – and should be held out as an example to those of you reading this who are not planning to pay. You know who you are. No stealing from the blind newsboy. If you wish to pay more than $1, you can either send a check to the address specified at Amazon.com Payments or pay multiple times with your credit card and then do not download the file.

53   King's Income/Expense Report on 'The Plant'. Deposits to Philtrum through December 2010 were $721,448.61. Net Profit was $463,832.27. From www.stephenking.com accessed in 2001.

54   Hillesund, T., 'Will E-books Change the World?', *First Monday Journal of the Internet*, 2001, http://firstmonday.org/issues/issue6_10/hillesund/index.html.

55   Rose, M. J., 'Authors, Agents on E-Books' Side', *Wired.com*, 2001, http://www.wired.com/news/culture/0,1284,43077,00.html.

56   Rose, M. J., '2001 Was a Tough Read for E-Books', *Wired*, 2001, http://www.wired.com/news/culture/0,1284,49297,00.html.

57   Guernsey, L., 'In Lean Times, E-Books Find a Friend: Libraries', *Nytimes*, 2002, http://www.nytimes.com/2002/02/21/technology/circuits/21BOOK.html; Reuters, 'Mystery of E-Books: Who Reads Them?', *USA Today*, 2002, http://www.usatoday.com/life/cyber/2002/05/08/ebooks.htm.

58   Thompson, J. B., *Books in the Digital Age*, Cambridge, Polity Press, 2005, p. 377.

59   Reuters, op. cit., 2002.

60   Associated Press, 'Gemstar-TV Guide Fires Former CEO', Associated Press, Los Angeles, 2003; Vogelstein, F., 'Meet the Bill Gates of TV. US', *News & World Report*, 2000; Writenews, 'Gemstar Closes Ebook Division', *Writenews.com*, http://www.writenews.com/deadzone/2003/arch0603.htm, 2003; Zeitchik, S., 'Gemstar E-books Shutdown', *Publishers Week*, 2003.

61   AAP, 'E-book Sales Lead Off 2003', Association of American Publishers, http://www.publishers.org/press/releases.cfm?PressReleaseArticleID=138.

62   Thompson, op. cit., p. 370.

63   In a co-venture with Phillips, the Boston-based E-Ink manufactured screens that reflected ambient light rather than being backlit like other computer screens. E-Ink's approach emulated print pages. As the screen image was stable and not reconfigured constantly, usability experts believed it would relieve or even remove eyestrain.

64  Sarah Prediletto, 'eBooks: Death to Print and Bind', *The Racquette*, 29 September 2010, http://media.www.theracquette.com/media/storage/paper1301/news/2010/10/29/Ae/Ebooks.Death.To.Print.And.Bind-3951690.shtml.

65  E-book Sales Rose 167% in May', *Publishers Weekly*, 14 July 2010.

66  Claire Cain Miller, 'E-Books Top Hardcovers at Amazon', *New York Times*, 19 July 2010, http://www.nytimes.com/2010/07/20/technology/20kindle.html.

67  Jim Milliot, 'Print, Digital Book Sales Accelerated in 3rd Quarter.', *Publishers Weekly*, 21 October 2010.

68  Rachel Deahl, 'How E-book Sales Compare To Print … So Far', *Publishers Weekly*, 1 November 2010.

69  Levison, P., *Digital McLuhan*, London, Routledge, 1999, pp. 14–15.

70  James McQuivey, 'eBooks Ready to Climb Past $1 Billion', 8 November 2010, http://blogs.forrester.com/james_mcquivey/10-11-08-ebooks_ready_to_climb_past_1_billion.

71  Allen Lane priced his paperbacks at one-twelfth of the hardcover price. One-twelfth of a hardcover today, on average, is between $2 and $2.50, even lower.

72  Bob Minzesheimer, 'More Bibliophiles Get on the Same Page with Digital Readers', *USA Today*, October 20, 2010.

# INDEX